D00932898

Wins, Losses, and Human Ties

Daniel R. Gilbert, Jr.

UNIVERSITY PRESS OF AMERICA,® INC.
Lanham • Boulder • New York • Toronto • Plymouth, UK

Copyright © 2008 by
University Press of America,® Inc.
4501 Forbes Boulevard
Suite 200
Lanham, Maryland 20706
UPA Acquisitions Department (301) 459-3366

Estover Road
Plymouth PL6 7PY
United Kingdom

Library of Congress Control Number: 2008922660
ISBN-13: 978-0-7618-4030-5 (paperback : alk. paper)
ISBN-10: 0-7618-4030-3 (paperback : alk. paper)

This book is dedicated to:
Joan T. Gilbert and Daniel R. Gilbert, Sr., my parents,
R. Edward Freeman, my teacher,
and Kate Rogers, my wife, my best friend, and my teaching colleague.

Contents

Preface

One of the privileges and pleasures of writing a book is naming the origins of the work. It is a privilege to claim that there is a coherent pathway that runs from origins to a published work. It is a pleasure to acknowledge companions who were present along the way. It is my privilege to name three origins of *Wins, Losses, and Human Ties*. It is my pleasure to dedicate this book to four persons in whose company I worked out a line of thinking that became this book. This book is dedicated to: Joan T. Gilbert and Daniel R. Gilbert, Sr., my parents; R. Edward Freeman, my teacher; and Kate Rogers, my wife, my best friend, and my teaching colleague.

One origin of this work was my good fortune to grow up in the Moravian College community in Bethlehem, Pennsylvania. I have my parents to thank for their decision to join that community in the early 1950s. In my grade-school years, I came to associate a college with visitors and visitation. Visitors to Moravian in those years included lecturers, performing arts groups, foreign dignitaries, a Presidential candidate (John F. Kennedy), and athletes and coaches who represented other colleges. (Later, I had the good fortune to be one of those visiting intercollegiate athletes.) This book is anchored in an idea that I can trace to those years in the Moravian College community: colleges are places where human beings, and their distinctive projects, come together in the joint act of visitation.

A second origin of this work is the liberal education that has both enabled and empowered me to keep asking questions about the world. I launched my liberal education at Dickinson College in Carlisle, Pennsylvania. That education received an enormous boost when I began working with R. Edward Freeman in my doctoral studies at the University of Minnesota. Ed introduced me to the thrill of formulating questions.

A decade into my life work as a teacher, I realized that I was working out questions that linked ethics, competition, and civil society. (I was reflecting at the same time on my intercollegiate basketball career.) In this time, Kate Rogers and I became life partners. I have been inspired by Kate's life work as a teacher and by the life of liberal education that she leads. She and Ed Freeman taught me that liberal education is a life of asking questions that come from living fully engaged in the world. Donald Hall (in *Life Work*) calls this a life of *absorbedness*. Kate and Ed are exemplars.

A third origin of this book is anchored in fifteen pairs of numbers: 73-47; 72-51; 73-43; 89-42; 60-40; 76-36; 73-47; 62-60; 69-54; 57-51; 84-49; 71-45; 42-30; 74-55; 57-39. These pairs of numbers are the final scores of the first fifteen games in which I played as a member of the Nitschmann Junior High School varsity basketball team in the mid-1960s. In each pair, the second number was the (lesser) Nitschmann point total. My basketball career began with a fifteen-game losing streak.

What do I recall about that losing streak? I was thrilled to wear a basketball uniform. I was thrilled to run on the hardwood floors in four distinctive gymnasiums and to see point totals illuminated on a scoreboard. I was thrilled to see my last name in the Nitschmann scorebook, preceded by my uniform number (5) and the abbreviation "F" for my position (Forward). I had already begun watching the "big boys" at Moravian College engage in basketball competition with their counterparts from Albright College, Elizabethtown College, Lebanon Valley College, and the University of Scranton, among others. Now I was playing the game!

I recall sensing, even then, that something connective was underway. In our twelve-game, junior high school basketball season, I quickly came to know my peers clad in the school colors of the Broughal, Northeast, and Washington teams. Three games into our ninth-grade season, my second varsity season, I had reunited with numerous acquaintances from the year before.

Years later, I marvel at connective experiences in my playing career. Three top the list. In eighth grade, Dan Woodard and I embarked on a playing relationship that spanned three sports and nine years, concluding in an intercollegiate basketball game in 1974. As "jayvee" basketball players in tenth grade, Al Sincavage and I embarked on a basketball playing relationship that spanned seven years, concluding in an intercollegiate basketball game at Muhlenberg College (his team) in 1974. In March, 1968, Danny Joseph and I embarked on a basketball playing relationship that spanned five high school and college seasons. In the final season, he wore the Moravian College colors. If not for a shoulder injury (mine) one week earlier, he and I would have met for a sixth year in a February, 1973, game in Bethlehem. Danny's name appears in this book, for his football accomplishments.

These are recollections about persons, places, relationships, and the game. These are the building blocks of *wins, losses, and human ties*. Coming full circle, I am grateful that my parents encouraged my athletic interests, entrusted no small part of my worldly education to my coaches, and drove many miles to witness that unfolding education.

Daniel R. Gilbert, Jr.
Gettysburg, Pennsylvania, December, 2007

Acknowledgments

Librarians have been enormously helpful in my research for this book. At the top of the list is Mary Johnston at the National Collegiate Athletic Association (NCAA) Library in Indianapolis. Mary was generous with her time, experience, and advice. Lisa Greer Douglass found work space for me on my numerous visits to the NCAA Library. I can always say that I once joined NCAA staff members in seeking shelter during a tornado warning.

Janelle Wertzberger, Musselman Library at Gettysburg College, pointed me in the direction of the National Climatic Data Center in Asheville, North Carolina. I am grateful to Bethlehem (Pennsylvania) Public Library staff members who patiently retrieved microfilm that contained thirty-plus years of the *Bethlehem Globe-Times* newspaper, and who kept the microfilm readers in working condition. Staff members at the Allentown (Pennsylvania) Public Library helped me find microfilm containing forty-plus years of the *Morning Call* newspaper.

At the National Climatic Data Center, Scott Stephens and Jan Carpenter pointed me to National Weather Service historical data and processed my orders for that data.

Scrapbooks assembled by Clifford Koch, longtime Sports Information Director at Moravian College in Bethlehem, Pennsylvania, were invaluable. These materials are held in the Reeves Library at Moravian. I am grateful that my father, Dr. Daniel R. Gilbert, Sr., while serving as the Moravian College Archivist, brought Cliff's materials to my attention.

I am pleased to acknowledge the influence of those with whom I have conversed about competition, ethics, and intercollegiate athletics. My brother Chris Gilbert has been a long-running conversation partner on these subjects. Chris is one of numerous former intercollegiate athletes who have shared their recollections: Rick Falk, Karl Gilbert, Steven Gimbel, Rick Hartzell, Tom Ilgen, Peter Johnson, Jeff Martinson, William Parker, George Petrie, Julienne Simpson, Barry Streeter, Andy Wicks, and Dave Wright (listed alphabetically).

My conversations with numerous coaches helped sharpen my thinking about competition relationships: John Campo, Terry Conrad, Carl Danzig, Gene Evans, Sid Jamieson, Glenn Robinson, Paul Seybold, and Michael Simpson. Others with whom I have enjoyed discussions on these subjects include: Michael Birkner, Daniel Butin, Douglas Candland, Gerry Commerford, Daniel DeNicola, R. Edward Freeman, Gordon Meyer, Kate Rogers, William Rosenbach, Tim Sweeney, Baird Tipson, and Steve Ulrich.

I am also grateful to John Feinstein, a man whom I have never met. Feinstein has created a narrative in which he portrays competitors as partners working through complex relationships. I drew inspiration and encouragement to write this book after reading and teaching Feinstein's work about intercollegiate athletic competition, most notably *A Civil War: Army vs. Navy*.

I am likewise grateful to John Edgar Wideman (*Hoop Roots*) and Pat Conroy (*My Losing Season*) for their portrayals of basketball players immersed in human ties with their competitors. I reflected a great deal on my own intercollegiate basketball career to develop the central themes of this book. I drew inspiration from Wideman's reflections on the blank pages in a basketball scorebook and from Conroy's assertion that an athlete learns more from the experience of losing than from winning. I have met neither Conroy nor Wideman. Still, I want to count them, along with Feinstein, as partners in a conversation about wins, losses, and human ties.

In the end, I alone am responsible for any errors that remain in the book. There are places where the data is thinner than I would have liked. Still, the data is here in sufficient quantity and variety to demonstrate the points that I want to make about intercollegiate athletic competition. The search for this data, and the interpretation of it, has been an enormous pleasure.

I acknowledge the following assistance in my use of copyrighted materials.

Moravian College granted me permission to cite photographic material published in *Benigna*, the Moravian yearbook, annually from 1958 through 2007, and to cite sports information material that appears online at the Moravian College Athletics web site. Copyright, Moravian College. I thank Dennis A. Domchek for processing this permission.

Muhlenberg College in Allentown, Pennsylvania, granted me permission to cite photographic material published in *Ciarla*, the Muhlenberg yearbook, from 1958 through 2002. Copyright, Muhlenberg College. I thank Michael Bruckner for processing this permission.

The National Collegiate Athletic Association granted me permission to reprint intercollegiate football schedules that appeared in *The Official National Collegiate Athletic Association Football Guide* (and variations on this name) in 1947 and annually from 1957 through 2001. Copyright, National Collegiate Athletic Association, 2007. All rights reserved. I thank Ellen Summers and Diane Young for processing this permission.

The *Morning Call*, published in Allentown, Pennsylvania, granted me permission to cite copyrighted material (Copyright, *Morning Call*) published in selected editions from 1958 through 2006. I thank Betty Kern for processing this permission.

I am grateful to Jim Deegan, Managing Editor at the *Express-Times*, published in Easton, Pennsylvania, for facilitating my use of copyrighted material published in the *Bethlehem Globe-Times* from 1958 through 1990 and the *Express-Times* from 1991 through 2006 (Copyright, *Express-Times*).

Meteorological data obtained from the National Climatic Data Center (NCDC), part of the National Oceanic and Atmospheric Administration, is in the public domain. Nonetheless, I am pleased to honor the NCDC request that I acknowledge their assistance.

Introduction

This book is about the competitive relationship involving the men who represented Moravian College (Bethlehem, Pennsylvania) and the men who represented Muhlenberg College (Allentown, Pennsylvania) in intercollegiate varsity football competition between 1958 and 2006. Over this span of forty-nine years, Moravian football team members and Muhlenberg football team members were scheduled to meet every year. Each Moravian-and-Muhlenberg football game was scheduled for a Saturday afternoon in November. On forty-eight of those Saturdays, the scheduled game was played. On the other Saturday, the members of the Moravian team and the members of Muhlenberg team did not assemble on the playing field. That Saturday was November 23, 1963. Representatives of Moravian College and Muhlenberg College agreed that it was inappropriate to honor the agreement to play that year's scheduled football game, in view of events on the previous day in Dallas, Texas.

This book is an expression of my passion for teaching and my passion for intercollegiate athletic competition. Accordingly, the book contains a set of teachings about intercollegiate athletic competition and a compilation of detailed information about the Moravian-and-Muhlenberg football playing relationship. My purpose in writing this book is to encourage you to attach new meaning to the experience of intercollegiate athletic competition, meaning that is centered in the relationships among the competitors. I argue that the parties responsible for sustaining the Moravian-and-Muhlenberg football relationship have joined in a remarkable ethical accomplishment.

The Moravian-and-Muhlenberg football playing relationship inspired me, beginning in my grade-school years, to imagine joining teammates and competitors in the experience of intercollegiate athletic competition. A decade later, I had the good fortune to experience a four-year, intercollegiate basketball playing career. Years later, the Moravian-and-Muhlenberg football playing relationship inspired me to imagine and then to experience teaching college students about competition as a thoroughly collaborative human experience.

I wish you a comparable prospect of inspiration and of journey into new projects.

FOUR PROPOSITIONS ABOUT INTERCOLLEGIATE ATHLETIC COMPETITION

Writing this book as a teacher first, I develop four propositions about intercollegiate athletic competition as an experience shared by competitors. Writing this book as a student of intercollegiate athletics, I develop these points by digging into statistical reports about what happened on the field of play when the men who represented the Moravian and Muhlenberg football teams, respectively, joined to play a football game. Accordingly, the book consists of four concurrent story lines about the Moravian-and-Muhlenberg football playing relationship from 1958 through 2006.

Since I write as a teacher, not as a sportswriter, these four story lines will not look exactly like what is customarily reported in the newspaper (and now online) about an intercollegiate football game. Still, I write this book with the sports fan in mind. Thus, you readers who thirst for the facts about a football game can rest assured that pertinent game statistics are provided in ample supply. Similarly, for you readers who thirst for the chronological record of a football rivalry, I accommodate that need, too.

For each year in the Moravian-and-Muhlenberg football playing relationship, I work with a standard compilation of game statistics.[1] The compilation includes team statistics and the line score, a quarter-by-quarter depiction of team scoring. Table Intro.1 contains this information for the 1965 Moravian-and-Muhlenberg football game.

Table Intro.1.   Team Statistics and Line Score for 1965 Game

1965	Moravian	Muhlenberg
First downs	17	11
Yards rushing	205	13
Yards passing	70	170
Passes completed-attempted	5-13	16-36
Pass attempts intercepted	0	3
Fumbles lost	2	0
Punts	6	6
Yards penalized	75	15

Moravian	7	3	0	7	—17
Muhlenberg	0	0	0	8	—8

ONE PROPOSITION

One proposition that I develop in this book is that intercollegiate athletic competition unfolds as an enduring relationship that is shared and shaped jointly by the human beings who participate as competitors. Competitors achieve their relationship through acts of visitation. In their visitation, competitors come together in ways that preserve their different approaches to playing the game.[2]

This is a point about what human beings accomplish together even though their interests are, in one respect, sharply at odds.[3] Competitors seek an outcome (a victory in a football game) that some of them will not be able to attain. I signaled my intention to develop this story line about collaboration through visitation in the very first paragraph. The hyphenated reference to "Moravian-and-Muhlenberg" is deliberate.[4]

I develop this proposition in Chapter 1. The excerpt below is a sneak preview. In it, I translate a section of the 1965 game statistics into a narrative about competitors bringing their distinctive projects, including uniform styles, onto the field of play.

They Visited in 1965

Moravian Coach Rocco Calvo, RBs Hank Nehilla and Brian Parry, and their teammates visited with Muhlenberg Coach Ray Whispell, QB Ron Henry, receiver Charlie Woginrich, and their teammates at Muhlenberg Field on November 20, 1965.

Nehilla and his teammates dressed for the occasion in blue jerseys, white pants trimmed with a blue stripe, and knee-length blue socks under white crew socks. The white Moravian helmet had two blue stripes and numerals. Henry and his teammates dressed for the occasion in white jerseys, white pants, and white knee-length socks with three cardinal stripes. The new Muhlenberg jersey had numbers on both upper arms and a cardinal cuff at the elbow. The Muhlenberg helmet was cardinal with the white swath.

Moravian rushers gained 205 yards. Muhlenberg rushers gained 13 yards. These totals are shown in Table Intro.1. Nehilla of Moravian was the center of attention in the rushing game. He met Muhlenberg tacklers on 42 occasions. Nehilla gained 124 yards in those encounters and scored one rushing touchdown.

The two teams scored three touchdowns, creating three extra-point opportunities.

Moravian—Shipley 30 run with blocked punt (Parry kick)
Moravian—Parry 22 FG
Muhlenberg—Woginrich 41 pass from Henry (Henry run)

Moravian—Nehilla 3 run (Parry kick)

Twice, Moravian Coach Calvo elected a "point after touchdown" (PAT) attempt. Both attempts by Parry were successful. After the Muhlenberg touchdown, Whispell elected a two-point conversion attempt. Henry rushed for the two points. In the second quarter, Calvo called on Parry to attempt a 22-yard field goal. The kick was successful for 3 Moravian points.

An Ethic

This is an excerpt from a story line about human beings who do something together on the field of football competition in one another's company. Moreover, it is an example of human beings practicing an ethic of tolerance of one another's projects.

SECOND PROPOSITION

A second proposition in this book is that any particular intercollegiate athletic competition lasts only if human beings periodically commit to sustaining their playing relationship. The endurance of a competitive playing relationship is not a given. Competitors are always going in different directions. It takes mutual agreement to continue an intercollegiate athletic playing relationship from year to year.[5] Sometimes, this makes mutual agreement an extraordinary accomplishment. A story line about reaffirmed agreements is plain to see in the Moravian-and-Muhlenberg relationship.

I develop this story line in Chapter 2. The excerpt below is a sneak preview. In the excerpt, I expand upon the final score of the 1965 game to create a narrative about the lengths to which the Moravian team and the Muhlenberg team went to meet on November 20, 1965.

They Sought One Another

On November 20, 1965, Calvo and members of the Moravian 1965 football team traveled ten miles from Bethlehem to Allentown and the Muhlenberg campus. There they met Whispell and members of the Muhlenberg 1965 team. Together, the two teams played to a 17-8 Moravian win and Muhlenberg loss. Together, these persons deserve credit for traversing a boundary that separated two leagues and two circles of competitors.

Moravian belonged to the Middle Atlantic Conference Northern Division (MAC North) for the 1965 football season. Muhlenberg belonged to the Middle Atlantic Conference Southern Division (MAC South) for the 1965 season. The capitalized entries in the Moravian schedule indicate other members of

Table Intro.2. Football Schedules for 1965

	Moravian 1965	Muhlenberg 1965
September 25	at Delaware Valley	DICKINSON*
October 2	at WILKES	at URSINUS*
October 9	at WAGNER	at PENNSYLVANIA MILITARY*
October 16	Pennsylvania Military	LEBANON VALLEY*
October 23	at Lebanon Valley	Wilkes
October 30	ALBRIGHT	at Upsala
November 6	UPSALA	Lycoming
November 13	JUNIATA	at FRANKLIN & MARSHALL*
November 20	at Muhlenberg	Moravian

the MAC North. The capitalized entries marked with an asterisk in the Muhlenberg schedule indicate other members of the MAC South. These schedules are shown in Table Intro.2.

The scheduling of this game enabled Calvo, Whispell and their respective team members to span jointly a boundary between the MAC North and MAC South and a boundary between a Moravian competition circle (with Delaware Valley and Pennsylvania Military College) and the Muhlenberg-and-Lycoming football relationship.

An Ethic

Here is a story line about competitors voluntarily creating an obligation to sustain a relationship. Neither team was obligated to schedule this game, because the Moravian and Muhlenberg football programs belonged to different leagues in 1965. Nonetheless, these competitors accepted an extra duty to find one another, reaching across a boundary between affiliations, for most of the years since the Moravian-and-Muhlenberg football relationship resumed in 1958.[6] This is a sneak preview of an ethical proposition about competitors taking extra steps to remain in one another's company.

THIRD PROPOSITION

A third proposition that I develop in this book is that competitors join in belonging to two places simultaneously. One place is their playing relationship. The second place is the natural setting, the football field and its surroundings, where they meet to play the game. With every play of a football game, competitors join to reaffirm their willful belonging to a place that they share in the world.

It is here that competitors experience an irony that is built into any inter-collegiate athletic competition. Athletes and coaches prepare diligently for competition, knowing full well that they are ignorant of the circumstances in which the game will actually be played.[7] One example is the weather on the day of a football game. Moravian-and-Muhlenberg football games are played in Pennsylvania in mid-November. This is a time of year when weather variations are considerable from week to week, and year to year.

I develop this story line in Chapter 3. The excerpt below is a sneak preview. In the excerpt, I translate a section of the 1965 game statistics into a narrative about passers and pass receivers moving through sun and shade, wind and rain, high pressure and low pressure, to create the artistry of (and the frequent failures in) the football passing game.[8]

They Passed Through the Weather

By the hour before sundown in Allentown on Saturday, November 20, 1965, skies were clear. The dew point held steady at 30 degrees. The temperature remained at 47. Air pressure was steady. Visibility was 13 miles. A "sun dog" was noted at 3:53 p.m.

As high clouds filtered the sunshine, Muhlenberg QB Ron Henry and Moravian QB John Petley used the pass differently. Henry filled the breezy (12 knots) air with 36 passes, completing 16 for 170 yards. (Table Intro.1) Petley threw 13 passes, completing 5 for 70 yards. In the fourth quarter, Henry connected with Charlie Woginrich on a 41-yard touchdown pass. On a subsequent touchdown drive, John Shipley caught a 28-yard Petley pass.

Shortly after sundown on November 20, 1965, skies were clear over Muhlenberg Field. The south wind eased to 8 knots. Air pressure fell to 29.88 inches in the evening.

An Ethic

Here is a story line about competitors belonging together to the natural space where they play the game, linked in their uncertainty about the natural conditions. It is a story about competitors practicing an ethic of imagination, seeking the perfect pass play, at the same time they practice an ethic of humility. With every forward pass, lofted into air and sky, these players hopefully and humbly reaffirm their belonging in this place.

FOURTH PROPOSITION

A fourth proposition in this book is that competitors jointly write their own unique chapter in the history of intercollegiate athletic competition as they play their game on a given day. By playing the game, competitors become co-authors. The text that they write is one part of an accumulating history of an intercollegiate athletic playing relationship, a story in which each competitor can claim a place.[9] The central point of Chapter 4 is that this achievement does not end with co-authorship of a particular game.

In the course of playing their game, competitors leave a unique story that others can use to assess their own participation in the playing relationship. Once they played the 1965 game to a conclusion, the Moravian team members and Muhlenberg team members had left a legacy that participants in the 1958 game, for example, could use to reflect on the football game that they had co-authored. So, too, participants in the 1975 and 1985 games could look to the 1965 game story to chart their accomplishments as football competitors.

In this book, I celebrate what two groups of men, the players and coaches for Moravian and Muhlenberg, respectively, together created each year on the field of play. These games were entertaining expressions of talent and strategy. These games were filled with surprises. The football games that I recount and interpret are narratives that belong to these men, who literally made these games their own, and that also belong to their heirs in the playing relationship.

I develop this story line in Chapter 4. The excerpt below is a sneak preview. In the excerpt, I translate a section of the 1965 game statistics into a narrative about defensive accomplishments, unusual plays, dramatic performances, and playing careers coming to a conclusion in the Moravian-and-Muhlenberg playing relationship.

They Left a Legacy

The Moravian defense and the Muhlenberg defense achieved a combined 17 changes of ball possession on November 20, 1965. Each defense forced 6 punts. Meanwhile, the Moravian offense, guided by John Petley, retained possession with 17 first downs, rushing for much of the necessary yardage. Team statistics are shown in the upper section of Table Intro.1.

Newcomers to the playing relationship in 1966 joined with returning players who helped create two precedents in the 1965 game at Muhlenberg Field. First, most of the penalty yardage (75 of 90) was assessed to Moravian. Second, the Muhlenberg offense rallied late in the game.

Earlier, Moravian led Muhlenberg by 7-0 at the end of the first quarter and by 10-0 at halftime. The line score is depicted in the lower section of Table Intro.1. The third quarter was scoreless. The scoring flow in the fourth quarter was:

Muhlenberg—Woginrich 41 pass from Henry (Henry run)
Moravian—Nehilla 3 run (Parry kick)

The Muhlenberg touchdown and two-point conversion cut the Moravian lead to 10-8. The Moravian touchdown drive and PAT kick squelched the Muhlenberg comeback.

In other ways, the 1965 chapter is available for all members of the playing relationship, before and since. The Moravian defense scored a touchdown when John Shipley blocked a punt and returned the ball 30 yards for a touchdown. "Special teams" accounted for all the first-half scoring. The field goal by Brian Parry of Moravian was the first in the modern Moravian-and-Muhlenberg football relationship. Unlike in previous years, Moravian rushing (205 yards) was nearly unstoppable, and Muhlenberg rushing was almost non-existent (13 yards) in the same game. Twice in the third quarter, the Muhlenberg defense stopped the Moravian offense inside the Muhlenberg 5-yard line. The 36 passing attempts by Ron Henry of Muhlenberg were the most thus far in the playing relationship since 1958.

The game marked the third straight year of change in the Moravian quarterback position. John Petley played in his only Moravian-and-Muhlenberg game in 1965.

Lastly, Petley and other players participating in their final Moravian-and-Muhlenberg game joined to conclude an era in the playing relationship: Charlie Woginrich of Muhlenberg scored a touchdown in each of three games.

One More Ethic

Here is a story line about human beings together creating a football game with their "signatures" affixed. The game played on November 20, 1965, was contested to the very end. The fourth-quarter drama was one part of what other participants in the Moravian-and-Muhlenberg playing relationship inherit from participants in the 1965 game. The 1965 co-authors thus accomplished an ethical act of leaving a legacy.

COMPETITION AND CIVIL SOCIETY

I weave these propositions into a depiction of competitors contributing jointly to American civil society. It is a story about civil society, because the characters are human beings routinely doing things together peaceably year after year, voluntarily honoring agreements of their own making. There is delicious irony in telling a story about civil society through the example of an intercollegiate football playing relationship. After all, we might not at first praise football players as agents of civil society, playing a game in which high-speed physical contact is routine. I provide four examples, the four chapters, of their collaborative civility.

There is a larger reason why I develop this ironic point. Many persons are pessimistic about American civil society. There is much complaint about decline in civic engagement. One image of such discontent is "bowling alone," a civic flaw that Robert Putnam names in a book. Pauline Vaillancourt Rosenau (*The Competition Paradigm*) fingers competition as a culprit in the erosion of civil society. Still others, James Shulman and William Bowen (*The Game of* Life) among them, argue that intercollegiate athletic competition has a corrosive influence on civic life on many American college campuses.

With this book, I raise my voice in response to such pessimism. There is another story to be told about American civil society. In tracing an ethical, historical record of the modern Moravian-and-Muhlenberg football playing relationship, I praise hundreds of human beings who have had a hand in strengthening American civil society. These human beings have accomplished this simply by going about their routine activities, playing football in the Moravian-and-Muhlenberg football relationship. They did so without much fanfare. In a context where wins and losses are counted, their accomplishments can be measured in their human ties.

This particular story of civic engagement has been unfolding for years on football fields in Bethlehem, Pennsylvania, and Allentown, Pennsylvania. This story unfolds all across the land. Each Saturday during the football regular season, more than two hundred intercollegiate football games are created by players and coaches. Every game marks an achievement of civic ties, human ties to be counted among the wins and losses.

If we can observe the participants in the Moravian-and-Muhlenberg football competition, and their contemporaries and ancestors, contributing to the fabric of American civil society, in what other unexpected places might we observe human beings working together to contribute to American civil society? Writing as a teacher and writing as someone who joined with competitors to play an intercollegiate sport, this is the larger question that I pose with *Wins, Losses, and Human Ties.*

NOTES

1. The data reported here and in Chapters 1 through 4 is drawn primarily from the *Allentown Morning Call*. I supplemented this extensive amount of data with selected data (twenty-two pieces, in all) from the *Bethlehem Globe-Times* and the *Express-Times*. The complete list of newspaper sources is in the Bibliography. For years since 1999, I added nine pieces of data from the official statistics reported online at moravian.edu/athletics/football.

2. An inspiration for this proposition comes from the writing of John Edgar Wideman. Wideman goes into considerable detail about the distinctive playing styles of his playground associates. John E. Wideman, *Hoop Roots: Playground Basketball, Love, and Race* (Boston: Houghton Mifflin, 2001), 46–49, 55, 172–79.

3. An inspiration for this point comes from the writings of sports journalist John Feinstein (*A March to Madness*, e.g.). Feinstein pioneered a nonfiction genre in which he takes readers inside competitive athletic relationships. Another inspiration comes from the writing of former intercollegiate basketball player Pat Conroy. In *My Losing Season*, his memoir about playing basketball for The Citadel, Conroy develops an account about men's college basketball as the game was played in the South in the 1960s.

4. The listing of the two colleges in this hyphenated form is merely alphabetical.

5. An inspiration for this proposition comes from what sports historian John Sayle Watterson writes about league formation in the history of intercollegiate football. John Sayle Watterson, *College Football: History, Spectacle, Controversy* (Baltimore, Md.: Johns Hopkins University Press, 2000), 241–59.

6. Throughout the book, I refer to the playing relationship that resumed in 1958 as the "modern" Moravian-and-Muhlenberg football playing relationship.

7. An inspiration for this proposition comes again from Wideman. Referring to the blank pages of a basketball scorebook, Wideman reflects on a pair of stark truths known to any intercollegiate athlete. At the outset of a competition, the line in the scorebook next to his or her name is blank. At the same time, the player has no idea what data will be entered on that line by the end of the game. Wideman, *Hoop Roots*, 51–52.

8. This data was collected by the National Weather Service at the Allentown-Bethlehem-Easton Airport. The airport is located 9 driving miles from Muhlenberg.

9. My inspiration here is once again Conroy's *My Losing Season*.

Chapter One

They Visited and Visited Again

Intercollegiate athletic competition begins when two parties agree to spend time in one another's company in the role of opponents. They visit. Soon after they join on the playing field, intercollegiate athletic competitors are doing something together. They move and respond to one another's moves, moving within the conventions of the game. Their time together is a visit. Then they conclude their time together. On another day, they might return to the playing field. In their time away, each competitor has changed. Back together again, they now move and respond as parties to a relationship. They visit anew in the present and in their growing togetherness.

I write this chapter to introduce a connection between intercollegiate athletic competition and the experience of wins, losses, and human ties. *Visit*, the verb and the noun, is the thread with which I make this connection. I use *visit*, the verb and the noun, to weave forty-nine scheduled visits in the modern Moravian-and-Muhlenberg football relationship into a narrative about athletic competitors jointly accomplishing both a resilient relationship and an ethic of tolerance.

ACTS OF VISITATION AND THE MODERN MORAVIAN-AND-MUHLENBERG FOOTBALL RELATIONSHIP

Visit is a versatile concept. *Visit*, the verb, is something that human beings do. *Visit*, the noun, is something that human beings experience. In both regards, *visit* draws our attention to human ties. Visit is something that human beings do together in one another's company. In this chapter, I use six connections between *visit*, the verb and the noun, and intercollegiate football competition to tell a story about the modern Moravian-and-Muhlenberg football relationship.

First, intercollegiate football competitors customarily meet on a playing field that is the "home" field for one of the teams. The members of one team travel, as guests, to that site to visit their hosts. *Visit*, the verb, signals that the competitors put some effort into establishing human ties. *Visit* encompasses the actions that guest and host agree to take.

It is common practice for football competitors to institutionalize these efforts in the practice known as "home-and-home" scheduling. In the modern Moravian-and-Muhlenberg football relationship, the two teams have engaged in this reciprocal act of *visit* from the very beginning. On November 22, 1958, the Muhlenberg team members traveled to the home field of the Moravian team members. On November 21, 1959, the Moravian team members traveled to the home field of the Muhlenberg team members. This reciprocal scheduling pattern has been in place ever since. In this chapter, I begin each episode in my narrative with a statement about guest and host joining to visit.

Second, intercollegiate football players enjoy the privilege of returning to the playing relationship multiple times. Under National Collegiate Athletic Association (NCAA) rules, for example, athletes are eligible to compete for four years. There is no such time limit for football coaches. In this context, *visit*, the verb, is an act of reuniting with members of other teams.

At the intersection of NCAA eligibility rules and home-and-home scheduling, the Moravian-and-Muhlenberg football relationship has long been a place where players and coaches visited and reunited. Since 1958, three men have coached Moravian teams and six men have coached Muhlenberg teams. Two pairs of head coaches revisited annually for more than a decade. In my narrative, I introduce an annual accounting of players and coaches who visit and revisit in the Moravian-and-Muhlenberg football relationship.[1]

Third, intercollegiate football competitors bring distinctive characteristics to the time that they spend together. Their joining on the field enhances their respective identities as competitors. *Visit*, the noun, refers to the space where each competitor can stake a claim to an identity. A *visit* is a display of difference. These differences are vivid in football uniform fashions. In intercollegiate football competition, the members of the opposing teams are identifiable by their uniform colors and designs. It is customary that the members of one team wear a uniform that displays comparatively more of their principal school color. This practice accentuates different approaches to the game.

In the modern Moravian-and-Muhlenberg football relationship since the 1969 game, it has been customary for the home team members to wear their more colorful football jersey and for members of the guest team to wear their less colorful (white) football jersey. Moravian school colors are blue and gray. Muhlenberg school colors are cardinal and gray. In the narrative of this chapter, each visit becomes a spectacle in which different colors and uniform designs, coupled with the convention about home jerseys, are evidence that the two teams maintain their distinctive identities as competitors.

Fourth, intercollegiate football competitors engage in certain recurring activities in every game. Their time together is a *visit* that is synonymous with these activities. Two such activities are commonplace. One is the act of rushing. Rushing is a central part of every football game *visit*. Certain members of each team take turns running ("rushing") with the ball until they fall down, are tackled, or cross a boundary line.

A second commonplace activity is placekicking. Placekicking is the act of kicking the ball, held in place by another player, in search of a "point after touchdown" (PAT, for short) or a three-point field goal. A PAT "place kick" is successful when the ball travels approximately 20 yards and clears a horizontal crossbar suspended ten feet off the ground. A successful field goal often covers a longer distance. The PAT is a strategic option. After a team scores a touchdown, it has the privilege of attempting to score an "extra point." The coach can elect to attempt a PAT kick for one point, or a try for two points by either rushing or passing the ball across the other team's goal line. In the narrative of this chapter, I provide an annual review of the rushing game and the kicking game in the modern Moravian-and-Muhlenberg football relationship. I use *visit*, the noun, to anchor intercollegiate football competition in a structure of routine activities. Within this structure, I interpret two more layers of human ties.

Fifth, intercollegiate football teams are always works-in-progress. This means that each *visit*, the noun, is unique. The lesson is vivid for players and coaches who return to a playing relationship. Even as the collective identity of a team remains more or less stable, team membership changes every year. Reasons for this include the four-year eligibility limit, career-ending injuries, and the annual arrival of new players. Players and coaches return to a playing relationship that they once knew, only to discover the presence of new participants. *Visit*, the noun, becomes a shared journey into the unknown for returnee and newcomer alike. In the narrative of this chapter, I name the prominent rushing and kicking performers. The names and the performance levels vary from year to year. With *visit*, the noun, I show that structured human ties are infused with unknowns.

Sixth, intercollegiate football competitors participate in something larger than their visit on a given day. Playing football within a structure of rules, conventions, and time-honored strategies, players and coaches create their version of football on their day together. When they first walk onto the field, the score is 0-0. Sixty minutes of playing time later, the players and coaches have created one more football game.[2] Together, players and coaches simultaneously preserve the game and create the game anew.[3] Their *visit*, the noun, is a civic project akin to family reunions and holiday celebrations. Each of these civic projects serves to solidify and to refresh human visitation and human ties.

In intercollegiate football, this meaning of *visit* is vivid in the kicking game. With the appearance of two innovations in the 1960s, competitors began testing a new strategy for the kicking game. One innovation was the soccer-style kicking technique. With this technique, longer and more accurate placekicking became routine. A second innovation was the artificial playing surface. Artificial turf contributed to surer footing and ball handling, particularly in wet weather. At the convergence of these innovations, some coaches opted for frequent placekicking attempts. How much would these innovations alter college football? By this sixth meaning of *visit*, this question is answered, game by game, in playing relationships such as Moravian-and-Muhlenberg football.

Visits Celebrated

I follow in the footsteps of observers who long ago noted that layers of *visit* were in place in the modern Moravian-and-Muhlenberg football relationship. Sports journalists began using *rivalry* to describe the annual renewal of the game. In 1965, still early in the renewed playing relationship, one journalist elicited this acknowledgment from one of the head coaches:[4]

> "By far it was one of the best games we've ever played against each other." Those were the words of Ray Whispell, head football coach at Muhlenberg as he met Moravian Coach Rocco Calvo at midfield after the Greyhounds stung the Mules, 17-8.

Forty-one years later, a journalist quoted a Moravian player about the importance of the game:[5]

> "What inspired us was [playing] Muhlenberg, of course. The seniors were playing their last game and even the younger players played better."

In this chapter, I celebrate something "best" and inspirational in each act of visitation in the modern Moravian-and-Muhlenberg football relationship. *Visit*, the verb and the noun, makes possible this connection between football competition and human ties.

THE ETHICAL ACCOMPLISHMENT

Forty-eight wins and forty-eight losses after the opening kickoff of the 1958 Moravian-and-Muhlenberg football game, the distinctive identities of the two teams have been preserved in layers of visits.[6] The human beings who visited over the years are joined in an achievement of diversity. In visiting, they created room for one another's individuality in their shared place. They are joined as participants in an ongoing ethical act of tolerance. Over forty-nine years, the two teams and their members have had room to be themselves, in the uniforms that they wore, in the rushing strategies that they used, and in the kicking strategies that they elected. They did this voluntarily, as private citizens, without the direction of a central authority. This is an impressive story about civil society as a place where different human beings can get along with one another.

Some observers might struggle to accept a claim that intercollegiate football competition is a place where an ethic of tolerance is routinely practiced. Football involves physical collision. Football strategy legitimates the act of impeding the progress of human beings who are called "opponents." Golf and cross-country, for example, might sooner come to mind as athletic competitions worthy of celebration as acts of civility among human beings whose interests are opposed. Anticipating such skepticism, I present here an ethical, historical narrative, forty-nine episodes in all, about an ethical accomplishment of tolerance in a football playing relationship.

Data and the Narrative

I begin this narrative about the modern Moravian-and-Muhlenberg football relationship by reporting two sets of data that are customarily reported about every college football game: rushing yardage totals; and the summary of scoring plays. For each Moravian-and-Muhlenberg game, I report this data and then proceed to report the names of coaches, principal performers who scored in each game, principal rushing performers, and the placekickers who attempted to score (or "convert") one point on a PAT kick and to score 3-point field goals. For each game after the 1958 game, I note reunions among principal performers who met in prior games.

Having attached names to the raw statistical data of football, I then describe the football uniforms worn by Moravian players and Muhlenberg players. Uniform styles are the principal data with which I argue that this playing relationship has long been a place where human beings have been tied in their tolerance. The point about tolerance is reinforced with data about changes in uniform styles. These changes have been annual events in Moravian-and-Muhlenberg football.

Finally, I group these forty-nine episodes into periods in which the kicking game was used more and less often, and more and less capably. I interpret a theme of *cautious adaptation* to describe placekicking in the forty-eight Moravian-and-Muhlenberg games played from 1958 through 2006. Unlike in "big time" college football, placekicking has occupied a lesser place in Moravian-and-Muhlenberg football. Soccer-style kicking and artificial turf eventually arrived. Still, the longest field goal (42 yards) was recorded in the 1981 game. Never have there been three field goals in one game. The kicking game jointly created by Moravian and Muhlenberg coaches and players in the 2000s is much like the 1970s kicking game, I conclude.

A Word to Readers

There is repetition and redundancy in the narrative that follows. This is necessary. This chapter is an introduction to a different way of talking about intercollegiate athletic competition. It takes practice to talk in new ways. In this chapter, there are forty-nine opportunities, the forty-nine games scheduled, to practice connecting intercollegiate athletics and ethics through the efforts that competitors make to tolerate one another's differences. Be patient as you read. Immerse yourself in this new way of talking. Midway through the chapter, I streamline the narrative. By then, the changes will likely escape your detection.

THE TWO-POINT CONVERSION IS THE PREFERRED OPTION, 1958-1965

The kicking game is now so commonplace in college football that it is difficult to imagine a time when the game was played differently. The early history of the modern Moravian-and-Muhlenberg football relationship will thus appeal to active imaginations. In the first three years of the relationship, only one PAT kick was successful. Through the 1964 game, the two teams combined for twelve two-point conversions and only five PAT kicks. No one kicked a PAT successfully for a Moravian team until the 1965 game. In that same game, the first field goal was kicked. That kick carried 22 yards, only two yards longer than the customary distance of a PAT kick. It was not until 1972 that the second field goal was kicked in a Moravian-and-Muhlenberg football game.

This sporadic and unproductive use of the kicking game came at a time when college football news headlines were increasingly filled with the names of soccer-style kickers such as the Gogolak brothers.[7] There were several reasons why the kicking game came slowly to the Moravian-and-Muhlenberg football relationship. One of the puzzles faced jointly by Muhlenberg Coach Ray Whispell and Moravian Coach Rocco Calvo was where to find competent kickers. In those years, it was rare that a kicking specialist would develop at the high school level. Some coaches turned to their best athletes, usually quarterbacks, to do double duty (even triple duty) and handle the placekicking chores. Whispell employed this strategy through the 1963 game. Some coaches turned to their heavier players, usually linemen and fullbacks, to do the kicking, on the premise that those men could combine their heft and the traditional straight-ahead kicking technique to boot the ball at least 20 yards for a PAT.[8] Calvo used this strategy through the 1967 game.

There were other factors contributing to the kicking puzzle in these early years. College football substitution rules were quite restrictive. The "unlimited substitution" era had not begun. Coaches could not afford to allocate a substitution to a kicking specialist. Team rosters were often small. Only 20 Moravian players took part in the 1958 game, for example. In the 2006 game, that many players took part for each team in the first two plays of the game, the opening kickoff and the first play from scrimmage!

This opening section of my narrative covers the first seven games in the modern Moravian-and-Muhlenberg football relationship. Each game is interpreted with the layers of *visit* that I introduced above. I connect these seven games with a theme of periodic use and erratic performance in the kicking game. Whispell and Calvo and their respective players were at work, using the opportunities available to them, to take their place in defining the college kicking game. As the kicking game was becoming established on the national scene, the opposite was happening in this particular intercollegiate football playing relationship.

In 1958, At Moravian Field

Muhlenberg Coach Ray Whispell, quarterback (QB) Ralph Borneman, running back (RB) Herb Owens, end Bob Pearsons, and their teammates visited with Moravian Coach Rocco Calvo, QB Tony Matz, RBs George Hollendersky and Dave Coe, and their teammates at Moravian Field on Saturday, November 22, 1958.

Borneman and his Muhlenberg teammates dressed for the occasion in white jerseys, white football pants, and white, knee-length socks.[9] Cardinal stripes were prominent on the Muhlenberg 1958 uniform. Two stripes circled each shoulder, and three circled the socks. Matz and his Moravian teammates dressed for the occasion in dark blue jerseys, white football pants, and white crew socks.[10] A blue stripe ran the length of each pant leg.[11] On the white Moravian football helmet, a single blue stripe ran from front to back. Borneman and his teammates wore all-cardinal helmets with numerals placed on each side.[12]

Muhlenberg rushers gained 74 yards in the game. Moravian rushers gained 164 yards. Hollendersky of Moravian was the center of attention in the rushing game. He met Muhlenberg tacklers 28 times, gaining 104 yards in those encounters. Hollendersky scored two rushing touchdowns. One of Borneman's rushes ended badly for Muhlenberg. He was tackled in his own end zone for a two-point Moravian safety.

During their visit that afternoon, the two teams scored seven touchdowns and thus created seven extra-point opportunities. (Extra-point results are indicated in parentheses.)

Moravian—Olson 8 pass from Matz (run failed)

Moravian—Hollendersky 7 run (Coe pass from Matz)

Muhlenberg—Yost 82 kickoff return (Pearsons pass from Owens)

Muhlenberg—Pearsons 10 pass from Borneman (kick failed)

Moravian—Olson 64 pass interception (Hollendersky run)

Muhlenberg—Wargo 4 run (run failed)

Moravian—Safety, Borneman tackled in end zone

Moravian—Hollendersky 1 run (pass failed)

For one of the Muhlenberg three extra-point occasions, Coach Whispell elected a PAT attempt. The Muhlenberg placekicker was Borneman. His kick failed. On another extra-point attempt, Owens completed a pass to Pearsons for two points. For all four Moravian extra-point attempts, Coach Calvo elected a two-point conversion attempt. On the second one, Matz completed a pass to Coe for the two points. Hollendersky ran for two points after the next Moravian touchdown.

In 1959, At Muhlenberg Field

Moravian Coach Calvo, RBs Dave Coe and Jeff Gannon, and their teammates visited with Muhlenberg Coach Whispell, RBs Herb Owens and Ed Yost, and their teammates at Muhlenberg Field on November 21, 1959. Their visit marked a reunion of 1958 game participants, when Coe, Owens, and Yost each took part in a scoring play.

Coe and his teammates dressed for the occasion in blue jerseys, white football pants with a blue stripe, and white knee-length socks. A blue stripe adorned the white Moravian helmet. The 1959 Moravian uniform included three blue stripes on the socks. Owens and his teammates dressed for the occasion in white jerseys with two shoulder stripes, white football pants, and white, knee-length socks with three stripes. The stripes were cardinal. The all-cardinal Muhlenberg helmet was redesigned with a broad, white swath running from front to back.

Moravian rushers gained 82 yards in the game. Muhlenberg rushers gained 315 yards. Yost and Owens of Muhlenberg were the center of attention in the rushing game. Yost and Owens met Moravian tacklers on 31 occasions. Yost gained 114 yards in those encounters and scored one rushing touchdown. Owens gained 113 yards.

During their visit that afternoon, the two teams scored four touchdowns and thus created four extra-point opportunities.

Muhlenberg—Dymond 5 run (pass failed)

Moravian—Coe 1 run (Coe pass from Gannon)

Muhlenberg—Owens 71 pass from Houseknecht (run failed)

Muhlenberg—Yost 1 plunge (Owens run)[13]

No PAT kicks were attempted. After the Moravian touchdown, Coe caught a pass from Gannon for the two extra points. On the third Muhlenberg extra-point try, Owens rushed for two points.

In 1960, At Moravian Field

Muhlenberg Coach Whispell, QB Rollie Houseknecht, RB Ed Yost, end Bob Butz, and their teammates visited with Moravian Coach Calvo, RBs Dave Coe and Jim Kelyman and Dick Ritter, QB Andy Semmel, end Jim Kritis, and their teammates at Moravian Field on November 19, 1960. Their visit marked a reunion of 1959 game participants, when Coe, Houseknecht, and Yost each took part in a scoring play and when each, along with Semmel and Kritis, played on both offense and defense.

Houseknecht and his Muhlenberg teammates dressed for the occasion in cardinal jerseys, white football pants, cardinal jersey, white pants, and white knee-length socks. On the sleeves was a white, three-stripe pattern, two narrow ones flanking a broad stripe. The Muhlenberg helmet was cardinal with a white swath. Coe and his teammates dressed for the occasion in white jerseys and white pants with a blue stripe. The white crew socks worn by the Moravian players stood apart from the knee-length socks with three cardinal stripes worn by the Muhlenberg players. The white Moravian helmet had a blue stripe.

Muhlenberg rushers gained 314 yards. Moravian rushers gained 144 yards. Yost of Muhlenberg was again at the center of attention in the rushing game. He was joined by Coe of Moravian. Yost and Moravian tacklers met on 17 occasions. He gained 75 yards there and scored two rushing touchdowns. Moravian rusher Coe gained 70 yards in 9 carries.

During their visit that afternoon, the two teams scored seven touchdowns and thus created seven extra-point opportunities.

Muhlenberg—Wolfe 24 run (Houseknecht kick)
Muhlenberg—Kuntzleman 10 pass from Houseknecht (kick failed)
Muhlenberg—Yost 9 run (run failed)
Moravian—Insinga 33 pass from Semmel (Kritis pass from Semmel)
Muhlenberg—Yost 3 run (Butz pass from Houseknecht)
Muhlenberg—Houseknecht 1 plunge (pass failed)
Moravian—Coe 3 plunge (Kelyman pass from Ritter)

Twice, Muhlenberg Coach Whispell elected a PAT attempt. Houseknecht was the Muhlenberg kicker.[14] He succeeded on the first try and missed on the second. Later, Butz caught a two-point pass from Houseknecht. Both Moravian two-point attempts succeeded. Semmel passed to Kritis, and Ritter passed to Kelyman.

In 1961, At Muhlenberg Field

Moravian Coach Calvo, QB Andy Semmel, and his teammates visited with Muhlenberg Coach Whispell, QB Rollie Houseknecht, RB Charlie Kuntzleman, and their teammates at Muhlenberg Field on November 18, 1961. Their visit was a reunion from 1960, when Semmel, Houseknecht, and Kuntzleman each took part in a scoring play.

Semmel and his teammates dressed for the occasion in blue jerseys, white pants with a blue stripe, and knee-length blue socks underneath white crew socks. The white Moravian helmet bore a blue stripe. Houseknecht and his teammates dressed for the occasion in cardinal helmets topped by a white swath. They wore white jerseys, pants (with one stripe), and knee-length socks, all trimmed in cardinal. Two stripes circled the shoulders. Three cardinal stripes encircled the knee-length white socks.

Moravian rushers gained 164 yards. Muhlenberg rushers gained 173 yards. Kuntzleman of Muhlenberg was the center of attention in the rushing game. He met Moravian tacklers on 22 occasions. Kuntzleman gained 150 yards in those encounters and scored one rushing touchdown. He also returned a punt for a touchdown.

During their visit, the two teams scored six touchdowns and thus created six extra-point opportunities.

Muhlenberg—Houseknecht 1 run (Houseknecht kick)
Muhlenberg—Lowe 26 pass from Houseknecht (Houseknecht kick)
Muhlenberg—Kuntzleman 29 run (pass failed)

Muhlenberg—Donmoyer 1 run (pass failed)
Muhlenberg—Kuntzleman 55 punt return (Houseknecht kick)
Moravian—Riccardi 13 pass from Semmel (Semmel run)
Three times, Muhlenberg Coach Whispell elected a PAT attempt. House-knecht made all three PATs. After the Moravian touchdown, Semmel rushed for the two extra points.

In 1962, At Moravian Field

Muhlenberg Coach Whispell, QB Terry Haney, back Charlie Woginrich, and their teammates visited with Moravian Coach Calvo, QB Bob Mushrush, end Pat Mazza, RB Marc Morganstine, and their Moravian teammates at Moravian Field on November 17, 1962.

Haney and his teammates dressed for the occasion in cardinal jerseys, white pants, and white knee-length socks. On the sleeves was a white, three-stripe pattern, two narrow stripes flanking a broad one. The Muhlenberg helmet was cardinal with the white swath. Mushrush and his teammates dressed for the occasion in white helmets with a dark blue stripe.[15] Their jerseys and pants were white. Both teams wore white crew socks.

Muhlenberg rushers gained 66 yards. Moravian rushers gained 120 yards. The rushing game took a backseat to the passing game during this visit. The only rushing touchdown was a 1-yard run by Moravian rusher Morganstine.

The two teams scored six touchdowns and created six extra-point opportunities.

Muhlenberg—Brown 40 pass from Haney (kick blocked)
Muhlenberg—Woginrich 17 pass from Haney (pass failed)
Muhlenberg—Lowe 37 pass from Haney (pass failed)
Muhlenberg—Hiller 69 pass interception (Woginrich pass from Haney)
Moravian—Morganstine 1 plunge (P. Mazza pass from Mushrush)
Muhlenberg—Barlok 12 pass interception (pass failed)
Muhlenberg Coach Whispell elected one PAT attempt by Haney. The kick was blocked. Later, Haney passed to Woginrich for two points. Three other Muhlenberg two-point passes were unsuccessful. After the only Moravian touchdown, Calvo elected a two-point attempt. Mushrush passed to Mazza for the two points.

In 1963, A Cancelled Visit at Muhlenberg Field

Moravian Coach Calvo, QB Andy Semmel, and his teammates did not visit with Muhlenberg Coach Whispell, QB Terry Haney, back Charlie Woginrich, and their teammates at Muhlenberg Field on November 23, 1963. The game was cancelled. Their visit would have marked a reunion of 1962 participants, when Haney, Woginrich, Mushrush, and Mazza took part in scoring plays.

Their visit would have been memorable for a new contrast in uniform styles. Large numerals were added to the Moravian helmet for the 1963 season. Muhlenberg players wore two different jersey designs in 1963.[16] At times, they wore uniforms with double stripes over each shoulder. Muhlenberg players also wore a uniform with a three-stripe design on the sleeve.

In 1964, At Moravian Field

Muhlenberg Coach Whispell, QBs Terry Haney and Ron Henry, receiver Charlie Woginrich, receiver Dave Binder, RBs Lee Berry and Dave Brown, and their teammates visited with Moravian Coach Calvo, lineman Vince Seaman, and his teammates at Moravian Field on November 21, 1964.

Haney and his teammates dressed for the occasion in cardinal jersey, white pants, and white knee-length socks. The three-stripe pattern appeared on the sleeves. The Muhlenberg helmet was cardinal with the white swath. Seaman and his Moravian teammates dressed for the occasion in a new uniform design.[17] The white jersey had two blue stripes on each sleeve. A blue stripe returned to the white pants. Moravian players wore blue, knee-length socks under white crew socks. The white Moravian helmet was redesigned with two blue stripes and numerals.[18]

Muhlenberg rushers gained 141 yards. Moravian rushers gained 160 yards. Brown of Muhlenberg was the center of attention on one rushing play. He eluded Moravian tacklers for a 49-yard run from scrimmage in the fourth quarter.

The two teams scored four touchdowns and created four extra-point opportunities.

Muhlenberg—Woginrich 68 punt return (Berry kick)
Moravian—Todd 6 run (kick failed)
Muhlenberg—Capobianco 19 run (Binder pass from Henry)
Muhlenberg—Gould 10 run (pass failed)

Muhlenberg Coach Whispell elected one PAT attempt. Berry scored the point. Later, Henry completed a two-point conversion pass to Binder. After the Moravian touchdown, Calvo elected a PAT attempt. The kick by Seaman was unsuccessful.

In 1965, At Muhlenberg Field

Moravian Coach Calvo, RBs Hank Nehilla and Brian Parry, and their teammates visited with Muhlenberg Coach Whispell, QB Ron Henry, receiver

Charlie Woginrich, and their teammates at Muhlenberg Field on November 20, 1965.

Nehilla and his teammates dressed for the occasion in blue jerseys, white pants trimmed with a blue stripe, and knee-length blue socks under white crew socks. The white Moravian helmet had two blue stripes and numerals. Henry and his teammates dressed for the occasion in white jerseys, white pants, and white knee-length socks with three cardinal stripes. The new Muhlenberg jersey had numbers on both upper arms and a cardinal cuff at the elbow. The Muhlenberg helmet was cardinal with the white swath.

Moravian rushers gained 205 yards. Muhlenberg rushers gained 13 yards. Nehilla of Moravian was the center of attention in the rushing game. He met Muhlenberg tacklers on 42 occasions. Nehilla gained 124 yards in those encounters and scored one rushing touchdown.

The two teams scored three touchdowns, creating three extra-point opportunities.

Moravian—Shipley 30 run with blocked punt (Parry kick)

Moravian—Parry 22 FG

Muhlenberg—Woginrich 41 pass from Henry (Henry run)

Moravian—Nehilla 3 run (Parry kick)

Twice, Moravian Coach Calvo elected a PAT attempt. Both attempts by Parry were successful. After the Muhlenberg touchdown, Whispell elected a two-point conversion attempt. Henry rushed for the two points. In the second quarter, Calvo called on Parry to attempt a 22-yard field goal. The kick was successful for 3 Moravian points.

MULTIPLES OF SEVEN, 1966–1972

The final point total for a football team is one indicator of how well the kickers are doing. Multiples of seven (7, 14, 21, etc.) typically indicate that kickers routinely convert PAT opportunities. Combinations of sevens and three (10, 17, 24, etc.) are likely indicators that kickers succeed in their PAT kicks and in a field goal attempt.

There are exceptions, of course, to how much we can deduce from final scores. The final score in the 2004 game, for example, did not include six PATs. Still, starting with the 1966 game, the next seven Moravian-and-Muhlenberg football games were marked by frequent and accurate PAT kicking and by the second field goal. I leave it to the reader to deduce the final scores and the multiples of seven attributable to PATs.

In 1966, At Moravian Field

Muhlenberg Coach Whispell, RBs Dave Yoder and Lee Berry, and their team-mates visited with Moravian Coach Calvo, QB Greg Seifert, RB Hank Ne-hilla, lineman Norm Linker, and their teammates at Moravian Field on No-vember 19, 1966.

Yoder and his teammates dressed for the occasion in the new Muhlenberg white helmet with numerals. The cardinal helmet would not be seen again. Muhlenberg players wore cardinal jerseys, white pants, and white knee-length socks. Each sleeve had a white elbow cuff. Seifert and his teammates dressed for the occasion in white jerseys with two blue stripes on the upper arms and a blue pants stripe. The white Moravian helmet bore a double blue stripe and numerals. Seifert and his teammates wore blue, knee-length socks, trimmed with two white stripes, under white crew socks, in contrast to the familiar cardinal-striped knee-length socks worn by Yoder and his teammates.

Muhlenberg rushers gained 124 yards. Moravian rushers gained 266 yards. Yoder of Muhlenberg and Seifert and Nehilla of Moravian were the center of attention in the rushing game. Yoder and Moravian tacklers met 21 times. He gained 100 yards in those encounters. Seifert and Nehilla met Muhlenberg tacklers on 19 and 20 occasions, respectively. In those encounters, Seifert gained 119 yards rushing, and Nehilla gained 85 yards.

The two teams scored three touchdowns, creating three extra-point oppor-tunities.

Muhlenberg—Fischer 1 run (Berry kick)
Moravian—Eltringham 37 pass from Dietz (N. Linker kick)
Moravian—Horn fumble recovery in end zone (N. Linker kick)
After the Muhlenberg touchdown, Coach Whispell elected a PAT attempt. Berry kicked the extra point. Twice, Moravian Coach Calvo elected a PAT kick. Linker made both.

In 1967, At Muhlenberg Field

Moravian Coach Calvo, RB Hugh Gratz, lineman Norm Linker, and their teammates visited with Muhlenberg Coach Whispell, QB Ron Henry, and his teammates at Muhlenberg Field on November 18, 1967.

Gratz and his teammates dressed for the occasion in blue jerseys, white pants with a blue stripe, and knee-length blue socks encircled by two white stripes. For 1967, the image of a striding greyhound was added to the white Moravian helmet. Two blue stripes and numerals remained on the helmet. Henry and his teammates dressed for the occasion in white jerseys, pants, and knee-length socks. Three cardinal stripes encircled the knee-length white socks. The Muhlenberg helmet was white with numerals.

Moravian rushers gained 214 yards. Muhlenberg rushers gained 143 yards. Hugh Gratz of Moravian and Henry of Muhlenberg were the center of attention in the rushing game.[19] Hugh Gratz and Muhlenberg tacklers met 28 times. He gained 165 yards in those encounters and scored one rushing touchdown. Henry and Moravian tacklers met 20 times. He gained 55 yards in those encounters.

The two teams scored four touchdowns and created four extra-point opportunities.

Moravian—Gratz 2 run (Linker kick)

Moravian—Martinelli 65 pass from Dietz (kick failed)

Moravian—Wilson 2 run with blocked kick (kick failed)

Muhlenberg—Saeger 32 pass from Evans (DiPanni run)

Three times, Moravian Coach Calvo elected a PAT attempt. Linker converted only the first kick. The Muhlenberg two-point conversion attempt was successful.

In 1968, At Steel Field

Muhlenberg Coach Whispell, placekicker (PK) Tryg Kleppinger, and his teammates visited with Moravian Coach Calvo, RBs Jack Iannantuono and Glenn Overk, PK Jack Regan, and their teammates at Moravian's new Steel Field on November 23, 1968.

Kleppinger and his teammates dressed for the occasion in cardinal jerseys with white cuffs, white pants, and white knee-length socks. New in the Muhlenberg uniform were two cardinal stripes on the pants and two stripes, separated by gray, on the white helmet. Numerals reappeared on the helmet. Iannantuono and his teammates dressed for the occasion in white jerseys with blue cuffs and white pants newly designed with two blue stripes. The white Moravian crew socks stood apart from the knee-length socks with three cardinal stripes worn by Muhlenberg players. On the redesigned Moravian helmet, the letters MC replaced the greyhound image. The numerals had disappeared.

Muhlenberg rushers gained 96 yards. Moravian rushers gained 369 yards. Iannantuono and Overk of Moravian were the center of attention in the rushing game. Iannantuono and Muhlenberg tacklers met 21 times. He gained 190 yards in those encounters and scored two rushing touchdowns. Overk and Muhlenberg tacklers met 13 times. He gained 97 yards there.

The two teams scored nine touchdowns, creating nine extra-point opportunities.

Moravian—H. Gratz 2 run (Regan kick)
Muhlenberg—Gonzalez 1 run (Kleppinger kick)
Moravian—Iannantuono 35 run (Regan kick)
Moravian—H. Gratz 11 pass from Dietz (Regan kick)
Moravian—Iannantuono 60 run (kick failed)
Moravian—H. Gratz 5 run (Regan kick)
Muhlenberg—Gonzalez 3 run (Harding pass from Uhrich)
Moravian—Martinelli 24 pass from Dietz (Regan kick)
Moravian—Smith 3 run (run failed)

Six times, Moravian Coach Calvo elected a PAT attempt. Regan made 5 of 6 kicks. Muhlenberg Coach Whispell elected one PAT attempt. Kleppinger scored the point.

In 1969, At Muhlenberg Field

Moravian Coach Calvo, RBs Bob Smith, Jack Iannantuono, and Glenn Overk, PK Ed Schedler, and their teammates visited with Muhlenberg Coach Whispell, RB Leon Gonzalez, and his teammates at Muhlenberg Field on November 22, 1969. Their visit was a reunion from the 1968 game, when Iannantuono, Overk, Smith, and Gonzalez each took part in a scoring play.

Smith and his teammates dressed for the occasion in white jerseys with blue cuffs and white pants with two blue stripes. Moravian players wore knee-length blue socks, with two white stripes, under white crew socks. The white Moravian helmet was trimmed with two blue stripes. Gonzalez and his teammates dressed for the occasion in cardinal jersey with white cuffs, white pants with two cardinal stripes, and white knee-length socks. The three-stripe sock design was replaced with two stripes surrounding a gray stripe. On the white Muhlenberg helmet, gray appeared between the two cardinal stripes.

The 1969 football season was celebrated nationwide as the 100th anniversary of intercollegiate football. To mark the occasion, an oval *100* decal appeared on the sides of the helmets. On the Muhlenberg helmet, the decal appeared above the cardinal numerals.

Moravian rushers gained 420 yards. Muhlenberg rushers gained 106 yards. Iannantuono and Overk of Moravian were again the center of attention in the rushing game. Iannantuono and Muhlenberg tacklers met 26 times. He gained 184 yards in those encounters and scored two rushing touchdowns. Overk and Muhlenberg tacklers met 12 times. He gained 118 yards in those encounters and scored one rushing touchdown.

The Moravian team scored six touchdowns, creating six extra-point opportunities.

Moravian—Iannantuono 1 run (run failed)
Moravian—Iannantuono 77 run (run failed)
Moravian—Smith 1 run (pass failed)
Moravian—H. Gratz 4 run (kick failed)
Moravian—Overk 42 run (run failed)
Moravian—Smith 31 run (Schedler kick)

Twice, Moravian Coach Calvo elected a PAT attempt. Schedler was 1-for-2 in his kicks. The Moravian offense converted none of their four two-point attempts.

In 1970, At Steel Field

New Muhlenberg Coach Frank Marino, QB Randy Uhrich, PK George Wheeler, and their teammates visited with Moravian Coach Calvo, RBs Jack Iannantuono and Wayne Marish, and their teammates at Steel Field on November 19, 1970. Their visit was a reunion from 1968, when Iannantuono and Uhrich each took part in a scoring play.

Uhrich and his teammates dressed for the occasion in white jerseys with cardinal cuffs and white pants with two cardinal stripes. The white Muhlenberg helmet was trimmed with numerals and gray between two cardinal stripes. Iannantuono and his teammates dressed for the occasion in blue jerseys with white cuffs, white pants with two blue stripes. Moravian players wore white helmets trimmed with two blue stripes and the letters MC on each side.[20] White crew socks completed the uniforms for both teams.

Muhlenberg rushers "gained" minus-2 yards. Moravian rushers gained 362 yards. Iannantuono of Moravian was again the center of attention in the rushing game, joined this time by Marish. Iannantuono and Muhlenberg tacklers met 26 times. He gained 134 yards in those encounters and scored two rushing touchdowns. Marish and Muhlenberg tacklers met 13 times. He gained 94 yards in those encounters and scored one rushing touchdown.

The two teams scored nine touchdowns, creating nine extra-point opportunities.

Moravian—Iannantuono 8 run (Marish kick)
Moravian—Roll 11 run (Marish kick)
Moravian—Gastmeyer 47 pass interception (kick failed)
Muhlenberg—C. Evans 35 pass from Uhrich (Wheeler kick)
Moravian—Marish 71 run (Marish kick)
Moravian—D. Joseph 9 pass from Dowling (Marish kick)
Moravian—Iannantuono 4 run (Marish kick)
Moravian—Martell 27 run (Marish kick)
Moravian—Youmans 1 run (Marish kick)

After all eight Moravian touchdowns, Coach Calvo elected a PAT attempt. Marish succeeded seven times. Wheeler converted the lone Muhlenberg PAT attempt.

In 1971, At Muhlenberg Field

Moravian Coach Calvo, QB Gary Martell, RB Wayne Marish, and their teammates visited with Muhlenberg Coach Marino, PK George Wheeler, and his teammates at Muhlenberg Field on November 20, 1971. Their visit marked a reunion from the 1970 game, when Martell, Marish, and Wheeler each took part in a scoring play.

Martell and his teammates dressed for the occasion in white jerseys with blue cuffs and white pants with two blue stripes. The white Moravian helmet had two blue stripes and the letters MC. Moravian players wore white crew socks. Wheeler and his teammates dressed for the occasion in cardinal jerseys with white cuffs, white pants with two cardinal stripes, and white knee-length socks with a gray stripe between two cardinal stripes. The white Muhlenberg helmet was trimmed with gray between cardinal stripes.

Moravian rushers gained 236 yards. Muhlenberg rushers gained 50. Martell of Moravian was the center of attention in the rushing game. He ran 15 times for 107 yards and a touchdown.

The two teams scored three touchdowns, creating three extra-point opportunities.

Muhlenberg—Dufford 41 pass interception (Wheeler kick)

Moravian—Marish 1 run (Marish kick)

Moravian—Martell 5 run (Marish kick)

After the lone Muhlenberg touchdown, Wheeler kicked the PAT. Moravian Coach Calvo elected two PAT attempts. Marish made both kicks.

In 1972, At Steel Field

Muhlenberg Coach Marino, PK Tryg Kleppinger, and his teammates visited with Moravian Coach Calvo, QB Gary Martell, lineman Jim Waradzyn, and their teammates at Steel Field on November 18, 1972.

Kleppinger and his teammates dressed for the occasion in white jerseys with cardinal cuffs and white pants with two cardinal stripes. On the white Muhlenberg helmet were numerals, two cardinal stripes, and gray between the stripes. Martell and his teammates dressed for the occasion in blue jerseys with white cuffs and white pants with two blue stripes. The greyhound returned to the white, two-striped Moravian helmet. Players on both teams wore white crew socks. The greyhound image disappeared from the Moravian helmet after 1972.

Muhlenberg rushers gained 2 yards. Moravian rushers gained 326 yards. Martell of Moravian was again the center of attention in the rushing game. He met Muhlenberg tacklers 15 times. Martell gained 75 yards in those encounters and scored a rushing touchdown.

The two teams combined for seven touchdowns and seven extra-point attempts.

Moravian—Waradzyn 28 FG
Moravian—Martell 7 run (Waradzyn kick)
Moravian—Porcarro 72 punt return (Waradzyn kick)
Moravian—Waradzyn 32 FG
Moravian—Steinberger 30 blocked punt return (kick failed)
Muhlenberg—Boll 53 pass from Reid (Kleppinger kick)
Moravian—B. Gratz 19 run (kick failed)
Muhlenberg—Hedden 55 pass from Shirvanian (Kleppinger kick)
Moravian—Ferratti 2 run (kick failed)

On five occasions, Moravian Coach Calvo elected a PAT attempt. Waradzyn converted 2 of his 5 attempts. Twice, Muhlenberg Coach Marino elected a PAT attempt. Kleppinger made both. In the first half, Calvo called on Waradzyn to attempt field goals from 28 yards and 32 yards. Both kicks were successful, adding 6 points to the Moravian total.

SURER FOOTING, 1973–1979

A period of reliable kicking marked the next seven years in the modern Moravian-and-Muhlenberg football relationship. There were several two-point conversion attempts. These occurred either after the failure of an earlier PAT attempt by the same team, or after the touchdown still left the scoring team well behind in the game score. The two placekickers in the 1974 game went 9-for-9 in their PAT attempts.

In 1973, At Muhlenberg Field

Moravian Coach Calvo, RB Bob Gratz, QB Fred Ferratti, PK Bob Richards, and their teammates visited with Muhlenberg Coach Marino, QBs Mike Reid and Bob Shirvanian, RB John Salley, receiver Randy Boll, PK Sam Stovall, and their teammates at Muhlenberg Field on November 17, 1973. Their visit was a reunion of participants in the 1972 game, when Bob Gratz, Ferratti, Reid, Shirvanian, and Boll each took part in a scoring play.

Bob Gratz and his teammates dressed for the occasion in white jerseys with blue cuffs, white pants with two blue stripes, and knee-length white socks with two stripes. Their white helmets had two blue stripes and the MC. Reid and his teammates dressed for the occasion in cardinal jerseys with white cuffs, white pants with two cardinal stripes, and white knee-length socks with two cardinal stripes.[21] The white Muhlenberg helmet was trimmed with numerals, two cardinal stripes, and gray between the stripes.

Moravian rushers gained 126 yards. Muhlenberg rushers gained 198 yards. Bob Gratz of Moravian and Salley of Muhlenberg were the center of attention in the rushing game.[22] Bob Gratz and Muhlenberg tacklers met 27 times. He gained 95 yards. Salley and Moravian tacklers met 22 times. He gained 112 yards in those encounters.

The two teams scored five touchdowns and created five extra-point opportunities.

Muhlenberg—Shirvanian 4 run (Stovall kick)

Muhlenberg—Butler 73 pass from Shirvanian (Stovall kick)

Moravian—Kasky 54 pass from Ferratti (Richards kick)

Muhlenberg—Boll fumble recovery in end zone (Stovall kick)

Moravian—Ferratti 1 run (kick failed)

On three occasions, Muhlenberg Coach Marino elected a PAT attempt. Stovall made all three kicks. After the first Moravian score, Calvo elected a PAT. Richards made the kick.

In 1974, At Steel Field

Muhlenberg Coach Marino, QB Mike Reid, PK Sam Stovall, receiver Randy Boll, and their teammates visited with Moravian Coach Calvo, QB Jon Van Valkenburg, RB Kenny King, PK Bob Richards, and their teammates at Steel Field on November 23, 1974. Their visit marked a reunion of participants in the 1973 game, when Stovall, Boll, and Richards each took part in a scoring play.

Reid and his teammates dressed for the occasion in white jerseys with cardinal cuffs and white pants with two cardinal stripes. The white Muhlenberg helmet had two cardinal stripes, gray between the stripes, and numerals. Van Valkenburg and his teammates dressed for the occasion in blue jerseys with white cuffs, white pants with two stripes, and white helmets with two blue stripes and the letters MC.[23] Players on both teams wore knee-length white socks with two stripes in their respective school colors.

Muhlenberg rushers gained 71 yards. Moravian rushers gained 368 yards. Van Valkenburg and King of Moravian were the center of attention in the rushing game. Van Valkenburg and Muhlenberg tacklers met 21 times. He gained 126 yards in those encounters and scored one rushing touchdown. King and Muhlenberg tacklers met 17 times. He gained 163 yards in those encounters and scored two rushing touchdowns.

The two teams scored ten touchdowns and created ten extra-point opportunities.

Muhlenberg—Reid 1 plunge (Stovall kick)
Moravian—Claudia 28 pass from Van Valkenburg (Richards kick)
Moravian—Claudia 9 pass from Van Valkenburg (Richards kick)
Muhlenberg—Boll 36 pass from Reid (Stovall kick)
Moravian—King 11 run (Richards kick)
Moravian—Van Valkenburg 1 plunge (Richards kick)
Muhlenberg—Mill 20 pass from Reid (Stovall kick)
Muhlenberg—Boll 14 pass from Reid (pass failed)
Moravian—King 40 run (Richards kick)
Moravian—Gratz 1 plunge (Richards kick)

Three times, Muhlenberg Coach Marino elected a PAT attempt. Stovall made all three. Six times, Moravian Coach Calvo elected a PAT attempt. Richards was 6-for-6.

In 1975, At Muhlenberg Field

Moravian Coach Calvo, QB Jon Van Valkenburg, RBs Kenny King and Bob Ternosky, PK Leon Finch, and their teammates visited with Muhlenberg Coach Marino, QB Mike Reid, and RB Jerry Fahy, and their teammates at Muhlenberg Field on November 22, 1975. Their visit marked a reunion of participants in the 1974 game, when King, Reid, and Van Valkenburg each took part in a scoring play.

Van Valkenburg and his teammates dressed for the occasion in white jerseys with blue cuffs and white pants with two blue stripes. Moravian players wore knee-length white socks with two blue stripes. The white Moravian helmet was redesigned to display two blue stripes and block letter M. Reid and his teammates dressed for the occasion in cardinal jerseys with white cuffs, white pants, and white knee-length socks. Two cardinal stripes adorned the pants and the socks. The white Muhlenberg helmet was trimmed with numerals, two cardinal stripes, and gray between the stripes.

Moravian rushers gained 241 yards. Muhlenberg rushers gained 151 yards. King and Ternosky of Moravian and Fahy of Muhlenberg were the center of attention in the rushing game. King and Muhlenberg tacklers met 23 times. He gained 84 yards. Ternosky and Muhlenberg tacklers met 16 times. He gained 141 yards in those encounters and scored one rushing touchdown. Fahy and Moravian tacklers met 17 times. He gained 116 yards in those encounters.

The two Moravian touchdowns created two extra-point opportunities.
Moravian—Finch 24 FG
Moravian—Ternosky 64 run (kick failed)
Moravian—G. Feinberg 16 pass from Van Valkenburg (Finch kick)
Twice, Moravian Coach Calvo elected a PAT attempt. Finch missed his first
kick and made the second one. In the second quarter, Calvo called on Finch
to attempt a 24-yard field goal. The kick cleared the crossbar for 3 Moravian
points.

In 1976, At Steel Field

Muhlenberg Coach Marino, PK Sam Stovall, and his teammates visited with
Moravian Coach Calvo, QB Jon Van Valkenburg, RBs Bob Ternosky and
Kenny King, PK Leon Finch, and their teammates at Steel Field on Novem-
ber 20, 1976. Their visit was a reunion of participants in the 1974 game, when
Stovall, Van Valkenburg, and King each took part in a scoring play.

Stovall and his teammates dressed for the occasion in white jerseys and
white pants trimmed with two cardinal stripes. Muhlenberg players wore
white crew socks with cardinal stripes. Their white helmets were trimmed
with numerals, two cardinal stripes, and gray between the stripes. Van
Valkenburg and his teammates dressed for the occasion in blue jerseys with
white cuffs and white pants with two blue stripes. Moravian players wore
knee-length white socks with two blue stripes. They also wore white shoes.
The Moravian helmet design remained white with two-stripes and the block
M.[24]

Muhlenberg rushers gained 63 yards. Moravian rushers gained 450 yards.
Ternosky, King, and Van Valkenburg of Moravian were again the center of attention in the rushing game. Ternosky and Muhlenberg tacklers met 16 times.
He gained 167 yards in those encounters. King and Muhlenberg tacklers met
16 times. He gained 143 yards. Van Valkenburg and Muhlenberg tacklers met
14 times. He gained 121 yards. King scored two rushing touchdowns, and
Van Valkenburg scored three rushing touchdowns.

The two teams combined for seven touchdowns and seven extra-point at-
tempts.
Moravian—King 9 run (Finch kick)
Moravian—King 1 run (Finch kick)
Moravian—Van Valkenburg 1 run (kick failed)
Moravian—Van Valkenburg 17 run (pass failed)
Muhlenberg—Sartori 9 pass from Sommerville (Stovall kick)
Moravian—Finch 29 FG
Muhlenberg—Sartori 8 pass from Schlecter (Stovall kick)

Moravian—Van Valkenburg 33 run (Finch kick)

On four occasions, Moravian Coach Calvo elected a PAT attempt. Finch was successful on three of the four attempts. Twice, Muhlenberg Coach Marino elected a PAT attempt. Stovall made both kicks. In the third quarter, Calvo called on Finch to attempt a 29-yard field goal. The kick was successful for 3 Moravian points.

In 1977, At Muhlenberg Field

New Moravian Coach Ed Little, QB Jack Bradley, PK Ed Jasiewicz, and their teammates visited with Muhlenberg Coach Marino, QB Don Sommerville, RB John Sules, PK Tom Weller, and their teammates at Muhlenberg Field on November 19, 1977.

Bradley and his teammates dressed for the occasion in white jerseys with blue cuffs and white pants with two blue stripes. The Moravian helmet was white with two blue stripes and the block M. Sommerville and his teammates dressed for the occasion in cardinal jerseys, white pants with two cardinal stripes, and white crew socks.[25] The Muhlenberg crew socks stood apart from the new, white, knee-length Moravian socks trimmed in blue and gray stripes. Muhlenberg players wore white helmets redesigned to include a block M and the image of a kicking mule superimposed on the M.

Moravian rushers gained 233 yards. Muhlenberg rushers gained 140 yards. Sules of Muhlenberg was the center of attention in the rushing game. Sules and Moravian tacklers met 27 times. He gained 140 yards in those encounters and scored three rushing touchdowns.

The two teams combined for seven extra-point attempts.

Muhlenberg—Sules 56 run (kick failed)

Moravian—Meyer 74 run (Jasiewicz kick)

Moravian—Ternosky 24 run (Jasiewicz kick)

Moravian—G. Feinberg 10 pass from Bradley (Jasiewicz kick)

Muhlenberg—Nivison 82 pass from Sommerville (pass failed)

Muhlenberg—Sules 5 run (Weller kick)

Muhlenberg—Sules 1 run (run failed)

Twice, Muhlenberg Coach Marino elected a PAT attempt. Weller missed his first kick, but made the second one. Three times, Moravian Coach Little elected a PAT attempt. Jasiewicz made all three kicks.

In 1978, At Steel Field

Muhlenberg Coach Marino, RBs John Sules and Brian Bodine, PK Mike Hiller, and their teammates visited with Moravian Coach Little, QB Jack

Bradley, and his teammates at Steel Field on November 11, 1978. Their visit marked a reunion of participants in the 1977 game, when Sules and Bradley each took part in a scoring play.

Sules and his teammates dressed for the occasion in white jerseys and white pants with two cardinal stripes. The Muhlenberg helmet was white with no trim. Bradley and his teammates dressed for the occasion in blue jerseys and white pants with two blue stripes.[26] The white Moravian helmet had two blue stripes and the block M. White knee-length socks and white shoes accompanied both uniforms.

Muhlenberg rushers gained 176 yards. Moravian rushers gained 65 yards. Bodine of Muhlenberg was the center of attention in the rushing game. He met Moravian tacklers 35 times. Bodine gained 121 yards in those encounters and scored two rushing touchdowns.

The Muhlenberg team had five extra-point opportunities.

Muhlenberg — Bodine 2 run (Hiller kick)

Muhlenberg — Fahy 1 run (Hiller kick)

Muhlenberg — Bodine 1 run (Hiller kick)

Muhlenberg — Sules 1 run (kick failed)

Muhlenberg — Albanese 20 run (Hiller kick)

All five times, Muhlenberg Coach Marino elected a PAT kick. Hiller was 4-for-5. In the fourth quarter, Marino called on Hiller to try a 25-yard field goal. The attempt failed.

In 1979, At Muhlenberg Field

Moravian Coach Little, QB Jack Bradley, PK Jim Roberts, and their teammates visited with Muhlenberg Coach Marino, PK Mike Hiller, RBs Marc Albanese and Jeff Finley, and their teammates at Muhlenberg Field on November 10, 1979.

Bradley and his teammates dressed for the occasion in white jerseys, white pants with two blue stripes, and knee-length white socks with two blue stripes. The white Moravian helmet had two blue stripes and the M. Hiller and his teammates dressed for the occasion in cardinal jerseys, white pants with two cardinal stripes, and white socks with two cardinal stripes. The mule-over-M returned to the white Muhlenberg helmet.

Moravian rushers gained 67 yards. Muhlenberg rushers gained 66 yards. Albanese and Finley of Muhlenberg were the center of attention in the rushing game. They gained 75 yards in their encounters with Moravian tacklers.

The two teams scored three touchdowns and created three extra-point opportunities.

Muhlenberg—Sartori 9 pass from Schulte (Hiller kick)
Moravian—Bradley 1 run (kick blocked)
Muhlenberg—Sartori 10 pass from Schulte (Hiller kick)

Twice, Muhlenberg Coach Marino elected a PAT attempt. Hiller made both kicks. After the Moravian touchdown, Moravian Coach Little elected a PAT attempt. The kick by Roberts was blocked.

TWICE ESCHEWING THE GAME-TYING KICK, 1980–81

Overtime had not yet arrived in intercollegiate football during the consecutive years when Moravian Coach Ed Little faced a pair of tough decisions. Each time, in the closing minutes of the fourth quarter, Little had to decide between a game-tying PAT attempt or a two-point try for the lead. Twice, Little elected to "go for two."

In 1980, At Steel Field

Muhlenberg Coach Marino, RB Marc Spatidol, PK Victor Lea, and their teammates visited with Moravian Coach Little, PK Jim Roberts, and his teammates at Steel Field on November 15, 1980.

Spatidol and his teammates dressed for the occasion in white jerseys and white pants with two cardinal stripes. Their white helmets were adorned with the mule-over-M design. Roberts and his teammates dressed for the occasion in blue jerseys with white cuffs, white pants with two blue stripes, and white, knee-length socks with a gray stripe between two blue stripes.[27] The white Moravian helmets were trimmed with two blue stripes, gray between the stripes, and the block M. Muhlenberg players wore knee-length socks, with and without cardinal stripes.

Muhlenberg rushers gained 123 yards. Moravian rushers gained 90 yards. Spatidol of Muhlenberg was the center of attention in the rushing game. He carried the ball for 81 yards.

The two teams scored six touchdowns and created six extra-point opportunities.

Moravian—Laverty 13 pass from Bradley (Roberts kick)
Moravian—Roberts 42 FG
Muhlenberg—DiDio 11 pass from Greb (Lea kick)
Muhlenberg—Lea 21 FG
Muhlenberg—Spatidol 11 pass from Greb (Lea kick)
Moravian—McAnany 1 run (Roberts kick)

Muhlenberg—Smith 30 pass interception (Lea kick)

Moravian—Nimphius 23 pass from Bradley (run failed)

Twice, Moravian Coach Little elected a PAT attempt. Roberts made both kicks. Three times, Muhlenberg Coach Marino elected a PAT attempt. Lea was 3-for-3 in his kicks. In the first quarter, Little called on Roberts to attempt a 42-yard field goal. The kick was good, adding 3 points to the Moravian total. In the second quarter, Marino called on Lea to attempt a 21-yard field goal. The kick was good for 3 Muhlenberg points.

In 1981, At Muhlenberg Field

Moravian Coach Little, PK Jim Roberts, and his teammates visited with new Muhlenberg Coach Ralph Kirchenheiter, QB Gary Greb, RB Mike Bailey, PK Victor Lea, and their teammates at Muhlenberg Field on November 14, 1981. Their visit marked a reunion of participants in the 1980 game, when Roberts, Greb, and Lea each took part in a scoring play.

Roberts and his teammates dressed for the occasion in white jerseys and white pants with two blue stripes. The white helmets had two blue stripes and the block M. Greb and his teammates dressed for the occasion in cardinal jerseys, white pants with two cardinal stripes, and white knee-length socks.[28] The white Muhlenberg helmets were trimmed with a mule superimposed on the M. Returning to the Muhlenberg uniform was a three-stripe, knee-length sock. Moravian players wore knee-length white socks, trimmed in blue-gray-blue striping. White shoes were worn by players on both teams.

Moravian rushers gained 86 yards. Muhlenberg rushers gained 177 yards. Bailey of Muhlenberg was the center of attention in the rushing game. He carried the ball for 89 yards.

The two teams scored two touchdowns and created two extra-point opportunities.

Muhlenberg—Lea 25 FG

Moravian—Roberts 33 FG

Muhlenberg—Hiller 5 pass from Greb (Lea kick)

Moravian—T. Ulicny 1 run (pass failed)

Muhlenberg Coach Kirchenheiter elected the only PAT attempt. Lea converted. In the second quarter, Kirchenheiter sent in Lea to attempt a 25-yard field goal. The kick was good for 3 Muhlenberg points. On the opening possession, Little called on Roberts to attempt a 42-yard field goal. The attempt failed. In the third quarter, Little called on Roberts to attempt a 33-yard field goal. The kick was good for 3 Moravian points.

THE FIELD GOAL MAKES
REGULAR APPEARANCES, 1982–1990

In time, the field goal attempt became a regular feature part of the Moravian-and-Muhlenberg playing relationship. A field goal attempt was successfully kicked in seven of the nine games played from 1982 through 1990. Moravian and Muhlenberg coaches showed growing confidence in the field goal as a scoring strategy. Two games (1985 and 1990) were played in rain and mud, but the conditions did not deter field goal attempts. In the 1984 game, Moravian Coach Rocco Calvo sent Shawn Phillips into the game in the closing minute with the scored tied, 14-14. Phillips' successful field goal kick was the first game-winning field goal in the modern Moravian-and-Muhlenberg football relationship. It remains the only such kick.

In 1982, At Steel Field

Muhlenberg Coach Kirchenheiter, PK Victor Lea, and his teammates visited with returning Moravian Coach Rocco Calvo, RB Jim Joseph, PK Jim Roberts, and their teammates at Steel Field on November 13, 1982. Their visit marked a reunion of participants in the 1981 game, when Lea and Roberts each took part in a scoring play.

Lea and his teammates wore white jerseys, white pants with two cardinal stripes, and white, knee-length socks with three cardinal stripes. Their white helmets bore the mule-over-M design. Joseph and his teammates wore blue jerseys, white pants with two blue stripes, and white, knee-length socks. Moravian players wore white helmets with two blue stripes and the M. White shoes were worn by players on both teams.

Muhlenberg rushers gained 122 yards. Moravian rushers gained 331 yards. Joseph of Moravian was the center of attention in the rushing game. Joseph and Muhlenberg tacklers met 17 times. He gained 126 yards and scored a rushing touchdown.

The two teams scored three touchdowns, creating three extra-point opportunities.

Moravian—Joseph 6 run (kick blocked)
Muhlenberg—Mottola 11 run (kick blocked)
Moravian—Roberts 29 FG
Moravian—Rhinehart 6 run (Roberts kick)

Twice, Moravian Coach Calvo elected a PAT attempt. After his first kick was blocked, Roberts made the second kick. After the Muhlenberg touchdown, Kirchenheiter elected a PAT attempt. The attempt by Lea was blocked.[29] Kirchenheiter called on Lea to attempt a 44-yard field goal just before halftime. The kick was unsuccessful. In the fourth quarter, Calvo called on Roberts to attempt a 29-yard field goal. The kick was successful for 3 Moravian points.

In 1983, At Muhlenberg Field

Moravian Coach Calvo, RB Jim Joseph, PK John Messemer, and their teammates visited with Muhlenberg Coach Kirchenheiter, PK Tom Mulroy, and his teammates at Muhlenberg Field on November 12, 1983.

Joseph and his teammates wore white jerseys, white pants with two blue stripes, and a redesigned helmet of solid blue with a white block letter M. White shoes and knee-length white socks completed the uniform. Mulroy and his teammates wore cardinal jerseys and white pants with two stripes. The white Muhlenberg helmet was trimmed with the mule-over-M design. White shoes and white knee-length socks bearing three cardinal stripes completed the Muhlenberg uniform.

Moravian rushers gained 221 yards. Muhlenberg rushers gained 52 yards. Joseph of Moravian was again the center of attention in the rushing game. Joseph and Muhlenberg tacklers met 25 times. He gained 106 yards in those encounters and scored three rushing touchdowns.

The two teams had four extra-point opportunities during the visit.

Muhlenberg—Mei 95 kickoff return (Mulroy kick)

Moravian—Joseph 1 run (Messemer kick)

Moravian—Messemer 36 FG

Moravian—Joseph 6 run (Messemer kick)

Moravian—Joseph 2 run (Messemer kick)

After the Muhlenberg touchdown, Kirchenheiter elected a PAT kick. Mulroy scored the point. Three times, Moravian Coach Calvo elected a PAT attempt. Messemer was 3-for-3. In the second quarter, Calvo called on Messemer to attempt a 36-yard field goal. The kick was successful for 3 Moravian points.

In 1984, At Steel Field

Muhlenberg Coach Kirchenheiter, PK Tom Mulroy and his teammates visited with Moravian Coach Calvo, RB Jim Joseph, PK Shawn Phillips, and their teammates at Steel Field on November 10, 1984. Their visit marked a reunion of participants in the 1983 game, when Mulroy and Joseph each took part in a scoring play.

Mulroy and his teammates wore white jerseys, white pants with two cardinal stripes, and white, knee-length socks with two cardinal stripes around a gray stripe. The gray Muhlenberg helmets had the mule-over-M design. Joseph and his teammates wore redesigned blue jerseys with a broad gray-and-white stripe on the sleeve. The white pants featured a wide blue stripe. The blue Moravian helmet was redesigned with "Hounds" in script. The blue helmet with block M was gone. White shoes completed both uniforms.

Muhlenberg rushers gained 33 yards. Moravian rushers gained 170 yards. Joseph of Moravian was again the center of attention in the rushing game. Joseph and Muhlenberg tacklers met 31 times. He gained 144 yards in those encounters and scored one rushing touchdown.

The two teams had four extra-point opportunities during the visit.

Moravian—Danna 2 run (Phillips kick)

Moravian—Joseph 1 run (Phillips kick)

Muhlenberg—Peischl 71 pass from Broas (Mulroy kick)

Muhlenberg—Mann 2 run (Mulroy kick)

Moravian—Phillips 33 FG

Twice, Moravian Coach Calvo elected a PAT attempt. Phillips made both kicks. Twice, Muhlenberg Coach Kirchenheiter elected a PAT. Mulroy made both. In the final minute, Calvo called on Phillips for a 33-yard field goal. The kick was successful.

In 1985, At Muhlenberg Field

Moravian Coach Calvo, RB Jim Joseph, PK Scott Perry, and their teammates visited with Muhlenberg Coach Kirchenheiter, PK Mike Tremblay, and his teammates at Muhlenberg Field on November 16, 1985.

Joseph and his teammates wore white jerseys with two blue stripes on each sleeve, white pants, and white socks. Moravian players wore blue helmets adorned with script "Hounds." Tremblay and his teammates wore cardinal jerseys and white pants with two stripes. Their white, knee-length socks had two cardinal stripes flanking a gray stripe. The Muhlenberg helmet was redesigned with a cardinal stripe and "Mules" in script.

Moravian rushers gained 114 yards. Muhlenberg rushers gained 53 yards. Joseph of Moravian was once again the center of attention in the rushing game. Joseph and Muhlenberg tacklers met 24 times. He gained 79 yards and scored one rushing touchdown.

The two teams had three extra-point opportunities during the visit.

Moravian—Joseph 2 run (Perry kick)

Muhlenberg—Tremblay 25 FG

Muhlenberg—Concordia 10 pass from Giordano (Tremblay kick)

Moravian—McLaughlin 9 pass from Godshall (Lasko run)

After the first Moravian touchdown, Perry converted the PAT. After the Muhlenberg touchdown, Tremblay converted the PAT. In the third quarter, Tremblay kicked a 25-yard field goal.

In 1986, At Steel Field

Muhlenberg Coach Kirchenheiter, QB Chris Elser, and his teammates visited with Moravian Coach Calvo, RB Mark Masessa, PK Scott Perry, and their teammates at Steel Field on November 15, 1986.

Elser and his teammates wore white jerseys and white pants with two cardinal stripes. The gray Muhlenberg helmet had a cardinal stripe and "Mules" in script. Masessa and his teammates wore blue jerseys with a white-and-gray sleeve stripe and white pants with a blue stripe. "Hounds" in script adorned the blue Moravian helmet. Both teams wore white, knee-length socks.

Muhlenberg rushers gained 24 yards. Moravian rushers gained 218 yards. Masessa of Moravian was the center of attention in the rushing game. Masessa and Muhlenberg tacklers met 31 times. He gained 136 yards in those encounters and rushed for both touchdowns in the game.

The Moravian team had two extra-point opportunities.

Moravian—Masessa 24 run (Perry kick)

Moravian—Masessa 4 run (Perry kick)

On both occasions, Coach Calvo elected a PAT attempt. Perry made both kicks.

In 1987, At Muhlenberg Field

New Moravian Coach Scot Dapp, PK Scott Perry, and his teammates visited with Muhlenberg Coach Kirchenheiter, RB Jeff Potkul, PK Bruce Hartman, and their teammates at Muhlenberg Field on November 14, 1987.

Perry and his teammates wore white jerseys with two blue sleeve stripes, white pants with a stripe, and white socks. On their blue helmets was "Hounds" in script. Potkul and his teammates wore cardinal jerseys, white pants, and white knee-length socks with cardinal stripes. Their gray helmets had a cardinal stripe and "Mules" in script.

Moravian rushers gained 154 yards. Muhlenberg rushers gained 115 yards. Potkul of Muhlenberg was the center of attention in the rushing game. Potkul and Moravian tacklers met 5 times in the two Muhlenberg touchdown drives. He gained 33 yards in those encounters.

The two teams had four extra-point opportunities during the visit.

Moravian—Light 1 run (kick failed)

Moravian—Light 1 run (pass failed)

Muhlenberg—Concordia 9 pass from Elser (Hartman kick)

Muhlenberg—Potkul 2 pass from Elser (Hartman kick)

After the first Moravian touchdown, Dapp elected a PAT attempt. Perry missed the kick. After both Muhlenberg touchdowns, Kirchenheiter elected a PAT. Hartman was 2-for-2.

In 1988, At Steel Field

Muhlenberg Coach Kirchenheiter, QB Chris Elser, receiver Tony Concordia, RB Jeff Potkul, PK Bob Powers, and their teammates visited with Moravian Coach Dapp, QB Rob Light, PKs Tim Cunniff and Scott Perry, and their teammates at Steel Field on November 12, 1988. Their visit marked a reunion of participants in the 1987 game, when Light, Elser, and Concordia each took part in a scoring play.

Elser and his teammates wore white jerseys and white pants. The Muhlenberg helmet was gray with one stripe and "Mules" in script. Light and his teammates wore blue jerseys and white pants with a broad stripe. The sleeve stripe was white between gray. The Moravian helmet was blue with "Hounds" in script. All wore white socks.

Muhlenberg rushers gained 86 yards. Moravian rushers gained 151 yards. Potkul of Muhlenberg was again the center of attention in the rushing game. He ran 21 times for 73 yards.

The two teams had ten extra-point opportunities during the visit.

Moravian—Krouse 2 run (Cunniff kick)
Moravian—Patrignani 51 punt return (Cunniff kick)
Moravian—Krouse 1 run (Cunniff kick)
Muhlenberg—DiGiorgio 16 pass from Elser (Powers kick)
Muhlenberg—Concordia 34 pass from Potkul (kick failed)
Moravian—Perry 29 FG
Muhlenberg—Aniello 3 pass from Elser (pass failed)
Moravian—Cara 48 pass from Light (kick failed)
Moravian—Reinhard blocked punt recovery in end zone (Cunniff kick)
Moravian—Cara 35 pass from Light (Cunniff kick)
Muhlenberg—Aniello 27 pass from Elser (pass failed)

On six occasions, Moravian Coach Dapp elected a PAT attempt. Cunniff made 5 of his 6 kicks. Twice, Muhlenberg Coach Kirchenheiter elected a PAT attempt. Powers made the first kick, but missed the second try. In the second quarter, Dapp called on Perry to attempt a 30-yard field goal. The kick was successful for 3 Moravian points.

In 1989, At Muhlenberg Field

Moravian Coach Dapp, QB Rob Light, PK Tim Cunniff, and their teammates visited with Muhlenberg Coach Kirchenheiter, RB Rob Paessler, PK Bob

Powers, and their teammates at Muhlenberg Field on November 11, 1989. Their visit was a reunion of 1988 participants, when Light, Cunniff, and Powers each took part in a scoring play.

Light and his teammates wore white jerseys and white pants with a broad blue stripe. The jersey sleeve had two blue stripes around a gray stripe. Moravian players wore white crew socks and blue helmets with "Hounds" in script. Paessler and his teammates wore cardinal jerseys, white pants trimmed with a double cardinal stripe, and white crew socks. Their gray helmets were trimmed with a cardinal stripe and "Mules" in script.

Moravian rushers gained 162 yards. Muhlenberg rushers gained 146 yards. Paessler of Muhlenberg was the center of attention in the rushing game. He carried 25 times for 116 yards and scored one rushing touchdown.

The two teams had three extra-point opportunities during the visit.

Moravian—Light 1 run (Cunniff kick)

Muhlenberg—Paessler 2 run (kick blocked)

Muhlenberg—Powers 35 FG

Moravian—Light 8 run (Cunniff kick)

After both Moravian touchdowns, Dapp elected a PAT attempt. Cunniff made both kicks. After the Muhlenberg touchdown, Kirchenheiter elected a PAT attempt. The kick by Powers was blocked. In the second quarter, Kirchenheiter called on Powers to attempt a 35-yard field goal. The kick was good for 3 Muhlenberg points.

In 1990, At Steel Field

New Muhlenberg Coach Fran Meagher, RB Rob Paessler, PK Bob Powers, and their teammates visited with Moravian Coach Dapp, QB Mike Harth, PK Tim Cunniff, and their teammates at Steel Field on November 10, 1990. Their visit marked a reunion of participants in the 1989 game, when Powers and Cunniff each took part in a scoring play.

Paessler and his teammates wore white jerseys and white pants trimmed with two cardinal stripes. The gray Muhlenberg helmet was redesigned with a mule superimposed on a cardinal M. Harth and his teammates wore blue jerseys and white pants with a wide stripe. Their blue helmets showed "Hounds" in script. Both teams wore white socks.

Muhlenberg rushers gained 20 yards. Moravian rushers gained 143 yards. Harth of Moravian and Paessler of Muhlenberg were the center of attention in the rushing game. Harth and Muhlenberg tacklers met 13 times. He gained 7 net yards, including 37 yards on a touchdown run. Paessler met Moravian tacklers 15 times and gained 36 yards.

The Moravian team had the only extra-point opportunity during the visit.

Moravian—Harth 37 run (Cunniff kick)
Muhlenberg—Powers 23 FG

Moravian Coach Dapp elected a PAT attempt. Cunniff scored the point. In the second quarter, Muhlenberg Coach Meagher called on Powers to attempt a 23-yard field goal. Powers made the kick for 3 Muhlenberg points.

ONE LATE-GAME COMEBACK, THEN PRECISION KICKING, 1991–2003

The next thirteen Moravian-and-Muhlenberg football games were marked by routine scoring through the kicking game. The exception came in 1991, when Moravian kicking problems early in the game prompted Coach Scot Dapp to choose two, two-point conversion tries in the second half.

In 1991, At Muhlenberg Field

Moravian Coach Dapp, RB Craig Cubbin, PK Jim Davis, and their teammates visited with Muhlenberg Coach Meagher, RB Rich Conte, PK Andy Gorman, and their teammates at Muhlenberg Field on November 16, 1991.

Cubbin and his teammates wore white jerseys, white pants with a wide stripe, and blue helmets with "Hounds" in script. Their blue, knee-length socks contrasted with the white crew socks worn by Muhlenberg players. Conte and his teammates wore cardinal jerseys, white pants with a double stripe, and gray helmets with a cardinal stripe and the mule superimposed on the cardinal M.[30]

Moravian rushers gained 166 yards. Muhlenberg rushers gained 114 yards. Conte of Muhlenberg and Cubbin of Moravian were the center of attention in the rushing game.[31] Conte carried 22 times for 67 yards. Cubbin scored the only rushing touchdown in the game.

The two teams had eight extra-point opportunities during the visit.

Moravian—Cubbin 2 run (kick blocked)
Muhlenberg—Conte 9 pass from McCullough (Gorman kick)
Muhlenberg—Callahan 5 pass from McCullough (Gorman kick)
Muhlenberg—Callahan 18 pass from McCullough (Gorman kick)
Moravian—Iasparro 64 punt return (Bagnaturo pass from Harth)
Muhlenberg—Slaton 56 pass from McCullough (Gorman kick)
Moravian—Durepo 26 pass from Keville (kick blocked)
Moravian—Hahn 13 pass from Keville (Durepo pass from Keville)

Twice, Moravian Coach Dapp elected a PAT attempt. Both attempts by Davis were blocked.[32] On four occasions, Muhlenberg Coach Meagher elected a

PAT attempt. Gorman was 3-for-4. Meagher called on Gorman to attempt a 42-yard field goal. The kick was unsuccessful.

In 1992, At Steel Field

Muhlenberg Coach Meagher, QB Sean McCullough, PK Gerry Scott, and their teammates visited with Moravian Coach Dapp, QB Sean Keville, RBs Jud Frank and Craig Cubbin, receiver Chris Iasparro, PKs Bill Koy and Jim Davis, and their teammates at Steel Field on November 14, 1992. Their visit marked a reunion of 1991 participants, when Keville, Cubbin, Iasparro, and McCullough each took part in a scoring play.

McCullough and his teammates wore white jerseys and white pants trimmed with two cardinal stripes. Their gray helmets had a cardinal stripe and a mule superimposed on a cardinal M. Keville and his teammates wore blue jerseys redesigned with a greyhound image, blue outlined in white, on the upper sleeve. Moravian players wore white pants and blue helmets with "Hounds" in script. Both teams wore white crew socks.

Muhlenberg rushers gained 59 yards. Moravian rushers gained 108 yards. Frank and Cubbin of Moravian were the center of attention in the rushing game. Frank met Muhlenberg tacklers 18 times and gained 40 yards. Cubbin carried 14 times for 41 yards and two touchdowns.

The two teams had seven extra-point opportunities during the visit.

Moravian—Keville 2 run (Koy kick)

Moravian—Iasparro 9 pass from Cubbin (kick blocked)

Moravian—Cubbin 1 run (Frank run)

Moravian—Anderko 14 pass from Mattes (Davis kick)

Muhlenberg—DeVirgilis 2 run (Scott kick)

Moravian—Cubbin 11 run (Koy kick)

Muhlenberg—Lokerson 60 pass from McCullough (Scott kick)

On four occasions, Moravian Coach Dapp elected a PAT attempt. Koy was 2-for-3. Davis made his one kick. Twice, Muhlenberg Coach Meagher elected a PAT. Scott made both kicks.

In 1993, At Muhlenberg Field

Moravian Coach Dapp, QB Sean Keville, RB Mike Natale, PK Chad Kurtz, and their teammates visited with Muhlenberg Coach Meagher, QB Sean McCullough, PK Jack Habash, and their teammates at Muhlenberg Field on November 13, 1993. Their visit marked a reunion of participants in the 1992 game, when Keville and McCullough each took part in a scoring play.

Keville and his teammates wore white jerseys and white pants. On their blue helmets was "Hounds" in script. McCullough and his teammates wore cardinal jerseys and white pants with a double stripe. Their gray helmets bore a cardinal stripe, but no M. Both teams wore white crew socks.

Moravian rushers gained 166 yards. Muhlenberg rushers gained 50 yards. Natale of Moravian was the center of attention in the rushing game. Natale and Muhlenberg tacklers met 19 times. He gained 134 yards and scored one rushing touchdown.

The two teams had five extra-point opportunities during the visit.

Moravian—Frank 72 pass from Keville (Kurtz kick)

Moravian—Kurtz 27 FG

Moravian—Anderko 25 pass from Keville (Kurtz kick)

Muhlenberg—Bokus 3 pass from McCullough (Habash kick)

Muhlenberg—Bokus 37 pass from McCullough (Habash kick)

Moravian—Natale 55 run (Kurtz kick)

Three times, Moravian Coach Dapp elected a PAT kick. Kurtz made all three. Twice, Muhlenberg Coach Meagher elected a PAT kick. Habash made both. In the first quarter, Dapp called on Kurtz to attempt a 27-yard field goal. The kick was good for 3 points.

In 1994, At Steel Field

New Muhlenberg Greg Olejack, PK Mark Mogavero, and his teammates visited with Moravian Coach Dapp, RB Mike Natale, PKs Chad Kurtz and Derek Stasiak, and their teammates at Steel Field on November 12, 1994.

Mogavero and his teammates wore white jerseys and white pants redesigned with a wide cardinal stripe. Their gray helmets, with the mule-over-M, were redesigned with a wide cardinal stripe. Natale and his teammates wore blue jerseys with the greyhound on the sleeve, white pants, and blue helmets with "Hounds" in script. All wore white socks.

Muhlenberg rushers gained 32 yards. Moravian rushers gained 221 yards. Natale of Moravian was again the center of attention in the rushing game. He carried 19 times for 84 yards.

The two teams had nine extra-point opportunities during the visit.

Muhlenberg—Mogavero 30 FG

Moravian—Keville 4 run (Kurtz kick)

Muhlenberg—Kern 6 pass from Jack (Mogavero kick)

Moravian—Breidinger 87 kickoff return (Kurtz kick)

Moravian—Roy 30 pass from Keville (Kurtz run)

Muhlenberg—Terpstra blocked punt recovery in end zone (Mogavero kick)

Moravian—Anderko 24 pass from Keville (Kurtz kick)
Moravian—Roy 8 pass from Keville (Kurtz kick)
Moravian—Bonsall 2 run (Stasiak kick)
Moravian—Paciulli 56 pass interception (Stasiak kick)

On seven occasions, Moravian Coach Dapp elected a PAT attempt. Kurtz was 5-for-5, and Stasiak made both his kicks. Twice, Muhlenberg Coach Olejack elected a PAT. Mogavero made both. In the first quarter, Olejack called on Mogavero to attempt a 30-yard field goal. The kick was successful for 3 Muhlenberg points.

In 1995, At Muhlenberg Field

Moravian Coach Dapp, RBs Brad Lower and Chad Breidinger, PK Chad Kutrz and their teammates visited with Muhlenberg Coach Olejack, RB Greg Bevan, PK Mark Mogavero, and their teammates at Muhlenberg Field on November 11, 1995. Their visit reunited 1994 participants Kurtz and Mogavero, who each had taken part in the scoring.

Lower and his teammates wore white jerseys, plain white pants, and blue helmets with "Hounds" in script. Bevan and his teammates wore cardinal jerseys, white pants with a wide stripe, and gray helmets with a wide cardinal stripe and the mule-over-M design. White crew socks completed the uniforms for both teams.

Moravian rushers gained 303 yards. Muhlenberg rushers gained 160 yards. Lower and Breidinger of Moravian and Bevan of Muhlenberg were the center of attention in the rushing game. Lower and Muhlenberg tacklers met 24 times. He gained 150 yards and scored one rushing touchdown. Breidinger and Muhlenberg tacklers met 20 times. He gained 109 yards. Bevan and Moravian tacklers met 10 times. He gained 75 yards in those encounters.

The two teams had six extra-point opportunities during the visit.

Moravian—Schroeder 6 run (run failed)
Moravian—Lower 21 run (Breidinger run)
Muhlenberg—Wohlbach 15 run (Mogavero kick)
Moravian—Pukszyn 11 pass interception (Kurtz kick)
Moravian—Schroeder 1 run (Kurtz kick)
Moravian—Kurtz 29 FG
Moravian—Scobo 1 run (Kurtz kick)

Three times, Moravian Coach Dapp elected a PAT attempt. Kurtz was 3-for-3. After the Muhlenberg touchdown, Mogavero made the kick. In the third quarter, Dapp called on Kurtz to attempt a 29-yard field goal. Kurtz made the kick for 3 Moravian points.

In 1996, At Steel Field

Muhlenberg Coach Olejack, PK Mark Mogavero, and his teammates visited with Moravian Coach Dapp, RB Brad Lower, PK Derek Stasiak, and their teammates at Steel Field on November 16, 1996. Their visit marked a reunion of participants in the 1994 game, when Stasiak, Mogavero, and Breidinger each took part in a scoring play.

Mogavero and his teammates wore white jerseys, white pants with a wide stripe, and gray helmets redesigned with the main cardinal stripe flanked by two black stripes. The mule-over-M remained on the helmet. Lower and his teammates wore blue jerseys with the greyhound on the sleeves, white pants, and blue helmets with "Hounds" in script. White crew socks completed the uniforms for both teams.

Muhlenberg rushers "gained" minus-2 yards. Moravian rushers gained 218 yards. Lower of Moravian was again the center of attention in the rushing game. He carried 25 times for 122 yards.

The Moravian team had three extra-point opportunities during the visit.

Moravian—Stasiak 37 FG
Moravian—Szabo 30 pass from Harrison (Stasiak kick)
Muhlenberg—Mogavero 23 FG
Moravian—Breidinger 2 run (Stasiak kick)
Moravian—Stasiak 27 FG
Moravian—Breidinger 2 run (Stasiak kick)

All three times, Coach Dapp elected a PAT try. Stasiak was 3-for-3. Stasiak scored 6 more Moravian points on two field goals. He made a 37-yard field goal in the first quarter and a 27-yard field goal in the third quarter. In the second quarter, Olejack called on Mogavero to attempt a 23-yard field goal. Mogavero's kick was good for 3 points.[33]

In 1997, At Muhlenberg Field

Moravian Coach Dapp, RB P. J. Jankowicz, PK Kevin Smith, and their teammates visited with new Muhlenberg Coach Mike Donnelly, RB Jason Brader, PK Dylan Sapir, and their teammates at Muhlenberg Field on November 15, 1997.

Jankowicz and his teammates wore white jerseys with the greyhound and blue collar, white pants, blue helmets with "Hounds" in script, and blue, knee-length socks. Brader and his teammates wore cardinal jerseys, white pants with a wide stripe, white socks, and gray helmets with a wide stripe and the mule-over-M.

Moravian rushers gained 122 yards. Muhlenberg rushers gained 164 yards. Brader of Muhlenberg and Jankowicz of Moravian were the center of attention in the rushing game. Brader and Moravian tacklers met on 32 occasions. He gained 144 yards. Jankowicz met Muhlenberg tacklers 27 times. He gained 116 yards and scored one rushing touchdown.

The two teams had five extra-point opportunities during the visit.

Muhlenberg—Lunn 2 pass from Fosdick (Sapir kick)

Muhlenberg—Lunn 3 pass from Fosdick (kick failed)

Moravian—Jankowicz 5 run (Smith kick)

Moravian—Petrosky 1 run (Smith kick)

Muhlenberg—Sapir 18 FG

Moravian—Campbell 21 pass interception (Smith kick)

Twice, Muhlenberg Coach Donnelly elected a PAT attempt. Sapir made the first kick, but missed the second attempt. Three times, Moravian Coach Dapp elected a PAT attempt. Smith converted all three kicks. In the fourth quarter, Donnelly sent Sapir to attempt an 18-yard field goal. The kick was good for 3 Muhlenberg points. The successful kick also gave Muhlenberg the lead.

In 1998, At Steel Field

Muhlenberg Coach Donnelly, RB Jason Brader, PK Michael Dickinson, and their teammates visited with Moravian Coach Dapp, PK Kevin Smith, and his teammates at Steel Field on November 14, 1998.

Brader and his teammates were recognizable in their white jerseys, white pants redesigned with a cardinal stripe edged in white, and gray helmets with a wide cardinal stripe and the mule-over-M. Smith and his teammates were recognizable in blue jerseys and blue "Hounds" helmets.

Muhlenberg rushers gained 210 yards. Moravian rushers gained 155 yards. Brader of Muhlenberg was again the center of attention in the rushing game. Brader and Moravian tacklers met 35 times. He gained 176 yards and scored a touchdown.

The two teams had six extra-point opportunities during the visit.

Moravian—Harryn 1 run (kick blocked)

Muhlenberg—Carter 40 pass from McCabe (Dickinson kick)

Moravian—Farkas 21 pass from Petrosky (Scott run)

Muhlenberg—Carter 9 run (Dickinson kick)

Muhlenberg—Dickinson 35 FG

Muhlenberg—Dickinson 41 FG

Muhlenberg—Arcuri 34 pass interception (run failed)

Muhlenberg—Brader 5 run (Dickinson kick)

Once, Moravian Coach Dapp elected a PAT attempt. Smith's kick was blocked. Three times, Muhlenberg Coach Donnelly elected a PAT attempt. Dickinson succeeded all three times. In the middle quarters, Donnelly twice called on Dickinson to attempt a field goal. Dickinson made the kicks from 35 yards and 41 yards, respectively, adding 6 points to the Muhlenberg scoring total.

In 1999, At Scotty Wood Stadium

Moravian Coach Dapp, QB Rob Petrosky, RB Josh Fick, PK Jim McIntyre, and their teammates visited with Muhlenberg Coach Donnelly, receiver Joshua Carter, PK Chris Reed, and their teammates at the renamed Scotty Wood Stadium on November 13, 1999. Their visit marked a reunion of 1998 participants, when Petrosky and Carter each took part in a scoring play.

Petrosky and his teammates were recognizable in white jerseys and blue "Hounds" helmets. Carter and his teammates were recognizable in cardinal jerseys, cardinal pants, and gray helmets with a wide cardinal stripe and the mule-over-M.

Moravian rushers gained 189 yards. Muhlenberg rushers gained 175 yards. Fick of Moravian was the center of attention in the rushing game. In the fourth quarter, he outran Muhlenberg pursuers on touchdown runs of 19 yards and 55 yards.

The two teams had eleven extra-point opportunities during the visit.
Muhlenberg—Carter 11 run (Reed kick)
Moravian—Buscio 29 pass from Petrosky (McIntyre kick)
Muhlenberg—Carter 47 pass from McCabe (Reed kick)
Muhlenberg—Carter 20 pass from McCabe (Reed kick)
Muhlenberg—McFarlane 24 pass from McCabe (Reed kick)
Moravian—Petrosky 1 run (kick blocked)
Muhlenberg—Carter 78 kickoff return (Reed kick)
Muhlenberg—Wolfsohn 9 pass from McCabe (Reed kick)
Muhlenberg—Steele 16 pass from McCabe (Reed kick)
Moravian—Fick 19 run (McIntyre kick)
Muhlenberg—Reed 19 FG
Moravian—Fick 55 run (kick failed)
On seven occasions, Muhlenberg Coach Donnelly elected a PAT attempt. Reed was 7-for-7 in his kicks. On four occasions, Moravian Coach Dapp elected a PAT attempt. McIntyre was 2-for-4 in his kicks. In the fourth quarter, Reed succeeded on a 19-yard field goal attempt, adding 3 Muhlenberg points.

In 2000, At Steel Field

Muhlenberg Coach Donnelly, QB Mike McCabe, receiver Joshua Carter, RB Matt Bernardo, PK Michael Dickinson, and their teammates visited with Moravian Coach Dapp, RB Josh Fick, PK Jim McIntyre, and their teammates at Steel Field on November 11, 2000. Their visit marked a reunion of participants in the 1999 game, when McCabe, Carter, and Fick each took part in a scoring play.

McCabe and his teammates were recognizable in white jerseys, cardinal pants, and gray helmets with a wide cardinal stripe and the mule-over-M. Fick and his teammates were recognizable in blue jerseys, newly-designed blue pants, and blue "Hounds" helmets. Players on both teams wore white, knee-length socks.

Muhlenberg rushers gained 317 yards. Moravian rushers gained 155 yards. Bernardo of Muhlenberg was the center of attention in the rushing game. He met Moravian tacklers 40 times. Bernardo gained 251 yards in those encounters and scored four rushing touchdowns.

The two teams had nine extra-point opportunities during the visit.

Muhlenberg—Bernardo 14 run (Dickinson kick)
Muhlenberg—Carter 41 pass from McCabe (Dickinson kick)
Moravian—Fick 3 run (kick failed)
Muhlenberg—Bernardo 1 run (Dickinson kick)
Moravian—Rhinehart 14 pass from Bowden (pass failed)
Muhlenberg—Carter 90 kickoff return (Dickinson kick)
Moravian—Barlok 36 run (Rhinehart pass from Bowden)
Muhlenberg—Bernardo 2 run (Dickinson kick)
Muhlenberg—Bernardo 1 run (Dickinson kick)
Muhlenberg—Dickinson 28 FG

Six times, Muhlenberg Coach Donnelly elected a PAT attempt. Dickinson was 6-for-6. Once, Moravian Coach Dapp elected a PAT kick. McIntyre did not convert. In the fourth quarter, Dickinson scored 3 more Muhlenberg points on a 28-yard field goal.

In 2001, At Scotty Wood Stadium

Moravian Coach Dapp, RB Tim Barlok, PKs Jim McIntyre and Marc Roesch, and their teammates visited with Muhlenberg Coach Donnelly, PK Chris Reed, and his teammates at Scotty Wood Stadium on November 10, 2001. Their visit marked a reunion from the 2000 game, when Barlok, McIntyre, and Reed each took part in a scoring play.

Barlok and his teammates were recognizable in white jerseys redesigned with "Moravian" above the front numerals, blue pants, and blue "Hounds" helmets. Reed and his teammates were recognizable in their cardinal jerseys and gray helmets had a wide cardinal stripe and the mule-over-M.

Moravian rushers gained 117 yards. Muhlenberg rushers gained 72 yards. Barlok of Moravian was the center of attention in the rushing game. He carried 24 times for 66 yards.

The two teams had three extra-point opportunities during the visit.

Muhlenberg—Stankowitz 3 pass from Jones (Reed kick)

Moravian—Roesch 20 FG

Moravian—Abbate 37 pass from Bowden (McIntyre kick)

Moravian—Abbate 11 run (McIntyre kick)

After the Muhlenberg touchdown, Donnelly elected a PAT attempt. Reed converted. Twice, Moravian Coach Dapp elected a PAT attempt. McIntyre was 2-for-2. In the second quarter, Roesch made a 20-yard field goal for 3 Moravian points.

In 2002, At Steel Field

Muhlenberg Coach Donnelly, RB Matt Bernardo, QB Justin Jones, and their teammates visited with Moravian Coach Dapp, QB Charlie Bowden, defensive back (DB) Jarrod Pence, and their teammates at Steel Field on November 16, 2002. Their visit marked a reunion from 2001, when Jones and Bowden each took part in a scoring play.

Bernardo and his teammates were recognizable in their white jerseys, cardinal pants, and gray helmets with a wide cardinal stripe and the mule-over-M. Bowden and his teammates wore blue from head to ankle (blue knee-length socks under white socks).

Muhlenberg rushers gained 163 yards. Moravian rushers gained 98 yards. Bernardo of Muhlenberg was again the center of attention in the rushing game. He ran 32 times for 129 yards.

The Muhlenberg team had the only extra-point opportunity during the visit.

Muhlenberg—Shay 29 pass from Jones (run failed)

Muhlenberg—Safety, Pence tackled in end zone

Muhlenberg Coach Donnelly elected a PAT attempt. The snap from center was fumbled, and the kick attempt did not materialize.

In 2003, At Scotty Wood Stadium

Moravian Coach Dapp, RB Chris Jacoubs, and his teammates visited with Muhlenberg Coach Donnelly, RB Matt Bernardo, PK Brian Hendershot, and their teammates at Scotty Wood Stadium on November 15, 2003.

Jacoubs and his teammates were recognizable in white jerseys, blue pants, and helmets redesigned in gray with "Hounds" in blue script. Bernardo and his teammates were recognizable in their cardinal outfits and gray helmets designed, as in the mid-1990s, to include a narrow black stripe on both sides of the main cardinal stripe. Already on the helmet, the mule-over-M was added to the jersey sleeve.

Moravian rushers gained 85 yards. Muhlenberg rushers gained 201. Bernardo of Muhlenberg and Jacoubs of Moravian were the center of attention in the rushing game. Bernardo ran 18 times for 127 yards and two rushing touchdowns. Jacoubs carried 29 times for 79 yards.

The Muhlenberg team had three extra-point opportunities during the visit.

Muhlenberg—Bernardo 30 run (Hendershot kick)

Muhlenberg—Hendershot 33 FG

Muhlenberg—Shay 45 run (Hendershot kick)

Muhlenberg—Bernardo 2 run (Hendershot kick)

On all three occasions, Muhlenberg Coach Donnelly elected a PAT attempt. Hendershot was 3-for-3. Late in the first half, Donnelly called on Hendershot to attempt a 33-yard field goal. The kick added 3 Muhlenberg points. Hendershot also missed a 37-yard try.

EXTRA-POINT ADVENTURES, 2004–2006

A fan of the kicking game could not ask for more variety than what happened in the three most recent Moravian-and-Muhlenberg football games. The multiples of seven in the 2004 final score suggested better kicking than what actually happened. The point totals that day included a safety and two failed two-point conversion attempts. In the fourth quarter of the 2005 game, one team failed in consecutive extra-point attempts. In the 2006 game, the kickers were a perfect 4-for-4 in PAT attempts, and the 3-3 halftime score was a first in the modern Moravian-and-Muhlenberg football relationship.

In 2004, At Steel Field

Muhlenberg Coach Donnelly, RB Jerome Beverly, PK Jordon Grube, and their teammates visited with Moravian Coach Dapp, RB Chris Jacoubs, PK Ken Macaulay, and their teammates at Steel Field on November 13, 2004.

Beverly and his teammates were recognizable in their white jerseys, cardinal pants, and gray helmets with black-red-black striping and the mule-over-

M. Jacoubs and his teammates were recognizable in their blue jerseys, blue pants, and the gray "Hounds" helmet.

Muhlenberg rushers gained 171 yards. Moravian rushers gained 94 yards. Beverly of Muhlenberg and Jacoubs of Moravian were the center of attention in the rushing game. Beverly and Moravian tacklers met 11 times. He gained 111 yards. Jacoubs met Muhlenberg tacklers 26 times. He gained 94 yards and scored one rushing touchdown.

The two teams had six extra-point opportunities during the visit.

Moravian—Safety, holding penalty in end zone

Muhlenberg—Montalto 28 pass from Rosetti (kick blocked)

Muhlenberg—Johnson 1 run (Grube kick)

Muhlenberg—Giannini 5 pass from Rosetti (Grube kick)

Moravian—Jacoubs 9 run (kick blocked)

Muhlenberg—Merrill blocked PAT return

Muhlenberg—Gasker 95 kickoff return (pass failed)

Moravian—Garr fumble recovery in end zone (run failed)

Muhlenberg Coach Donnelly elected three PAT attempts. Grube was 2-for-3. Dapp elected a PAT attempt after the first Moravian touchdown. The kick by Macaulay was blocked. Donnelly called on Grube to attempt a 36-yard field goal. The kick missed.

In 2005, At Scotty Wood Stadium

Moravian Coach Dapp, RB Chris Jacoubs, PK Brian Reckenbeil, and their teammates visited with Muhlenberg Coach Donnelly, DB Phil Gasker, PK Jordon Grube, and their teammates at Scotty Wood Stadium on November 12, 2005. Their visit was a reunion from 2004, when Jacoubs, Gasker, and Grube each took part in a scoring play.

Jacoubs and his teammates were recognizable in their white jerseys, blue pants, and gray "Hounds" helmets. The new Moravian jersey had a blue stripe on each side of the torso. Gasker and his teammates were recognizable in their cardinal jerseys and pants. Their gray helmets, striped in black-and-cardinal, were trimmed with the familiar mule.

Moravian rushers gained 193 yards. Muhlenberg rushers gained 111 yards. Jacoubs of Moravian was again the center of attention in the rushing game. He met Muhlenberg tacklers 34 times, gained 89 yards, and scored a rushing touchdown.

The two teams had six extra-point opportunities during the visit.

Moravian—Reckenbeil 37 FG

Muhlenberg—Gasker 94 kickoff return (Grube kick)

Moravian—Jacoubs 3 run (Reckenbeil kick)
Moravian—Hawkins 64 pass from Venturino (Reckenbeil kick)
Moravian—Lukich 10 run (Reckenbeil kick)
Muhlenberg—Santagato 4 run (kick failed)
Muhlenberg—Douglass 45 pass from Santagato (pass failed)
Muhlenberg Coach Donnelly elected two PAT attempts. Grube made the first kick and missed the second. Moravian Coach Dapp elected three PAT attempts. Reckenbeil made all three kicks. In the second quarter, Dapp called on Reckenbeil to attempt a 37-yard field goal. The kick was successful for 3 Moravian points.

In 2006, At Rocco Calvo Field

Muhlenberg Coach Donnelly, QB Eric Santagato, RB John DeLuca, PK Tim Hughes, and their teammates visited with Moravian Coach Dapp, PK Brian Reckenbeil, and his teammates at renamed Rocco Calvo Field on November 11, 2006. Their visit marked a reunion from 2005, when Santagato and Reckenbeil each took part in a scoring play.

Santagato and his teammates were recognizable in their white jerseys and gray helmets with three cardinal stripes (broadest in the middle) and the mule-over-M. Reckenbeil and his teammates were recognizable in their blue jerseys and gray "Hounds" helmets. Players on both teams wore knee-high socks. The Muhlenberg sock was black, and the Moravian sock was blue.

Muhlenberg rushers gained 182 yards. Moravian rushers gained 118 yards. DeLuca of Muhlenberg was the center of attention in the rushing game. He carried 10 times for 90 yards.

The two teams had four extra-point opportunities during the visit.
Muhlenberg—Hughes 31 FG
Moravian—Reckenbeil 27 FG
Muhlenberg—Doyle 51 pass interception (Hughes kick)
Moravian—Martell 54 pass from Braxmeier (Reckenbeil kick)
Muhlenberg—Santagato 1 run (Hughes kick)
Muhlenberg—Santagato 4 run (Hughes kick)
Three times, Muhlenberg Coach Donnelly elected a PAT attempt. Hughes was 3-for-3. After the Moravian touchdown, Dapp elected a PAT attempt. Reckenbeil converted. In the first quarter, Donnelly called on Hughes to attempt a 31-yard field goal. The kick was successful for 3 Muhlenberg points. In the second quarter, Dapp called on Reckenbeil to attempt a 27-yard field goal. The kick was successful for 3 Moravian points.

CONCLUSION

This chapter introduces the proposition that competitors are collaborators in one another's company. The narrative is an account of human beings accomplishing a human tie, one visit at a time. It is a story about civil society, the solid associations that human beings join voluntarily to construct for their own respective reasons. In this narrative, it so happens that human beings accomplish this while wearing fearsome-looking uniforms engaged in vigorous competition after which some of them will be labeled "losers." Civil society comes in many shapes and sizes.

This is also a story about competition that does not revolve around winning. No final scores are reported in this chapter. Instead, the modern Moravian-and-Muhlenberg football relationship emerges as an enduring and changing human tie. Each of these football games was played to a conclusion that could be defined as a win for one team and a loss for the other team. Still, there is a more interesting story unfolding than mere wins and losses. The wins and losses are counted only after human ties are in place. If you find this inconceivable, go back and read the chapter again.

This chapter is celebration of an ethic of tolerance that human beings routinely accomplished in the course of the sustaining the Moravian-and-Muhlenberg football competition. This ethic has been cumulatively enacted by football players and coaches who walk onto the playing field with sharply opposed interests. Each year, a new group of players and coaches jointly pursues victory on the field of play. They represent different colleges that compete for attention and for students. Their differences are prominent in their respective school colors and in their ever-changing uniform designs.

Still, these human beings stay together, for an afternoon, for a pair of years in a "home and home" scheduling cycle. They become parties to a figurative conversation. Each game is an exchange of ideas about uniform fashions and playing strategies. Before long, as their historical record of *visits* grew, members of the Moravian and Muhlenberg teams had created a tacit agreement to tolerate one another's quest for distinctiveness.

I have woven an ethic of tolerance, acts of visitation, and the civic spirit of conversation into a story in which each Moravian-and-Muhlenberg game stands as an achievement of human ties. I now move to show in Chapter 2 that every game in this competition relationship was accomplished in a wider context of human ties. This story of visits could have ended long ago. The next proposition about human ties is focused on the efforts that Moravian and Muhlenberg representatives made to arrange each year's visit. The Moravian and Muhlenberg campuses are ten miles apart. The distance between their respective circles of competitive relationships has often been much greater.

NOTES

1. I only *introduce* such an accounting. I do not attempt a complete accounting.

2. The playing time could extend beyond sixty minutes if overtime were required. Through 2006, no Moravian-and-Muhlenberg football game has gone to overtime.

3. Sometimes, a strategic initiative changes the way the game is played. A coach imports a new strategy into his game plan. Sometimes, the change is accidental. A veteran player is injured, and an untested player steps into the role. Both kinds of change occurred in Moravian-and-Muhlenberg football. In the 1958 game, Moravian Coach Rocco Calvo revived the "single wing" offense formation. The Muhlenberg defense struggled to contain Moravian rushers. In 2000, Muhlenberg Coach Mike Donnelly called on freshman Matt Bernardo to replace an injured rusher. Bernardo's performance in the 2000 game was unprecedented in the Moravian-and-Muhlenberg football relationship. Over Bernardo's playing years, his rushing diversified the Muhlenberg offense to a degree that Moravian defenses had not seen since the 1950s.

4. Jack Gray, "Muhlenberg Coach Says Game One of Best Yet," *Sunday Call-Chronicle*, 21 November 1965, D3.

5. John Heilig, "Mules End Season on Good Note, Beat Rival Moravian," *Morning Call*, 12 November 2006, CC8.

6. The 1963 game was cancelled, due to the death of President John F. Kennedy. Thus, forty-eight of the forty-nine scheduled games were played.

7. For an account about how Pete Gogolak and Charlie Gogolak changed Ivy League football, see Richard Goldstein, *Ivy League Autumns: An Illustrated History of College Football's Grand Old Rivalries* (New York: St. Martin's Press, 1996), 143-61.

8. This use of numbers (e.g., 20) is a sports journalism convention.

9. This uniform description, and all that follow, is fully my interpretation. No descriptions of football uniforms appear anywhere in published accounts of Moravian-and-Muhlenberg football games since 1958. In doing this interpretive work, I draw on data from three principal sources. One source is firsthand observation. I have attended fifteen Moravian-and-Muhlenberg football games, more than fifty other games involving a Moravian football team, and eight other football games involving a Muhlenberg team. A second source of data consists of photographs published in *Benigna*, the Moravian College yearbook, from 1958 through 2007, and in *Ciarla*, the Muhlenberg College yearbook, from 1959 through 2002. In endnotes below, I call attention to *Benigna* and *Ciarla* photographs in which the uniform contrasts are vivid. A third source is my own photographic work. I began creating a collection of Moravian-and-Muhlenberg game photographs in 2000. For several games, accessible data about uniforms was spotty. For several games, I had access to game programs, published by the host college, containing posed team photos. In other instances, I had to draw inferences.

10. For contrasts in uniforms, see *Benigna 1959*, 144-45; *Ciarla 1959*, 135.

11. In football pants design, stripes always appear on the outside length of the pant leg. Hereafter, I will simply refer to the number and color of the stripes.

12. Each player's uniform number appeared on the front and back of his jersey. Since this is a customary aspect of uniform design, I omit reference to these markings.

13. Through 1974, scoring summaries contained references to touchdown *runs* and *plunges*. The latter likely involved the player falling into the end zone.

14. Since all attempts to score by kicking were from a holder's placement of the ball on the ground (hence, "placekicker"), I hereafter refer to "kicker."

15. For contrasts in uniforms, see *Benigna 1963*, 176.

16. *Ciarla 1964*, 141–43.

17. For contrasts in uniforms, see *Ciarla 1965*, 152.

18. Hereafter, I note only the presence of numerals (always on both sides).

19. I list *Hugh* Gratz, because another Gratz will soon appear for Moravian.

20. For contrasts in uniforms, see *Benigna 1971*, 22, 26.

21. For contrasts in uniforms, see *Ciarla 1974*, 31.

22. This was one of eight games for which the Bethlehem (later, Easton) and Allentown newspaper accounts listed different rushing totals. The games are 1973, 1975, 1979, 1981, 1983, 1984, 1989, and 1991. Only in 1991 was the difference greater than ten yards, when Moravian rushing was reported as 138 yards and 166 yards. I follow the convention of citing the statistic that was reported in the "home team" newspaper. In 1973, this was the *Sunday Call-Chronicle*.

23. For contrasts in uniforms, see *Benigna 1975*, 101.

24. For contrasts in uniforms, see *Benigna 1977*, 118, 122–23.

25. For contrasts in uniforms, see *Benigna 1978*, 87; *Ciarla 1978*, 154.

26. For contrasts in uniforms, see *Benigna 1979*, 71.

27. For contrasts in uniforms, see *Ciarla 1981*, 162, 164-65.

28. For contrasts in uniforms, see *Ciarla 1982*, 71.

29. Lea was a soccer-style kicker. *Ciarla 1983*, 139.

30. For contrasts in uniforms, see *Benigna 1992*, 76.

31. The *Bethlehem Globe-Times* reported 28 yards fewer for Moravian and 32 fewer for Muhlenberg. This might reflect inclusion of yardage lost on quarterback sacks.

32. Davis was a soccer-style kicker. *Benigna 1992*, 83.

33. Three different distances for this kick can be found in published accounts of the game: 16, 23, and 27 yards. The first seems implausible. The 23-yard distance appears in a scoring summary that accompanied: Andre Williams, "Moravian Continues Its Domination of Muhlenberg," *Morning Call*, 17 November 1996, C4.

Chapter Two

Competitors Seek One
Another's Company

Intercollegiate athletics is the scene of some extraordinary efforts by competitors to find one another and then to meet on a field of play. Sometimes intercollegiate athletic competitors literally go to great lengths to meet. These lengths can be measured in miles traveled and in hours spent on bus rides. Sometimes intercollegiate athletic competitors figuratively go to great lengths to meet. This occurs when two competitors reach across a boundary that separates the circle of playing relationships to which each elects to belong. This latter extraordinary act of sustaining competitive relationships is the subject of this chapter. Through this act, competitors join in an ethical accomplishment.

IN ONE'S LEAGUE AND BEYOND ONE'S LEAGUE

Two competitors must sometimes go to great lengths to find and to engage one another, for the ironic reason that each already belongs to an institutionalized set of relationships called an intercollegiate athletic league (or conference).[1] Continuity and competitiveness are two reasons why competitors join and sustain membership in a league. League membership commits each league member to a schedule of competitions with the other league members. This commitment results in what is known as a "round robin" schedule. For any one league member, this commitment reduces the time and expense of constructing annually a schedule of competitions.[2] For any league member, too, the round robin provides an historical accumulation of competitive experiences. Each competitor can tap this history for purposes of assessing and devising playing strategies in relation to other league members. Through round robin competition, the reasoning goes, each competitor can aspire to become a smarter competitor.[3]

It is in this context of established relationships that extraordinary scheduling efforts are accomplished. The league round robin usually does not encompass the entire annual schedule for a league member.[4] Often, the league round robin commits each member to fewer games than the number of games a team is permitted to schedule.[5] This provides competitors with the impetus to begin the search for competitive relationships outside a competitor's circle of league partners. This is where some extraordinary things can be accomplished by two competitors seeking additional playing relationships.

Because league membership is a dominant feature of American intercollegiate athletic competition, it is easy to overlook these scheduling ventures. One such ongoing venture is the story line of this chapter. The story is about human beings who deserve continuing ethical praise for what they do together as competitors.

THE MODERN MORAVIAN-AND-MUHLENBERG PLAYING RELATIONSHIP

The modern Moravian-and-Muhlenberg football playing relationship, dating to 1958, is an instructive lesson about competitors reaching beyond formal circles of playing relationships to accomplish an ethical feat. The relationship is an ironic example of the lengths to which competitors can go to accomplish a human tie. The irony here is that Moravian College and Muhlenberg College are literally neighbors. The Moravian campus in Bethlehem, Pennsylvania and the Muhlenberg campus in Allentown, Pennsylvania are situated ten miles apart. The drive typically takes less than thirty minutes.

Still, for nearly three-quarters of the football seasons that comprise the modern history of this playing relationship, the Moravian football team and the Muhlenberg football team traveled in separate worlds of competition relationships. In a span of forty-nine autumns, the Moravian and Muhlenberg football teams, respectively, belonged to the same league for only fourteen seasons: the Middle Atlantic Conference Southern Division from 1969 through 1982. Moreover, from 1958 through 2006, the boundary between the Moravian and the Muhlenberg league memberships shifted six times.[6]

In 1958, Moravian joined the Middle Atlantic Conference College Division North (MAC North). In the same year, Muhlenberg left the Eastern Intercollegiate Football Association to join the Middle Atlantic Conference University Division.

In 1963, while Moravian continued as a MAC North member, Muhlenberg joined the Middle Atlantic Conference College Division South (MAC South).

In 1969, Moravian moved from the MAC North to the MAC South, while Muhlenberg continued to compete in the MAC South.

In 1983, Moravian competed in a newly-unified MAC, while Muhlenberg joined the newly-formed Centennial Football Conference.

In 1993, Moravian participated in the MAC Commonwealth League, when the MAC was split into the Commonwealth League and the Freedom League, while Muhlenberg continued in the re-named Centennial Conference.

In 2001, Moravian competed in a reunified MAC, while Muhlenberg continued in the Centennial Conference.

THE ETHICAL ACCOMPLISHMENT

On either side of the fourteen-season span from 1969 through 1982, the members of the Moravian and Muhlenberg football teams, respectively, were not required to meet on the field of play. The teams belonged to different leagues. In the modern history of the Moravian-and-Muhlenberg football relationship that continues uninterrupted from 1958 through 2006, the two colleges' representatives reached across a shifting divide to arrange for members of the two teams to engage year after year on the playing field.

These representatives—college presidents, athletic directors, and coaches—did this voluntarily, and they did it repeatedly.[7] This is the extraordinary act of human connection that I celebrate in this chapter. These human beings created and accepted an obligation to engage one another year after year. This deliberate enhancement of civic ties is an impressive ethical accomplishment.

Methodology and Data

This chapter contains an ethical, historical interpretation of scheduling in the modern Moravian-and-Muhlenberg football relationship. The principal evidence is drawn from nearly one hundred intercollegiate football schedules (two teams for the forty-nine years). I use this data to make annual comparisons of the Moravian football schedule and the Muhlenberg football schedule. Matching these schedules with league memberships, I create an account about competitors finding one another, year after year.

A Word to Readers

There is repetition and redundancy in the narrative that follows. This is necessary. This chapter is an introduction to a different way of talking about intercollegiate athletic competition. It takes practice to talk in new ways. In this chapter, there are forty-nine opportunities—the forty-nine games scheduled in the modern Moravian-and-Muhlenberg football relationship from 1958 through 2006—to practice connecting intercollegiate athletics and ethics through the duty that competitors accept to sustain their ties. Be patient. Immerse yourself in this new way of talking. Midway through the chapter, I will have streamlined the narrative. By then, the changes will likely escape your detection.

A COMPETITION RELATIONSHIP RESUMES

On November 16, 1946, in Allentown, Pennsylvania, Moravian Coach Larry Rosati and his team members visited Muhlenberg Coach Ben Schwartzwalder and his team members.[8] The Moravian-and-Muhlenberg football playing relationship was then dormant from 1947 through 1957. In that span, the two teams moved in different circles. This separation is depicted in the Moravian and Muhlenberg schedules for the 1947 and 1957 football seasons.[9]

Moravian 1947 Football

September 19—at West Chester; September 26—Buffalo; October 4—at Lebanon Valley; October 11—at Upsala; October 17—Ursinus; October 24—Albright; October 31—Ithaca; November 7—Pennsylvania Military College.

Muhlenberg 1947 Football

September 27—at Lafayette; October 4—Albright; October 11—at Swarthmore; October 17—at Temple; October 25—Upsala; November 1—at Lehigh; November 8—Gettysburg; November 15—Delaware; November 22—Bucknell; November 27—at Franklin & Marshall.

Moravian 1957 Football

October 5—at Lycoming; October 12—Juniata; October 19—Pennsylvania Military College; October 26—at Lebanon Valley; November 2—Albright; November 9—Upsala; November 16—at Wagner; November 23—at Wilkes.

Muhlenberg 1957 Football

September 28—at Lafayette; October 5—Albright; October 12—Scranton; October 19—Lebanon Valley; October 26—Gettysburg; November 2—at Temple; November 9—at Hofstra; November 16—at Franklin & Marshall.

In the 1947 season, for example, only Albright and Upsala appeared on both the Moravian football schedule and the Muhlenberg football schedule. In 1957, only Albright and Lebanon Valley appeared on both schedules.

November 22, 1958, Muhlenberg at Moravian

On November 22, 1958, Head Coach Ray Whispell and members of the Muhlenberg 1958 football team traveled ten miles from Allentown to Bethlehem and the Moravian campus. There they met Head Coach Rocco Calvo and members of the Moravian 1958 football team. Together, the two teams played to a 30-20 final score, a Moravian win and a Muhlenberg loss. Together, these persons deserve credit for doing something more than conducting this football game. On November 22, 1958, they traversed a boundary that separated two leagues and two circles of competitors.

Moravian belonged to the Middle Atlantic Conference College Division North (hereafter, MAC North) for the 1958 football season. Muhlenberg belonged to the Middle Atlantic Conference University Division (hereafter, MAC University) for the 1958 season. The capitalized entries in the Moravian 1958 schedule indicate other members of the MAC North. The capitalized entries marked with an asterisk in the Muhlenberg 1958 schedule indicate other members of the MAC University. These schedules are shown in Table 2.1.

Moravian College and Muhlenberg College officials were under no obligation to schedule the 1958 game. They did so, despite different league affiliations. Moreover, the scheduling of this game enabled participants to span jointly another boundary. Muhlenberg Coach Whispell and his players moved beyond a competition circle that included Hofstra and Franklin & Marshall, neither an MAC University member in 1958, and Moravian Coach Calvo and his players moved beyond a competition circle that included Pennsylvania Military College and Upsala, neither in the MAC North in 1958.[10] A separation had ended. A distance of eleven years and ten miles had been traversed,

Table 2.1.   Football Schedules for 1958

	Moravian 1958	*Muhlenberg 1958*
October 4	WILKES	at LAFAYETTE*
October 11	at JUNIATA	TEMPLE*
October 18	at Pennsylvania Military	at Lebanon Valley
October 25	LEBANON VALLEY	at GETTYSBURG*
November 1	at ALBRIGHT	Hofstra
November 8	at Upsala	at Albright
November 15	WAGNER	Franklin & Marshall
November 22	Muhlenberg	at Moravian

at least for one year, by two competitors voluntarily seeking one another's company on the field of play.

REAFFIRMATION BEGINS FOR A NEW
COMPETITION RELATIONSHIP

Rocco Calvo and Ray Whispell were parties to this ethical accomplishment from the 1958 football season through the 1968 season, accompanied each year by different groups of team members. In this span of eleven seasons, the representatives of the two colleges affirmed publicly a mutual desire to meet on the field of play. They reached across a divide that they were under no obligation to recognize, much less to span. The modern Moravian-and-Muhlenberg playing relationship unfolds from the outset as an ethical accomplishment. What follows is the year-by-year account of this civic feat.

November 21, 1959, Moravian at Muhlenberg

On November 21, 1959, Calvo and members of the Moravian 1959 football team traveled ten miles from Bethlehem to Allentown and the Muhlenberg campus. There they met Whispell and members of the Muhlenberg 1959 football team. Together, the two teams played to a 20-8 final score, a Muhlenberg win and a Moravian loss. Together, these persons deserve credit for doing something more than conducting this football game. They traversed a boundary that separated two leagues and two circles of competitors.

Moravian belonged to the MAC North for the 1959 football season. Muhlenberg belonged to the MAC University for the 1959 season. The capitalized entries in the Moravian 1959 schedule indicate other members of the MAC North. The capitalized entries marked with an asterisk in the Muhlenberg 1959 schedule indicate other members of the MAC University. These schedules are shown in Table 2.2.

The scheduling of this game enabled Calvo, Whispell, and their respective team members to span jointly a boundary between the MAC North and MAC University and a boundary between a Moravian competition circle (with Pennsylvania Military and Upsala) and a Muhlenberg competition circle (with Scranton, Hofstra, and Franklin & Marshall).

November 19, 1960, Muhlenberg at Moravian

On November 19, 1960, Whispell and members of the Muhlenberg 1960 football team traveled ten miles from Allentown to Bethlehem and the Moravian

Table 2.2. Football Schedules for 1959

	Moravian 1959	*Muhlenberg 1959*
September 26		at Scranton
October 3	at WILKES	LAFAYETTE*
October 10	JUNIATA	at TEMPLE*
October 17	Pennsylvania Military	Lebanon Valley
October 24	at LEBANON VALLEY	GETTYSBURG*
October 31	ALBRIGHT	at Hofstra
November 7	Upsala	Albright
November 14	at WAGNER	at Franklin & Marshall
November 21	at Muhlenberg	Moravian

campus. There they met Calvo and members of the Moravian 1960 football team. Together, the two teams played to a 33-16 final score, a Muhlenberg win and a Moravian loss. Together, these persons deserve credit for doing something more than conducting this football game. They traversed a boundary that separated two leagues and two circles of competitors.

Moravian belonged to the MAC North for the 1960 football season. Muhlenberg belonged to the MAC University for the 1960 season. The capitalized entries in the Moravian 1960 schedule indicate other members of the MAC North. The capitalized entries marked with an asterisk in the Muhlenberg 1960 schedule indicate other members of the MAC University. These schedules are shown in Table 2.3.

The scheduling of this game enabled Calvo, Whispell, and their respective team members to span jointly a boundary between the MAC North and MAC University and a boundary between the Moravian-and-Pennsylvania Military College football relationship, and a Muhlenberg competition circle (with Lycoming, Scranton, and Franklin & Marshall).[11]

Table 2.3. Football Schedules for 1960

	Moravian 1960	*Muhlenberg 1960*
September 24		Albright
October 1	WILKES	at LAFAYETTE*
October 8	at JUNIATA	TEMPLE*
October 15	at Pennsylvania Military	at Lebanon Valley
October 22	LEBANON VALLEY	at GETTYSBURG*
October 29	at ALBRIGHT	Lycoming
November 5	at UPSALA	at Scranton
November 12	WAGNER	Franklin & Marshall
November 19	Muhlenberg	at Moravian

November 18, 1961, Moravian at Muhlenberg

On November 18, 1961, Calvo and members of the Moravian 1961 football team traveled ten miles from Bethlehem to Allentown and the Muhlenberg campus. There they met Whispell and members of the Muhlenberg 1961 team. Together, the two teams played to a 33-8 Muhlenberg win and Moravian loss. Together, these persons deserve credit for doing something more than conducting this football game. They traversed a boundary that separated two leagues and two circles of competitors.

Moravian belonged to the MAC North for the 1961 football season. Muhlenberg belonged to the MAC University for the 1961 season. The capitalized entries in the Moravian schedule indicate other members of the MAC North. The capitalized entries marked with an asterisk in the Muhlenberg schedule indicate other members of the MAC University. These schedules are shown in Table 2.4.

The scheduling of this game enabled Calvo, Whispell, and their respective team members to span jointly a boundary between the MAC North and MAC University and a boundary between a Moravian competition circle (with C.W. Post and Pennsylvania Military College) and a Muhlenberg competition circle (with Kings Point and Franklin & Marshall).

November 17, 1962, Muhlenberg at Moravian

On November 17, 1962, Whispell and members of the Muhlenberg 1962 football team traveled ten miles from Allentown to Bethlehem. There they met Calvo and members of the Moravian 1962 team. Together, the two teams played to a 32-8 Muhlenberg win and Moravian loss. Together, these persons deserve credit for traversing a boundary that separated two leagues and two circles of competitors.

Table 2.4. Football Schedules for 1961

	Moravian 1961	*Muhlenberg 1961*
September 23	at C.W. Post	LAFAYETTE*
September 30	at WILKES	at Albright
October 7	JUNIATA	at TEMPLE*
October 14	Pennsylvania Military	Lebanon Valley
October 21	at LEBANON VALLEY	GETTYSBURG*
October 28	ALBRIGHT	at BUCKNELL*
November 4	UPSALA	at Kings Point
November 11		at Franklin & Marshall
November 18	at Muhlenberg	Moravian

Table 2.5.   Football Schedules for 1962

	Moravian 1962	Muhlenberg 1962
September 22		at LAFAYETTE*
September 29	WILKES	Albright
October 6	at JUNIATA	TEMPLE*
October 13	at Pennsylvania Military	at Lebanon Valley
October 20	LEBANON VALLEY	at GETTYSBURG*
October 27	at ALBRIGHT	BUCKNELL*
November 3	at UPSALA	King's (PA)
November 10	C.W. Post	Franklin & Marshall
November 17	Muhlenberg	at Moravian

Moravian belonged to the MAC North for the 1962 football season. Muhlenberg belonged to the MAC University in 1962. The capitalized entries in the Moravian schedule indicate other members of the MAC North. The capitalized entries marked with an asterisk in the Muhlenberg schedule indicate other MAC University members. These schedules are shown in Table 2.5.

The scheduling of this game enabled Calvo, Whispell, and their respective team members to span jointly a boundary between the MAC North and MAC University and a boundary between a Moravian competition circle (with Pennsylvania Military College and C.W. Post) and a Muhlenberg competition circle (with King's and Franklin & Marshall).

November 23, 1963, Moravian at Muhlenberg

Calvo, Whispell, and the members of their respective teams did not meet as scheduled on November 23, 1963, in Allentown. Due to events that occurred on the previous day in Dallas, Texas, representatives of Moravian College and Muhlenberg College agreed to cancel this scheduled football game.[12]

Moravian belonged to the MAC North for the 1963 football season. Muhlenberg joined the MAC South for the 1963 season. The capitalized entries in the Moravian schedule indicate other members of the MAC North. The capitalized entries marked with an asterisk in the Muhlenberg schedule indicate other members of the MAC South. These schedules are shown in Table 2.6.

The scheduling of this game indicated a mutual desire to span jointly a boundary between the MAC North and MAC South and a boundary between the Moravian-and-Pennsylvania Military College football relationship, and a Muhlenberg competition circle (with Lafayette, Temple, Gettysburg, and Lycoming).

Table 2.6.   Football Schedules for 1963

	Moravian 1963	*Muhlenberg 1963*
September 28		at Albright
October 5	at WILKES	Lafayette
October 12	at WAGNER	at Temple
October 19	Pennsylvania Military	LEBANON VALLEY*
October 26	Lebanon Valley	Gettysburg
November 2	ALBRIGHT	at Upsala
November 9	UPSALA	Lycoming
November 16		at FRANKLIN & MARSHALL*
November 23	at Muhlenberg	Moravian

November 21, 1964, Muhlenberg at Moravian

On November 21, 1964, Whispell and members of the Muhlenberg 1964 football team traveled ten miles from Allentown to Bethlehem. There they met Calvo and members of the Moravian 1964 team. Together, the two teams played to a 21-6 Muhlenberg win and Moravian loss. Together, these persons deserve credit for traversing a boundary that separated two leagues and two circles of competitors.

Moravian belonged to the MAC North for the 1964 football season. Muhlenberg belonged to the MAC South in 1964. The capitalized entries in the Moravian schedule indicate other members of the MAC North. The capitalized entries marked with an asterisk in the Muhlenberg schedule indicate other members of the MAC South. These schedules are shown in Table 2.7.

This scheduling of this game enabled Calvo, Whispell, and their respective team members to span jointly a boundary between the MAC North and MAC South and a boundary between a Moravian competition circle (with Delaware Valley and Pennsylvania Military College) and a Muhlenberg competition circle (with Gettysburg and Lycoming).

Table 2.7.   Football Schedules for 1964

	Moravian 1964	*Muhlenberg 1964*
September 26	at Delaware Valley	at DICKINSON*
October 3	WILKES	URSINUS*
October 10	WAGNER	PENNSYLVANIA MILITARY*
October 17	at Pennsylvania Military	at LEBANON VALLEY*
October 24	Lebanon Valley	at Gettysburg
October 31	at ALBRIGHT	Upsala
November 7	at UPSALA	at Lycoming
November 14		FRANKLIN & MARSHALL*
November 21	Muhlenberg	at Moravian

November 20, 1965, Moravian at Muhlenberg

On November 20, 1965, Calvo and members of the Moravian 1965 football team traveled ten miles from Bethlehem to Allentown. There they met Whispell and members of the Muhlenberg 1965 team. Together, the two teams played to a 17-8 Moravian win and Muhlenberg loss. Together, these persons deserve credit for traversing a boundary that separated two leagues and two circles of competitors.

Moravian belonged to the MAC North for the 1965 football season. Muhlenberg belonged to the MAC South for the 1965 season. The capitalized entries in the Moravian schedule indicate other members of the MAC North. The capitalized entries marked with an asterisk in the Muhlenberg schedule indicate other members of the MAC South. These schedules are shown in Table 2.8.

The scheduling of this game enabled Calvo, Whispell and their respective team members to span jointly a boundary between the MAC North and MAC South and a boundary between a Moravian competition circle (with Delaware Valley and Pennsylvania Military College) and the Muhlenberg-and-Lycoming football relationship.

November 19, 1966, Muhlenberg at Moravian

On November 19, 1966, Whispell and members of the Muhlenberg 1966 football team traveled ten miles from Allentown to Bethlehem. There they met Calvo and members of the Moravian 1966 team. Together, the two teams played to a 14-7 Moravian win and Muhlenberg loss. Together, these persons deserve credit for traversing a boundary that separated two leagues and two circles of competitors.

Moravian belonged to the MAC North for the 1966 football season. Muhlenberg belonged to the MAC South for the 1966 season. The capitalized en-

Table 2.8.   Football Schedules for 1965

	Moravian 1965	*Muhlenberg 1965*
September 25	at Delaware Valley	DICKINSON*
October 2	at WILKES	at URSINUS*
October 9	at WAGNER	at PENNSYLVANIA MILITARY*
October 16	Pennsylvania Military	LEBANON VALLEY*
October 23	at Lebanon Valley	Wilkes
October 30	ALBRIGHT	at Upsala
November 6	UPSALA	Lycoming
November 13	JUNIATA	at FRANKLIN & MARSHALL*
November 20	at Muhlenberg	Moravian

Table 2.9. Football Schedules for 1966

	Moravian 1966	*Muhlenberg 1966*
September 24	DELAWARE VALLEY	Upsala
October 1	WILKES	URSINUS*
October 8	WAGNER	PENNSYLVANIA MILITARY*
October 15	at Pennsylvania Military	at LEBANON VALLEY*
October 22	Lebanon Valley	at DICKINSON*
October 29	at ALBRIGHT	SWARTHMORE*
November 5	at UPSALA	at Lycoming
November 12	at JUNIATA	FRANKLIN & MARSHALL*
November 19	Muhlenberg	at Moravian

tries in the Moravian schedule indicate other members of the MAC North. The capitalized entries marked with an asterisk in the Muhlenberg schedule indicate other members of the MAC South. These schedules are shown in Table 2.9.

The scheduling of this game enabled Calvo, Whispell, and their respective team members to span jointly a boundary between the MAC North and MAC South and a boundary between the Moravian-and-Pennsylvania Military College football relationship and the Muhlenberg-and-Lycoming football relationship.

November 18, 1967, Moravian at Muhlenberg

On November 18, 1967, Calvo and members of the Moravian 1967 football team traveled ten miles from Bethlehem to Allentown. There they met Whispell and members of the Muhlenberg 1967 team. Together, the two teams played to a 19-8 Moravian win and Muhlenberg loss. Together, these persons deserve credit for traversing a boundary that separated two leagues and two circles of competitors.

Moravian belonged to the MAC North for the 1967 football season. Muhlenberg belonged to the MAC South for the 1967 season. The capitalized entries in the Moravian schedule indicate other members of the MAC North. The capitalized entries marked with an asterisk in the Muhlenberg schedule indicate other members of the MAC South. These schedules are shown in Table 2.10.

The scheduling of this game enabled Calvo, Whispell, and their respective team members to span jointly a boundary between the MAC North and MAC South; and a boundary between the Moravian-and-Pennsylvania Military College football relationship and the Muhlenberg-and-Lycoming football relationship.

Table 2.10. Football Schedules for 1967

	Moravian 1967	Muhlenberg 1967
September 23	DELAWARE VALLEY	
September 30	at WILKES	at URSINUS*
October 7	at WAGNER	at PENNSYLVANIA MILITARY*
October 14	Pennsylvania Military	LEBANON VALLEY*
October 21	at Lebanon Valley	DICKINSON*
October 28	ALBRIGHT	at SWARTHMORE*
November 4	UPSALA	Lycoming
November 11	JUNIATA	at FRANKLIN & MARSHALL*
November 18	at Muhlenberg	Moravian

November 23, 1968, Muhlenberg at Moravian

On November 23, 1968, Whispell and members of the Muhlenberg 1968 football team traveled ten miles from Allentown to Bethlehem. There they met Calvo and members of the Moravian 1968 team. Together, the two teams played to a 47-15 Moravian win and Muhlenberg loss. Together, these persons deserve credit for traversing a boundary that separated two leagues and two circles of competitors.

Moravian belonged to the MAC North for the 1968 football season. Muhlenberg belonged to the MAC South for the 1968 season. The capitalized entries in the Moravian schedule indicate other members of the MAC North. The capitalized entries marked with an asterisk in the Muhlenberg schedule indicate other members of the MAC South. These schedules are shown in Table 2.11.

The scheduling of this game enabled Calvo, Whispell, and their respective team members to span jointly a boundary between the MAC North and MAC South and a boundary between the Moravian-and-Pennsylvania Military Col-

Table 2.11. Football Schedules for 1968

	Moravian 1968	Muhlenberg 1968
September 28	at DELAWARE VALLEY	JOHNS HOPKINS*
October 5	WILKES	at HAVERFORD*
October 12	WAGNER	LEBANON VALLEY*
October 19	at Pennsylvania Military	URSINUS*
October 26	Lebanon Valley	at DICKINSON*
November 2	at ALBRIGHT	SWARTHMORE*
November 9	at UPSALA	at Lycoming
November 16	at JUNIATA	FRANKLIN & MARSHALL*
November 23	Muhlenberg	at Moravian

lege football relationship and the Muhlenberg-and-Lycoming football relationship.

IN THE SAME LEAGUE, STILL TRAVELING
IN DIFFERENT CIRCLES

Changes were underway in the second decade of the modern Moravian-and-Muhlenberg football relationship. In 1969, Moravian moved to the Middle Atlantic Conference South league. At first, the Moravian schedule gave little indication of this change in affiliation. Scheduling commitments to such MAC North members as Albright were honored for several years after Moravian formally departed the MAC North. Moravian football teams did not participate substantially in the MAC South round robin until the 1975 season.

Moravian and Muhlenberg both belonged to the MAC South through 1982. From the mid-1970s through 1982, there appeared another twist to the unfolding story of competitors traversing boundaries to sustain a playing relationship. The MAC South round robin schedule was not mandatory. Some MAC South members appeared in the Muhlenberg schedule but not in the Moravian schedule (e.g., Swarthmore in 1976). In effect, Moravian and Muhlenberg were members of different groups of MAC South members. There was now a new boundary to cross.

There were coaching changes, too. Frank Marino became Muhlenberg Head Coach in 1970. Ed Little became Moravian Head Coach in 1977. Marino and Little now joined the accomplishment of human ties that Rocco Calvo and Ray Whispell had been instrumental in establishing.

November 22, 1969, Moravian at Muhlenberg

On November 22, 1969, Calvo and members of the Moravian 1969 football team traveled ten miles from Bethlehem to Allentown. There they met Whispell and members of the Muhlenberg 1969 team. Together, the two teams played to a 37-0 Moravian win and Muhlenberg loss. Together, these persons deserve credit for traversing a boundary that separated two segments of the same league and two circles of competitors.

Moravian and Muhlenberg both belonged to the MAC South for the 1969 football season. The capitalized entries in the two schedules indicate other MAC South members. These schedules are shown in Table 2.12.

The scheduling of this game enabled Calvo, Whispell, and their respective team members to span jointly a boundary between one MAC South group (Moravian, Pennsylvania Military College, and Lebanon Valley) and a second

Table 2.12.   Football Schedules for 1969

	Moravian 1969	*Muhlenberg 1969*
September 27	Delaware Valley	at JOHNS HOPKINS
October 4	at Wilkes	HAVERFORD
October 11	at Wagner	at LEBANON VALLEY
October 18	PENN. MILITARY	at URSINUS
October 25	at LEBANON VALLEY	DICKINSON
November 1	Albright	at SWARTHMORE
November 8	Upsala	Lycoming
November 15	Juniata	at FRANKLIN & MARSHALL
November 22	at MUHLENBERG	MORAVIAN

MAC South group (Muhlenberg, Johns Hopkins, Haverford, Ursinus, Dickinson, Swarthmore, and Franklin & Marshall) and a boundary between a Moravian competition circle (with Delaware Valley, Wilkes, Wagner, Albright, Upsala, and Juniata) and the Muhlenberg-and-Lycoming football relationship.

November 21, 1970, Muhlenberg at Moravian

On November 21, 1970, new Head Coach Frank Marino and members of the Muhlenberg 1970 football team traveled ten miles from Allentown to Bethlehem. There they met Calvo and members of the Moravian 1970 team. Together, the two teams played to a 55-7 Moravian win and Muhlenberg loss. Together, these persons deserve credit for traversing a boundary separating two segments of the same league and two circles of competitors.

Moravian and Muhlenberg both belonged to the MAC South for the 1970 football season. The capitalized entries in the two schedules indicate other members of the MAC South. These schedules are shown in Table 2.13.

The scheduling of this game enabled Calvo, Marino, and their respective team members to span jointly a boundary between one MAC South group

Table 2.13.   Football Schedules for 1970

	Moravian 1970	*Muhlenberg 1970*
September 26	at Delaware Valley	JOHNS HOPKINS
October 3	Wilkes	at HAVERFORD
October 10	Wagner	LEBANON VALLEY
October 17	at PENN. MILITARY	URSINUS
October 24	LEBANON VALLEY	at DICKINSON
October 31	at Albright	SWARTHMORE
November 7	at Upsala	at PENNSYLVANIA MILITARY
November 14	at Juniata	FRANKLIN & MARSHALL
November 21	MUHLENBERG	at MORAVIAN

(Moravian, Pennsylvania Military College, and Lebanon Valley) and a second MAC South group (Muhlenberg, Johns Hopkins, Haverford, Ursinus, Dickinson, Swarthmore, and Franklin & Marshall) and a boundary between a Moravian competition circle (with Delaware Valley, Wilkes, Wagner, Albright, Upsala, and Juniata) and the Muhlenberg full MAC South schedule.[13]

November 20, 1971, Moravian at Muhlenberg

On November 20, 1971, Calvo and members of the Moravian 1971 football team traveled ten miles from Bethlehem to Allentown. There they met Marino and members of the Muhlenberg 1971 team. Together, the two teams played to a 14-7 Moravian win and Muhlenberg loss. Together, these persons deserve credit for traversing a boundary separating two segments of the same league and two circles of competitors.

Moravian and Muhlenberg both belonged to the MAC South for the 1971 football season. The capitalized entries in the two schedules indicate other MAC South members. These schedules are shown in Table 2.14.

The scheduling of this game enabled Calvo, Marino, and their respective team members to span jointly a boundary between one MAC South group (Moravian, Pennsylvania Military College, and Lebanon Valley) and a second MAC South group (Muhlenberg, Johns Hopkins, Haverford, Ursinus, Dickinson, Swarthmore, and Franklin & Marshall) and a boundary between a Moravian competition circle (with Delaware Valley, Wilkes, Wagner, Albright, Upsala, and Juniata) and the Muhlenberg-and-Lycoming football relationship.

November 18, 1972, Muhlenberg at Moravian

On Saturday, November 18, 1972, Marino and members of the Muhlenberg 1972 football team traveled ten miles from Allentown to Bethlehem. There they met Calvo and members of the Moravian 1972 team. Together, the two

Table 2.14.   Football Schedules for 1971

	Moravian 1971	*Muhlenberg 1971*
September 25	Delaware Valley	at JOHNS HOPKINS
October 2	at Wilkes	HAVERFORD
October 9	at Wagner	at LEBANON VALLEY
October 16	PENN. MILITARY	at URSINUS
October 23	at LEBANON VALLEY	DICKINSON
October 30	Albright	at SWARTHMORE
November 6	Upsala	Lycoming
November 13	Juniata	at FRANKLIN & MARSHALL
November 20	at MUHLENBERG	MORAVIAN

Table 2.15. Football Schedules for 1972

	Moravian 1972	Muhlenberg 1972
September 23	at Delaware Valley	JOHNS HOPKINS
September 30	at Upsala	at HAVERFORD
October 7	Wilkes	LEBANON VALLEY
October 14	at WIDENER	URSINUS
October 21	LEBANON VALLEY	at DICKINSON
October 28	at Albright	SWARTHMORE
November 4		at WIDENER
November 11	at Juniata	FRANKLIN & MARSHALL
November 18	MUHLENBERG	at MORAVIAN

teams played to a 38-14 Moravian win and Muhlenberg loss. Together, these persons deserve credit for traversing a boundary separating two segments of the same league and two circles of competitors.

Moravian and Muhlenberg both belonged to the MAC South for the 1972 football season. The capitalized entries in the two schedules indicate other MAC South members.[14] These schedules are shown in Table 2.15.

The scheduling of this game enabled Calvo, Marino, and their respective team members to span jointly a boundary between one MAC South (Moravian, Widener, and Lebanon Valley) and a second MAC South (Muhlenberg, Johns Hopkins, Haverford, Ursinus, Dickinson, Swarthmore, and Franklin & Marshall) and a boundary between a Moravian competition circle (with Delaware Valley, Upsala, Wilkes, Albright, and Juniata) and the Muhlenberg full MAC South schedule.[15]

November 17, 1973, Moravian at Muhlenberg

On November 17, 1973, Calvo and members of the Moravian 1973 football team traveled ten miles from Bethlehem to Allentown. There they met Marino and members of the Muhlenberg 1973 team. Together, the two teams played to a 21-13 Muhlenberg win and Moravian loss. Together, these persons deserve credit for traversing a boundary separating two segments of the same league and two circles of competitors.

Moravian and Muhlenberg both belonged to the MAC South for the 1973 football season. The capitalized entries in the two schedules indicate other MAC South members. These schedules are shown in Table 2.16.

The scheduling of this game enabled Calvo, Marino, and their respective team members to span jointly a boundary between one MAC South (Moravian, Widener, Lebanon Valley, and Franklin & Marshall) and a second MAC South (Muhlenberg, Johns Hopkins, Ursinus, Dickinson, and Swarthmore)

Table 2.16. Football Schedules for 1973

	Moravian 1973	Muhlenberg 1973
September 22	at Delaware Valley	at JOHNS HOPKINS
September 29	Upsala	Delaware Valley
October 6	at Wilkes	at LEBANON VALLEY
October 13	WIDENER	at URSINUS
October 20	at LEBANON VALLEY	DICKINSON
October 27	Albright	at SWARTHMORE
November 3	FRANK. & MARSHALL	WIDENER
November 10	at Juniata	at FRANKLIN & MARSHALL
November 17	at MUHLENBERG	MORAVIAN

and a boundary between a Moravian competition circle (with Upsala, Wilkes, Albright, and Juniata) and the Muhlenberg MAC South schedule.

November 23, 1974, Muhlenberg at Moravian

On November 23, 1974, Marino and members of the Muhlenberg 1974 football team traveled ten miles from Allentown to Bethlehem. There they met Calvo and the members of the Moravian 1974 team. Together, the two teams played to a 42-27 Moravian win and Muhlenberg loss. Together, these persons deserve credit for traversing a boundary separating two segments of the same league and two circles of competitors.

Moravian and Muhlenberg both belonged to the MAC South for the 1974 football season. The capitalized entries in the two schedules indicate other MAC South members. These schedules are shown in Table 2.17.

The scheduling of this game enabled Calvo, Marino, and their respective team members to span jointly a boundary between one MAC South (Moravian and

Table 2.17. Football Schedules for 1974

	Moravian 1974	Muhlenberg 1974
September 21	DICKINSON	
September 28	at Delaware Valley	JOHNS HOPKINS
October 5	Wilkes	at Rensselaer Polytechnic
October 12	at WESTERN MD.	LEBANON VALLEY
October 19	at WIDENER	URSINUS
October 26	LEBANON VALLEY	at DICKINSON
November 2	at Albright	SWARTHMORE
November 9	at FRANK. & MARSHALL	at WIDENER
November 16	at Juniata	FRANKLIN & MARSHALL
November 23	MUHLENBERG	at MORAVIAN

Western Maryland) and a second MAC South (Muhlenberg, Johns Hopkins, Ursinus, Dickinson, and Swarthmore) and a boundary between a Moravian competition circle (with Delaware Valley, Wilkes, Wagner, Albright, and Juniata) and the Muhlenberg-and-Rensselaer Polytechnic Institute relationship.

November 22, 1975, Moravian at Muhlenberg

On November 22, 1975, Calvo and members of the Moravian 1975 football team traveled ten miles from Bethlehem to Allentown. There they met Marino and members of the Muhlenberg 1975 team. Together, the two teams played to a 16-0 Moravian win and Muhlenberg loss. Together, these persons deserve credit for traversing a boundary separating two segments of the same league and two circles of competitors.

Moravian and Muhlenberg both belonged to the MAC South for the 1975 football season. The capitalized entries in the two schedules indicate other MAC South members. These schedules are shown in Table 2.18.

The scheduling of this game enabled Calvo, Marino, and their respective team members to span jointly a boundary between one MAC South (Moravian and Western Maryland) and a second MAC South (Muhlenberg and Swarthmore) and a boundary between a Moravian competition circle (with Delaware Valley and Upsala) and the Muhlenberg-and-Rensselaer Polytechnic Institute football relationship.

November 20, 1976, Muhlenberg at Moravian

On November 20, 1976, Marino and members of the Muhlenberg 1976 football team traveled ten miles from Allentown to Bethlehem. There they met Calvo and members of the Moravian 1976 team. Together, the two teams

Table 2.18. Football Schedules for 1975

	Moravian 1975	*Muhlenberg 1975*
September 20	at DICKINSON	
September 27	Delaware Valley	at JOHNS HOPKINS
October 4	Upsala	Rensselaer Polytechnic
October 11	WESTERN MARYLAND	at LEBANON VALLEY
October 18	WIDENER	at URSINUS
October 25	at LEBANON VALLEY	DICKINSON
November 1	JOHNS HOPKINS	at SWARTHMORE
November 8	FRANK. & MARSHALL	WIDENER
November 15	at URSINUS	at FRANKLIN & MARSHALL
November 22	at MUHLENBERG	MORAVIAN

Table 2.19.   Football Schedules for 1976

	Moravian 1976	*Muhlenberg 1976*
September 18	DICKINSON	
September 25	at Delaware Valley	JOHNS HOPKINS
October 2	Wilkes	at WESTERN MARYLAND
October 9	at WESTERN MD	LEBANON VALLEY
October 16	at WIDENER	URSINUS
October 23	LEBANON VALLEY	at DICKINSON
October 30	at JOHNS HOPKINS	SWARTHMORE
November 6	at FRANK. & MARSHALL	at WIDENER
November 13	URSINUS	FRANKLIN & MARSHALL
November 20	MUHLENBERG	at MORAVIAN

played to a 36-14 Moravian win and Muhlenberg loss. Together, these persons deserve credit for traversing a boundary separating two segments of the same league and two circles of competitors.

Moravian and Muhlenberg both belonged to the MAC South for the 1976 football season. The capitalized entries in the two schedules indicate other MAC South members. These schedules are shown in Table 2.19.

The scheduling of this game enabled Calvo, Marino, and their respective team members to span jointly a boundary between one MAC South (including Moravian) and a second MAC South (Muhlenberg and Swarthmore) and a boundary between a Moravian competition circle (with Delaware Valley and Wilkes) and the Muhlenberg full MAC South schedule.

November 19, 1977, Moravian at Muhlenberg

On November 19, 1977, new Head Coach Ed Little and members of the Moravian 1977 football team traveled ten miles from Bethlehem to Allentown. There they met Marino and members of the Muhlenberg 1977 team. Together, the two teams played to a 25-21 Muhlenberg win and Moravian loss. Together, these persons deserve credit for traversing a boundary separating two segments of the same league and two circles of competitors.

Moravian and Muhlenberg both belonged to the MAC South for the 1977 football season. The capitalized entries in the two schedules indicate other MAC South members. These schedules are shown in Table 2.20.

The scheduling of this game enabled Little, Marino, and their respective team members to span jointly a boundary between one MAC South (including Moravian) and a second MAC South (Muhlenberg, Ursinus, and Swarthmore) and a boundary between a Moravian competition circle (with Delaware Valley and Wilkes) and the Muhlenberg-and-Susquehanna relationship.

Table 2.20. Football Schedules for 1977

	Moravian 1977	*Muhlenberg 1977*
September 17	at DICKINSON	
September 24	Delaware Valley	at JOHNS HOPKINS
October 1	WIDENER	WESTERN MARYLAND
October 8	WESTERN MARYLAND	at LEBANON VALLEY
October 15	at Wilkes	at URSINUS
October 22	at LEBANON VALLEY	DICKINSON
October 29	JOHNS HOPKINS	at SWARTHMORE
November 5	FRANK. & MARSHALL	Susquehanna
November 12		at FRANKLIN & MARSHALL
November 19	at MUHLENBERG	MORAVIAN

November 11, 1978, Muhlenberg at Moravian

On November 11, 1978, Marino and members of the Muhlenberg 1978 football team traveled ten miles from Allentown to Bethlehem. There they met Little and members of the Moravian 1978 team. Together, the two teams played to a 34-0 Muhlenberg win and Moravian loss. Together, these persons deserve credit for traversing a boundary separating two segments of the same league and two circles of competitors.

Moravian and Muhlenberg both belonged to the MAC South for the 1978 football season. The capitalized entries in the two schedules indicate other MAC South members. These schedules are shown in Table 2.21.

The scheduling of this game enabled Little, Marino, and their respective team members to span jointly a boundary between one MAC South (Moravian, Widener, and Gettysburg) and a second MAC South (Muhlenberg, Ursinus, and Swarthmore) and a boundary between the Moravian-and-Delaware Valley relationship and Muhlenberg-and-Susquehanna relationship.

Table 2.21. Football Schedules for 1978

	Moravian 1978	*Muhlenberg 1978*
September 16	DICKINSON	FRANKLIN & MARSHALL
September 23	Delaware Valley	JOHNS HOPKINS
September 30	WIDENER	at WESTERN MARYLAND
October 7	at WESTERN MD.	LEBANON VALLEY
October 14	GETTYSBURG	URSINUS
October 21	LEBANON VALLEY	at DICKINSON
October 28	at JOHNS HOPKINS	SWARTHMORE
November 4	at FRANK. & MARSHALL	at Susquehanna
November 11	MUHLENBERG	at MORAVIAN

Table 2.22.   Football Schedules for 1979

	Moravian 1979	*Muhlenberg 1979*
September 15	at DICKINSON	at FRANKLIN & MARSHALL
September 22	at Delaware Valley	at JOHNS HOPKINS
September 29	WIDENER	WESTERN MARYLAND
October 6	WESTERN MARYLAND	at LEBANON VALLEY
October 13	at GETTYSBURG	at URSINUS
October 20	LEBANON VALLEY	DICKINSON
October 27	JOHNS HOPKINS	at SWARTHMORE
November 3	FRANK. & MARSHALL	Susquehanna
November 10	at MUHLENBERG	MORAVIAN

November 10, 1979, Moravian at Muhlenberg

On November 10, 1979, Little and members of the Moravian 1979 football team traveled ten miles from Bethlehem to Allentown. There they met Marino and members of the Muhlenberg 1979 team. Together, the two teams played to a 14-6 Muhlenberg win and Moravian loss. Together, these persons deserve credit for traversing a boundary separating two segments of the same league and two circles of competitors.

Moravian and Muhlenberg both belonged to the MAC South for the 1979 football season. The capitalized entries in the two schedules indicate other MAC South members. These schedules are shown in Table 2.22.

The scheduling of this game enabled Little, Marino, and their respective team members to span jointly a boundary between one MAC South (Moravian, Widener, and Gettysburg) and a second MAC South (Muhlenberg, Ursinus, and Swarthmore) and a boundary between the Moravian-and-Delaware Valley relationship and Muhlenberg-and-Susquehanna relationship.

November 15, 1980, Muhlenberg at Moravian

On November 15, 1980, Marino and members of the Muhlenberg 1980 football team traveled ten miles from Allentown to Bethlehem. There they met Little and members of the Moravian 1980 team. Together, the two teams played to a 24-23 Muhlenberg win and Moravian loss. Together, these persons deserve credit for traversing a boundary separating two segments of the same league and two circles of competitors.

Moravian and Muhlenberg both belonged to the MAC South for the 1980 football season. The capitalized entries in the two schedules indicate other MAC South members. These schedules are shown in Table 2.23.

Table 2.23. Football Schedules for 1980

	Moravian 1980	Muhlenberg 1980
September 20	DICKINSON	at FRANKLIN & MARSHALL
September 27	Delaware Valley	JOHNS HOPKINS
October 4	at WIDENER	at WESTERN MARYLAND
October 11	at WESTERN MD.	LEBANON VALLEY
October 18	GETTYSBURG	URSINUS
October 25	at LEBANON VALLEY	at DICKINSON
November 1	at JOHNS HOPKINS	SWARTHMORE
November 8	at FRANK. & MARSHALL	at Susquehanna
November 15	MUHLENBERG	at MORAVIAN

The scheduling of this game enabled Little, Marino, and their respective team members to span jointly a boundary between one MAC South (Moravian, Widener, and Gettysburg) and a second MAC South (Muhlenberg, Ursinus, and Swarthmore) and a boundary between the Moravian-and-Delaware Valley relationship and Muhlenberg-and-Susquehanna relationship.

November 14, 1981, Moravian at Muhlenberg

On November 14, 1981, Little and members of the Moravian 1981 football team traveled ten miles from Bethlehem to Allentown. There they met new Head Coach Ralph Kirchenheiter and members of the Muhlenberg 1981 team. Together, the two teams played to a 10-9 Muhlenberg win and Moravian loss. Together, these persons deserve credit for traversing a boundary separating two segments of the same league and two circles of competitors.

Moravian and Muhlenberg both belonged to the MAC South for the 1981 football season. The capitalized entries in the two schedules indicate other MAC South members. These schedules are shown in Table 2.24.

Table 2.24. Football Schedules for 1981

	Moravian 1981	Muhlenberg 1981
September 19	SWARTHMORE	at FRANKLIN & MARSHALL
September 26	at URSINUS	at GETTYSBURG
October 3	FRANK. & MARSHALL	WIDENER
October 10	at JOHNS HOPKINS	at Susquehanna
October 17	at WESTERN MD.	at LEBANON VALLEY
October 24	WIDENER	WESTERN MARYLAND
October 31	GETTYSBURG	DICKINSON
November 7	at Delaware Valley	at JOHNS HOPKINS
November 14	at MUHLENBERG	MORAVIAN

Table 2.25.   Football Schedules for 1982

	Moravian 1982	*Muhlenberg 1982*
September 18	at SWARTHMORE	FRANKLIN & MARSHALL
September 25	URSINUS	GETTYSBURG
October 2	at FRANK. & MARSHALL	at WIDENER
October 9	JOHNS HOPKINS	Susquehanna
October 16	WESTERN MARYLAND	LEBANON VALLEY
October 23	at WIDENER	at WESTERN MARYLAND
October 30	at GETTYSBURG	at DICKINSON
November 6	Delaware Valley	JOHNS HOPKINS
November 13	MUHLENBERG	at MORAVIAN

The scheduling of this game enabled Little, Kirchenheiter, and their respective team members to span jointly a boundary between one MAC South (Moravian and Swarthmore) and a second MAC South (Muhlenberg and Dickinson) and a boundary between the Moravian-and-Delaware Valley relationship and Muhlenberg-and-Susquehanna relationship.

November 13, 1982, Muhlenberg at Moravian

On November 13, 1982, Kirchenheiter and members of the Muhlenberg 1982 football team traveled ten miles from Allentown to Bethlehem. There they met returning Head Coach Rocco Calvo and members of the Moravian 1982 team. Together, the two teams played to a 16-6 Moravian win and Muhlenberg loss. Together, these persons deserve credit for traversing a boundary separating two segments of the same league and two circles of competitors.

Moravian and Muhlenberg both belonged to the MAC South for the 1982 football season. The capitalized entries in the two schedules indicate other MAC South members. These schedules are shown in Table 2.25.

The scheduling of this game enabled Calvo, Kirchenheiter, and their respective team members to span jointly a boundary between one MAC South (Moravian and Swarthmore) and a second MAC South (Muhlenberg and Dickinson) and a boundary between the Moravian-and-Delaware Valley relationship and Muhlenberg-and-Susquehanna relationship.

NEW LEAGUES, NEW CHALLENGES
TO REMAIN CONNECTED

Dramatic transformation came to the Middle Atlantic Conference football league in 1983. The representatives of Muhlenberg joined their counterparts at Dickinson, Franklin & Marshall, Gettysburg, Johns Hopkins, Swarthmore, Ursinus, and Western Maryland (listed alphabetically) to form the Centennial Football Conference. All eight of these institutions had been members of the MAC South. The MAC South disbanded.

The representatives of Moravian, Lebanon Valley, and Widener looked north, literally and figuratively, for a new community of football competitors. They joined with members of the MAC North to reconstitute the Middle Atlantic Conference football league for the 1983 football season. Moravian resumed football playing relationships with Albright, Juniata, and Wilkes.

This restructuring was the dawn of a new era for the representatives of the Moravian and Muhlenberg football programs. Continuing their football relationship would take some effort. The new MAC membership was large. Moravian's entire annual football schedule could now consist of MAC members.[16] The Centennial Football Conference presidents publicly promoted their venture as a statement about conducting football competition at the National Collegiate Athletic Association (NCAA) Division III level. This clearly was an act of distancing the Centennial league from its MAC roots.

More than two decades later, the Moravian-and-Muhlenberg football relationship continues uninterrupted. Scot Dapp at Moravian and Ralph Kirchenheiter, Fran Meagher, Greg Olejack, and Mike Donnelly at Muhlenberg formed a new generation of head coaches who joined their predecessors in sustaining this human tie. It is in these years, 1983 through 2006, that the remarkable achievement of this human tie comes fully into view.

November 12, 1983, Moravian at Muhlenberg

On November 12, 1983, Calvo and members of the Moravian 1983 football team traveled ten miles from Bethlehem to Allentown. There they met Kirchenheiter and members of the Muhlenberg 1983 team. Together, the two teams played to a 24-7 Moravian win and Muhlenberg loss. Together, these persons deserve credit for traversing a boundary separating two leagues and two circles of competitors.

Moravian belonged to the MAC for the 1983 football season. Muhlenberg belonged to the Centennial Football Conference (hereafter, Centennial) for the 1983 football season. The capitalized entries in the Moravian schedule indicate other MAC members. The capitalized entries marked with an asterisk in the Muhlenberg schedule indicate the other members of the Centennial.[17] These schedules are shown in Table 2.26.

The scheduling of this game enabled Calvo, Kirchenheiter, and their respective team members to span jointly a boundary between the MAC and Centennial and a boundary between the MAC and the Muhlenberg-and-Lebanon Valley football relationship.

Table 2.26.   Football Schedules for 1983

	Moravian 1983	*Muhlenberg 1983*
September 10	WIDENER	
September 17	JUNIATA	DICKINSON*
September 24		at FRANKLIN & MARSHALL*
October 1	at DELAWARE VALLEY	WESTERN MARYLAND*
October 8	WILKES	at SWARTHMORE*
October 15	at SUSQUEHANNA	JOHNS HOPKINS*
October 22	LYCOMING	at GETTYSBURG*
October 29	at ALBRIGHT	URSINUS*
November 5	at UPSALA	at Lebanon Valley
November 12	at Muhlenberg	Moravian

November 10, 1984, Muhlenberg at Moravian

On November 10, 1984, Kirchenheiter and members of the Muhlenberg 1984 football team traveled ten miles from Allentown to Bethlehem. There they met Calvo and members of the Moravian 1984 team. Together, the two teams played to a 17-14 Moravian win and Muhlenberg loss. Together, these persons deserve credit for traversing a boundary separating two leagues and two circles of competitors.

Moravian belonged to the MAC for the 1984 football season. Muhlenberg belonged to the Centennial league for the 1984 season. The capitalized entries in the Moravian schedule indicate other MAC members. The capitalized entries marked with an asterisk in the Muhlenberg schedule indicate the other Centennial members. These schedules are shown in Table 2.27.

The scheduling of this game enabled Calvo, Kirchenheiter, and their respective team members to span jointly a boundary between the MAC and Centennial and a boundary between the MAC and the Muhlenberg-and-Lebanon Valley football relationship.

Table 2.27.   Football Schedules for 1984

	Moravian 1984	*Muhlenberg 1984*
September 8	at WIDENER	
September 15	at JUNIATA	at DICKINSON*
September 22		FRANKLIN & MARSHALL*
September 29	DELAWARE VALLEY	at WESTERN MARYLAND*
October 6	at WILKES	SWARTHMORE*
October 13	SUSQUEHANNA	at JOHNS HOPKINS*
October 20	at LYCOMING	GETTYSBURG*
October 27	ALBRIGHT	at URSINUS*
November 3	UPSALA	Lebanon Valley
November 10	Muhlenberg	at Moravian

November 16, 1985, Moravian at Muhlenberg

On November 16, 1985, Calvo and members of the Moravian 1985 football team traveled ten miles from Bethlehem to Allentown. There they met Kirchenheiter and members of the Muhlenberg 1985 team. Together, the two teams played to a 15-10 Moravian win and Muhlenberg loss. Together, these persons deserve credit for traversing a boundary separating two leagues and two circles of competitors.

Moravian belonged to the MAC for the 1985 football season. Muhlenberg belonged to the Centennial league for the 1985 season. The capitalized entries in the Moravian schedule indicate other MAC members. The capitalized entries marked with an asterisk in the Muhlenberg schedule indicate the other Centennial members. These schedules are shown in Table 2.28.

The scheduling of this game enabled Calvo, Kirchenheiter, and their respective team members to span jointly a boundary between the MAC and Centennial and a boundary between the MAC and the Muhlenberg-and-Catholic football relationship.

November 15, 1986, Muhlenberg at Moravian

On November 15, 1986, Kirchenheiter and members of the Muhlenberg 1986 football team traveled ten miles from Allentown to Bethlehem. There they met Calvo and members of the Moravian 1986 football team. Together, the two teams played to a 14-0 Moravian win and Muhlenberg loss. Together, these persons deserve credit for traversing a boundary separating two leagues and two circles of competitors.

Moravian belonged to the MAC for the 1986 football season. Muhlenberg belonged to the Centennial league for the 1986 season. The capitalized entries in the Moravian schedule indicate other MAC members. The capitalized en-

Table 2.28.   Football Schedules for 1985

	Moravian 1985	Muhlenberg 1985
September 14	WIDENER	at Susquehanna
September 21	JUNIATA	DICKINSON*
September 28	at LEBANON VALLEY	at FRANKLIN & MARSHALL*
October 5	at DELAWARE VALLEY	WESTERN MARYLAND*
October 12	WILKES	at SWARTHMORE*
October 19	at SUSQUEHANNA	JOHNS HOPKINS*
October 26	LYCOMING	at GETTYSBURG*
November 2	at ALBRIGHT	URSINUS*
November 9	at UPSALA	at Catholic
November 16	at Muhlenberg	Moravian

Table 2.29. Football Schedules for 1986

	Moravian 1986	*Muhlenberg 1986*
September 13	at WIDENER	Susquehanna
September 20	at JUNIATA	at DICKINSON*
September 27	LEBANON VALLEY	FRANKLIN & MARSHALL*
October 4	DELAWARE VALLEY	at WESTERN MARYLAND*
October 11	at WILKES	SWARTHMORE*
October 18	SUSQUEHANNA	at JOHNS HOPKINS*
October 25	at LYCOMING	GETTYSBURG*
November 1	ALBRIGHT	at URSINUS*
November 8	UPSALA	Catholic
November 15	Muhlenberg	at Moravian

tries marked with an asterisk in the Muhlenberg schedule indicate the other members of the Centennial. These schedules are shown in Table 2.29.

The scheduling of this game enabled Calvo, Kirchenheiter, and their respective team members to span jointly a boundary between the MAC and Centennial and a boundary between the MAC and the Muhlenberg-and-Catholic relationship.

November 14, 1987, Moravian at Muhlenberg

On November 14, 1987, new Head Coach Scot Dapp and members of the Moravian 1987 football team traveled ten miles from Bethlehem to Allentown. There they met Kirchenheiter and members of the Muhlenberg 1987 team. Together, the two teams played to a 14-12 Muhlenberg win and Moravian loss. Together, these persons traversed a boundary separating two leagues and two circles of competitors.

Moravian belonged to the MAC for the 1987 football season. Muhlenberg belonged to the Centennial league for the 1987 season. The capitalized entries in the Moravian schedule indicate other MAC members. The capitalized entries marked with an asterisk in the Muhlenberg schedule indicate the other members of the Centennial. These schedules are shown in Table 2.30.

The scheduling of this game enabled Dapp, Kirchenheiter, and their respective team members to span jointly a boundary between the MAC and Centennial and a boundary between the MAC and the Muhlenberg-and-Hampden-Sydney football relationship.

November 12, 1988, Muhlenberg at Moravian

On November 12, 1988, Kirchenheiter and members of the Muhlenberg 1988 football team traveled ten miles from Allentown to Bethlehem. There they

Table 2.30.   Football Schedules for 1987

	Moravian 1987	*Muhlenberg 1987*
September 12	LEBANON VALLEY	at Susquehanna
September 19	at SUSQUEHANNA	DICKINSON*
September 26	WIDENER	at FRANKLIN & MARSHALL*
October 3	at WILKES	WESTERN MARYLAND*
October 10	at JUNIATA	at SWARTHMORE*
October 17	UPSALA	JOHNS HOPKINS*
October 24	at LYCOMING	at GETTYSBURG*
October 31	at DELAWARE VALLEY	URSINUS*
November 7	ALBRIGHT	at Hampden-Sydney
November 14	at Muhlenberg	Moravian

met Dapp and members of the Moravian 1988 team. Together, the two teams played to a 44-25 Moravian win and Muhlenberg loss. Together, these persons traversed a boundary between leagues and competition circles.

Moravian belonged to the MAC for the 1988 football season. Muhlenberg belonged to the Centennial league for the 1988 season. The capitalized entries in the Moravian schedule indicate other MAC members. The capitalized entries marked with an asterisk in the Muhlenberg schedule indicate the other members of the Centennial. These schedules are shown in Table 2.31.

The scheduling of this game enabled Dapp, Kirchenheiter, and their respective team members to span jointly a boundary between the MAC and Centennial and a boundary between the MAC and the Muhlenberg-and-Hampden-Sydney relationship.

November 11, 1989, Moravian at Muhlenberg

On November 11, 1989, Dapp and members of the Moravian 1989 football team traveled ten miles from Bethlehem to Allentown. There they met

Table 2.31.   Football Schedules for 1988

	Moravian 1988	*Muhlenberg 1988*
September 10	at LEBANON VALLEY	Susquehanna
September 17	SUSQUEHANNA	at DICKINSON*
September 24	at WIDENER	FRANKLIN & MARSHALL*
October 1	WILKES	at WESTERN MARYLAND*
October 8	JUNIATA	SWARTHMORE*
October 15	at UPSALA	at JOHNS HOPKINS*
October 22	at LYCOMING	GETTYSBURG*
October 29	DELAWARE VALLEY	at URSINUS*
November 5	at ALBRIGHT	Hampden-Sydney
November 12	Muhlenberg	at Moravian

Table 2.32.   Football Schedules for 1989

	Moravian 1989	*Muhlenberg 1989*
September 9	LEBANON VALLEY	at Susquehanna
September 16	at SUSQUEHANNA	DICKINSON*
September 23	WIDENER	at FRANKLIN & MARSHALL*
September 30	at WILKES	WESTERN MARYLAND*
October 7	at JUNIATA	at SWARTHMORE*
October 14	UPSALA	JOHNS HOPKINS*
October 21	LYCOMING	at GETTYSBURG*
October 28	at DELAWARE VALLEY	URSINUS*
November 4	ALBRIGHT	at FDU-Madison
November 11	at Muhlenberg	Moravian

Kirchenheiter and members of the Muhlenberg 1989 team. Together, the two teams played to a 14-9 Moravian win and Muhlenberg loss. Together, these persons traversed a boundary between leagues and competition circles.

Moravian belonged to the MAC for the 1989 football season. Muhlenberg belonged to the Centennial league for the 1989 season. The capitalized entries in the Moravian schedule indicate other MAC members. The capitalized entries marked with an asterisk in the Muhlenberg schedule indicate the other members of the Centennial. These schedules are shown in Table 2.32.

The scheduling of this game enabled Dapp, Kirchenheiter, and their respective team members to span jointly a boundary between the MAC and Centennial and a boundary between the MAC and the Muhlenberg-and-FDU-Madison football relationship.[18]

November 10, 1990, Muhlenberg at Moravian

On November 10, 1990, new Muhlenberg Head Coach Fran Meagher and members of the Muhlenberg 1990 football team traveled ten miles from Allentown to Bethlehem. There they met Dapp and the Moravian 1990 team members. Together, the two teams played to a 7-3 Moravian win and Muhlenberg loss. Together, these persons traversed a boundary between leagues and competition circles.

Moravian belonged to the MAC for the 1990 football season. Muhlenberg belonged to the Centennial league for the 1990 season. The capitalized entries in the Moravian schedule indicate other MAC members. The capitalized entries marked with an asterisk in the Muhlenberg schedule indicate the other members of the Centennial. These schedules are shown in Table 2.33.

The scheduling of this game enabled Dapp, Meagher, and their respective team members to span jointly a boundary between the MAC and Centennial

Table 2.33.   Football Schedules for 1990

	Moravian 1990	Muhlenberg 1990
September 8	at LEBANON VALLEY	Susquehanna
September 15	SUSQUEHANNA	at DICKINSON*
September 22	at WIDENER	FRANKLIN & MARSHALL*
September 29	WILKES	at WESTERN MARYLAND*
October 6	JUNIATA	SWARTHMORE*
October 13	at Wesley (DE)	at JOHNS HOPKINS*
October 20	at LYCOMING	GETTYSBURG*
October 27	DELAWARE VALLEY	at URSINUS*
November 3	at ALBRIGHT	FDU-Madison
November 10	Muhlenberg	at Moravian

and a boundary between the Moravian-and-Wesley football relationship and
the Muhlenberg-and-FDU-Madison relationship.

November 16, 1991, Moravian at Muhlenberg

On November 16, 1991, Dapp and members of the Moravian 1991 football
team traveled from Bethlehem to Allentown. There they met Meagher and
members of the Muhlenberg 1991 team. Together, the two teams played to a
28-27 Moravian win and Muhlenberg loss. Together, these persons traversed
a boundary between leagues and competition circles.

Moravian belonged to the MAC for the 1991 football season. Muhlenberg
belonged to the Centennial league for the 1991 season. The capitalized entries
in the Moravian schedule indicate other MAC members. The capitalized entries marked with an asterisk in the Muhlenberg schedule indicate the other
members of the Centennial. These schedules are shown in Table 2.34.

Table 2.34.   Football Schedules for 1991

	Moravian 1991	Muhlenberg 1991
September 14	at Franklin & Marshall	at Susquehanna
September 21	at SUSQUEHANNA	DICKINSON*
September 28	WIDENER	at FRANKLIN & MARSHALL*
October 5	at WILKES	WESTERN MARYLAND*
October 12	at JUNIATA	at SWARTHMORE*
October 19	LEBANON VALLEY	JOHNS HOPKINS*
October 26	LYCOMING	at GETTYSBURG*
November 2	at DELAWARE VALLEY	URSINUS*
November 9	ALBRIGHT	at Washington & Jefferson
November 16	at Muhlenberg	Moravian

The scheduling of this game enabled Dapp, Meagher, and their respective team members to span jointly a boundary between the MAC and Centennial and a boundary between the Moravian-and-Franklin & Marshall football relationship and the Muhlenberg-and-Washington & Jefferson football relationship.

November 14, 1992, Muhlenberg at Moravian

On November 14, 1992, Meagher and members of the Muhlenberg 1992 football team traveled from Allentown to Bethlehem. There they met Dapp and members of the Moravian 1992 team. Together, the two teams played to a 35-14 Moravian win and Muhlenberg loss. Together, these persons traversed a boundary between leagues and competition circles.

Moravian belonged to the MAC for the 1992 football season. Muhlenberg belonged to the Centennial league for the 1992 season. The capitalized entries in the Moravian schedule indicate other MAC members. The capitalized entries marked with an asterisk in the Muhlenberg schedule indicate the other members of the Centennial. These schedules are shown in Table 2.35.

The scheduling of this game enabled Dapp, Meagher, and their respective team members to span jointly a boundary between the MAC and Centennial and a boundary between the Moravian-and-Franklin & Marshall relationship and the Muhlenberg-and-Merchant Marine Academy football relationship.

November 13, 1993, Moravian at Muhlenberg

On November 13, 1993, Dapp and members of the Moravian 1993 football team traveled from Bethlehem to Allentown. There they met Meagher and members of the Muhlenberg 1993 team. Together, the two teams played to a

Table 2.35. Football Schedules for 1992

	Moravian 1992	*Muhlenberg 1992*
September 12	Franklin & Marshall	Susquehanna
September 19	SUSQUEHANNA	at DICKINSON*
September 26	at WIDENER	FRANKLIN & MARSHALL*
October 3	WILKES	at WESTERN MARYLAND*
October 10	JUNIATA	SWARTHMORE*
October 17	at LEBANON VALLEY	at JOHNS HOPKINS*
October 24	at LYCOMING	GETTYSBURG*
October 31	DELAWARE VALLEY	at Merchant Marine
November 7	at ALBRIGHT	at URSINUS*
November 14	Muhlenberg	at Moravian

Table 2.36. Football Schedules for 1993

	Moravian 1993	Muhlenberg 1993
September 11	Baldwin-Wallace	at Hampden-Sydney
September 18	at Delaware Valley	DICKINSON*
September 25	WIDENER	at FRANKLIN & MARSHALL*
October 2	at LEBANON VALLEY	WESTERN MARYLAND*
October 9	Lycoming	at SWARTHMORE*
October 16	at SUSQUEHANNA	JOHNS HOPKINS*
October 23	ALBRIGHT	at GETTYSBURG*
October 30	at JUNIATA	
November 6	King's	URSINUS*
November 13	at Muhlenberg	Moravian

24-14 Moravian win and Muhlenberg loss. Together, these persons traversed a boundary between leagues and competition circles.

Moravian joined the MAC Commonwealth League for the 1993 football season.[19] Muhlenberg belonged to the Centennial Conference for the 1993 season. The capitalized entries in the Moravian schedule are the other MAC Commonwealth teams in the full league round robin. The capitalized entries marked with an asterisk in the Muhlenberg schedule indicate the other members of the Centennial. These schedules are shown in Table 2.36.

The scheduling of this game enabled Dapp, Meagher, and their respective team members to span jointly a boundary between the MAC Commonwealth and Centennial and a boundary between a Moravian competition circle (with Baldwin-Wallace, Delaware Valley, Lycoming, and King's) and the Muhlenberg-and-Hampden-Sydney football relationship.

November 12, 1994, Muhlenberg at Moravian

On November 12, 1994, new Head Coach Greg Olejack and members of the Muhlenberg 1994 football team traveled from Allentown to Bethlehem. There they met Dapp and members of the Moravian 1994 team. Together, the two teams played to a 50-17 Moravian win and Muhlenberg loss. Together, these persons traversed a boundary between leagues and competition circles.

Moravian belonged to the MAC Commonwealth for the 1994 season. Muhlenberg belonged to the Centennial league for the 1994 season. The capitalized entries in the Moravian schedule are the other MAC Commonwealth teams. The capitalized entries marked with an asterisk in the Muhlenberg schedule indicate the other members of the Centennial. These schedules are shown in Table 2.37.

Table 2.37. Football Schedules for 1994

	Moravian 1994	Muhlenberg 1994
September 10	at Baldwin-Wallace	Hampden-Sydney
September 17	Delaware Valley	at DICKINSON*
September 24	at WIDENER	FRANKLIN & MARSHALL*
October 1	LEBANON VALLEY	at WESTERN MARYLAND*
October 8	at Lycoming	SWARTHMORE*
October 14		at JOHNS HOPKINS*
October 15	SUSQUEHANNA	
October 22	at ALBRIGHT	GETTYSBURG*
October 29	JUNIATA	Union (NY)
November 5	at King's	at URSINUS*
November 12	Muhlenberg	at Moravian

The scheduling of this game enabled Dapp, Olejack, and their respective team members to span jointly a boundary between the MAC Commonwealth and Centennial and a boundary between a Moravian competition circle (with Baldwin-Wallace, Delaware Valley, Lycoming, and King's) and a Muhlenberg competition circle (with Hampden-Sydney and Union).

November 11, 1995, Moravian at Muhlenberg

On November 11, 1995, Dapp and members of the Moravian 1995 football team traveled from Bethlehem to Allentown. There they met Olejack and members of the Muhlenberg 1995 team. Together, the two teams played to a 38-7 Moravian win and Muhlenberg loss. Together, these persons traversed a boundary between leagues and competition circles.

Moravian belonged to the MAC Commonwealth for the 1995 season. Muhlenberg belonged to the Centennial league for the 1995 season. The capitalized entries in the Moravian schedule are the other MAC Commonwealth teams. The capitalized entries marked with an asterisk in the Muhlenberg schedule indicate the other members of the Centennial. These schedules are shown in Table 2.38.

The scheduling of this game enabled Dapp, Olejack, and their respective team members to span jointly a boundary between the MAC Commonwealth and Centennial and a boundary between a Moravian competition circle (with King's, Delaware Valley, FDU-Madison, and Wilkes) and a Muhlenberg competition circle (with Catholic and Union).

November 16, 1996, Muhlenberg at Moravian

On November 16, 1996, Olejack and members of the Muhlenberg 1996 football team traveled from Allentown to Bethlehem. There they met Dapp and

Table 2.38. Football Schedules for 1995

	Moravian 1995	*Muhlenberg 1995*
September 9	King's	at Catholic
September 16	at JUNIATA	DICKINSON*
September 23	at ALBRIGHT	at FRANKLIN & MARSHALL*
September 30	Delaware Valley	WESTERN MARYLAND*
October 7	at WIDENER	at SWARTHMORE*
October 14	SUSQUEHANNA	JOHNS HOPKINS*
October 21	LEBANON VALLEY	at GETTYSBURG*
October 27	at FDU-Madison	
October 28		at Union (NY)
November 4	Wilkes	URSINUS*
November 11	at Muhlenberg	Moravian

the members of the Moravian 1996 team. Together, the two teams played to a 27-3 Moravian win and Muhlenberg loss. Together, these persons traversed a boundary between leagues and competition circles.

Moravian belonged to the MAC Commonwealth for the 1996 season. Muhlenberg belonged to the Centennial league for the 1996 season. The capitalized entries in the Moravian schedule are the other MAC Commonwealth teams. Capitalized entries marked with an asterisk in the Muhlenberg schedule indicate other Centennial members. These schedules are shown in Table 2.39.

The scheduling of this game enabled Dapp, Olejack, and their respective team members to span jointly a boundary between the MAC Commonwealth and Centennial and a boundary between a Moravian competition circle (with King's, Delaware Valley, FDU-Madison, and Wilkes) and a Muhlenberg competition circle (with Catholic and Carnegie Mellon).

Table 2.39. Football Schedules for 1996

	Moravian 1996	*Muhlenberg 1996*
September 14	at King's	Catholic
September 21	JUNIATA	at DICKINSON*
September 28	ALBRIGHT	FRANKLIN & MARSHALL*
October 5	at Delaware Valley	at WESTERN MARYLAND*
October 12	WIDENER	SWARTHMORE*
October 18		at JOHNS HOPKINS*
October 19	at SUSQUEHANNA	
October 26	at LEBANON VALLEY	GETTYSBURG*
November 2	FDU-Madison	at URSINUS*
November 9	at Wilkes	Carnegie Mellon
November 16	Muhlenberg	at Moravian

November 15, 1997, Moravian at Muhlenberg

On November 15, 1997, Dapp and the members of the Moravian 1997 football team traveled from Bethlehem to Allentown. There they met new Head Coach Mike Donnelly and the members of the Muhlenberg 1997 team. Together, Dapp and Donnelly and their respective team members played to a 21-16 Moravian win and Muhlenberg loss. Together, they traversed a boundary between leagues and circles of competitors.

Moravian belonged to the MAC Commonwealth for the 1997 season. Muhlenberg belonged to the Centennial league for the 1997 season. The capitalized entries in the Moravian schedule are other MAC Commonwealth teams. The capitalized entries marked with an asterisk in the Muhlenberg schedule indicate other Centennial members. These schedules are shown in Table 2.40.

The scheduling of this game enabled Dapp, Donnelly, and their respective team members to span jointly a boundary between the MAC Commonwealth and Centennial and a boundary between a Moravian circle (with Lycoming, Delaware Valley, FDU-Madison, and Wilkes) and a Muhlenberg circle (with Hartwick and Carnegie Mellon).

November 14, 1998, Muhlenberg at Moravian

On November 14, 1998, Donnelly and the members of the Muhlenberg 1998 football team traveled from Allentown to Bethlehem. There they met Dapp and the members of the Moravian 1998 team. Together, Donnelly and Dapp and their respective team members played to a 33-14 Muhlenberg win and Moravian loss. Together, these persons traversed a boundary between leagues and circles of competitors.

Table 2.40.   Football Schedules for 1997

	Moravian 1997	*Muhlenberg 1997*
September 6		at Hartwick
September 13	Lycoming	
September 20	at JUNIATA	DICKINSON*
September 27	at ALBRIGHT	at FRANKLIN & MARSHALL*
October 4	Delaware Valley	WESTERN MARYLAND*
October 11	at WIDENER	at SWARTHMORE*
October 18	SUSQUEHANNA	JOHNS HOPKINS*
October 25	LEBANON VALLEY	at GETTYSBURG*
November 1	at FDU-Madison	URSINUS*
November 8	Wilkes	at Carnegie Mellon
November 15	at Muhlenberg	Moravian

Table 2.41.   Football Schedules for 1998

	Moravian 1998	Muhlenberg 1998
September 5		Hartwick
September 12	at Lycoming	
September 19	JUNIATA	at DICKINSON*
September 26	ALBRIGHT	FRANKLIN & MARSHALL*
October 3	at Delaware Valley	at WESTERN MARYLAND*
October 10	WIDENER	SWARTHMORE*
October 16		at JOHNS HOPKINS*
October 17	at SUSQUEHANNA	
October 24	at LEBANON VALLEY	GETTYSBURG*
October 31	FDU-Madison	at URSINUS*
November 7	at Wilkes	Grove City
November 14	Muhlenberg	at Moravian

Moravian belonged to the MAC Commonwealth for the 1998 season. Muhlenberg belonged to the Centennial in 1998. The capitalized entries in the Moravian schedule are the other Commonwealth teams. Capitalized entries marked with an asterisk in the Muhlenberg schedule indicate other Centennial members. These schedules are shown in Table 2.41.

The scheduling of this game enabled Dapp, Donnelly, and their respective team members to span jointly a boundary between the MAC Commonwealth and Centennial and a boundary between a Moravian circle (with Lycoming, Delaware Valley, FDU-Madison, and Wilkes) and a Muhlenberg circle (with Hartwick and Grove City).

November 13, 1999, Moravian at Muhlenberg

On November 13, 1999, Dapp and the members of the Moravian 1999 football team traveled from Bethlehem to Allentown. There they met Donnelly and the members of the Muhlenberg 1999 team. Together, Dapp and Donnelly and their respective team members played to a 52-26 Muhlenberg win and Moravian loss. Together, these persons traversed a boundary between leagues and circles of competitors.

Moravian belonged to the MAC Commonwealth for the 1999 season. Muhlenberg belonged to the Centennial in 1999. The capitalized entries in the Moravian schedule are the other Commonwealth teams. Capitalized entries marked with an asterisk in the Muhlenberg schedule indicate other Centennial members. These schedules are shown in Table 2.42.

The scheduling of this game enabled Dapp, Donnelly, and their respective team members to span jointly a boundary between the MAC Commonwealth

Table 2.42.   Football Schedules for 1999

	Moravian 1999	*Muhlenberg 1999*
September 4		at Kings Point
September 11	Delaware Valley	
September 18	at ALBRIGHT	DICKINSON*
September 25	LEBANON VALLEY	at FRANKLIN & MARSHALL*
October 2	at WIDENER	WESTERN MARYLAND*
October 9	King's	at SWARTHMORE*
October 16	at JUNIATA	JOHNS HOPKINS*
October 23	at FDU-Madison	at GETTYSBURG*
October 30	SUSQUEHANNA	URSINUS*
November 6	Wilkes	at Grove City
November 13	at Muhlenberg	Moravian

and Centennial and a boundary between a Moravian circle (with Delaware Valley, King's, FDU-Madison, and Wilkes) and a Muhlenberg circle (with the Merchant Marine of Kings Point and Grove City).

November 11, 2000, Muhlenberg at Moravian

On November 11, 2000, Donnelly and the members of the Muhlenberg 2000 football team traveled from Allentown to Bethlehem, where they met Dapp and the members of the Moravian 2000 team. Together, Donnelly and Dapp and their respective team members played to a 45-20 Muhlenberg win and Moravian loss. Together, these persons traversed a boundary between leagues and circles of competitors.

Moravian belonged to the MAC Commonwealth for the 2000 season. Muhlenberg belonged to the Centennial in 2000. The capitalized entries in the Moravian schedule are the other Commonwealth teams. Capitalized entries marked with an asterisk in the Muhlenberg schedule indicate other Centennial members.[20] These schedules are shown in Table 2.43.

The scheduling of this game enabled Dapp, Donnelly, and their respective team members to span jointly a boundary between the MAC Commonwealth and Centennial and a boundary between a Moravian circle (with Delaware Valley, King's, FDU-Madison, and Wilkes) and a Muhlenberg circle (with Kings Point and Hartwick).

November 10, 2001, Moravian at Muhlenberg

On November 10, 2001, Dapp and the members of the Moravian 2001 football team traveled from Bethlehem to Allentown. There they met Donnelly

Table 2.43. Football Schedules for 2000

	Moravian 2000	*Muhlenberg 2000*
September 2		Kings Point
September 9	at Delaware Valley	
September 16	ALBRIGHT	at DICKINSON*
September 23	at LEBANON VALLEY	FRANKLIN & MARSHALL*
September 30	WIDENER	at WESTERN MARYLAND*
October 7	at King's	SWARTHMORE*
October 14	JUNIATA	at JOHNS HOPKINS*
October 21	FDU-Madison	GETTYSBURG*
October 28	at SUSQUEHANNA	at URSINUS*
November 4	at Wilkes	Hartwick
November 11	Muhlenberg	at Moravian

and the members of the Muhlenberg 2001 team. Together, Dapp and Donnelly and their respective team members played to a 17-7 Moravian win and Muhlenberg loss. Together, these persons traversed a boundary between leagues and circles of competitors.

Moravian belonged to the reunited Middle Atlantic Conference (MAC) in 2001. Muhlenberg belonged to the Centennial in 2001. The capitalized entries in the Moravian schedule are other MAC teams. The capitalized entries marked with an asterisk in the Muhlenberg schedule indicate the other Centennial members. These schedules are shown in Table 2.44.

Scheduling this game enabled Dapp, Donnelly, and their respective team members to span jointly a boundary between the MAC and Centennial and a boundary between the MAC and a Muhlenberg circle (with Kings Point, California Lutheran, and Hartwick).

Table 2.44. Football Schedules for 2001

	Moravian 2001	*Muhlenberg 2001*
September 1		at Kings Point
September 8	KING'S	at California Lutheran
September 15	at FDU-MADISON	DICKINSON*
September 22	at WIDENER	at FRANKLIN & MARSHALL*
September 29	LEBANON VALLEY	WESTERN MARYLAND*
October 6	at JUNIATA	
October 13	DELAWARE VALLEY	JOHNS HOPKINS*
October 20	WILKES	at GETTYSBURG*
October 27	at ALBRIGHT	URSINUS*
November 3	SUSQUEHANNA	at Hartwick
November 10	at Muhlenberg	Moravian

November 16, 2002, Muhlenberg at Moravian

On November 16, 2002, Donnelly and the members of the Muhlenberg 2002 football team traveled from Allentown to Bethlehem. There they Dapp and the members of the Moravian 2002 team. Together, Donnelly and Dapp and their respective team members played to an 8-0 Muhlenberg win and Moravian loss. Together, these persons traversed a boundary between leagues and circles of competitors.

Moravian belonged to the MAC for the 2002 season. Muhlenberg belonged to the Centennial in 2002. The capitalized entries in the Moravian schedule are other MAC teams. The capitalized entries marked with an asterisk in the Muhlenberg schedule indicate the other members of the Centennial.[21] These schedules are shown in Table 2.45.

Scheduling this game enabled Dapp, Donnelly, and their respective team members to span jointly a boundary between the MAC and Centennial and a boundary between the MAC and a Muhlenberg circle (with Kings Point, California Lutheran, and Union).

November 15, 2003, Moravian at Muhlenberg

On November 10, 2003, Dapp and the members of the Moravian 2003 football team traveled from Bethlehem to Allentown. There they met Donnelly and the Muhlenberg 2003 team members. Together, Dapp and Donnelly and their respective team members played to a 24-0 Muhlenberg win and Moravian loss. Together, these persons traversed a boundary between leagues and circles of competitors.

Table 2.45.   Football Schedules for 2002

	Moravian 2002	Muhlenberg 2002
September 1		Kings Point
September 7	FDU-FLORHAM	
September 14	at KING'S	California Lutheran
September 21		at DICKINSON*
September 28	WIDENER	FRANKLIN & MARSHALL*
October 5	at LEBANON VALLEY	at MCDANIEL*
October 12	JUNIATA	
October 19	at DELAWARE VALLEY	at JOHNS HOPKINS*
October 26	at WILKES	GETTYSBURG*
November 2	ALBRIGHT	at URSINUS*
November 9	at SUSQUEHANNA	Union (NY)
November 16	Muhlenberg	at Moravian

Table 2.46.   Football Schedules for 2003

	Moravian 2003	Muhlenberg 2003
September 6	FDU-FLORHAM	at Kings Point
September 13	JUNIATA	
September 20	at SUSQUEHANNA	at Christopher Newport
September 27	LEBANON VALLEY	MCDANIEL*
October 4	at KING'S	at FRANKLIN & MARSHALL*
October 11	WILKES	DICKINSON*
October 18		at URSINUS*
October 25	LYCOMING	JOHNS HOPKINS*
November 1	WIDENER	at GETTYSBURG*
November 8	at ALBRIGHT	at Union (NY)
November 15	at Muhlenberg	Moravian

Moravian belonged to the MAC in 2003. Muhlenberg belonged to the Centennial in 2003. The capitalized entries in the Moravian schedule are other MAC teams. The capitalized entries marked with an asterisk in the Muhlenberg schedule indicate the other members of the Centennial. These schedules are shown in Table 2.46.

Scheduling this game enabled Dapp, Donnelly, and their respective team members to span jointly a boundary between the MAC and Centennial and a boundary between the MAC and a Muhlenberg circle (with Kings Point, Christopher Newport, and Union).

November 13, 2004, Muhlenberg at Moravian

On November 13, 2004, Donnelly and the members of the Muhlenberg 2004 football team traveled from Allentown to Bethlehem. There they met Dapp and the Moravian 2004 team members. Together, Donnelly and Dapp and their respective team members played to a 28-14 Muhlenberg win and Moravian loss. Together, they traversed a boundary between leagues and circles of competitors.

Moravian belonged to the MAC in 2004. Muhlenberg belonged to the Centennial in 2004. The capitalized entries in the Moravian schedule are other MAC teams. The capitalized entries marked with an asterisk in the Muhlenberg schedule indicate the other members of the Centennial. These schedules are shown in Table 2.47.

Scheduling this game enabled Dapp, Donnelly, and their respective team members to span jointly a boundary between the MAC and Centennial and a boundary between the MAC and a Muhlenberg circle (with Kings Point, Union, and Grove City).

Table 2.47.   Football Schedules for 2004

	Moravian 2004	*Muhlenberg 2004*
September 4		Kings Point
September 11	at JUNIATA	
September 18	SUSQUEHANNA	at Union (NY)
September 25	at LEBANON VALLEY	Grove City
October 2	KING'S	FRANKLIN & MARSHALL*
October 9	at WILKES	at DICKINSON*
October 16	FDU-FLORHAM	URSINUS*
October 23	at LYCOMING	at JOHNS HOPKINS*
October 30	at WIDENER	GETTYSBURG*
November 6	ALBRIGHT	at MCDANIEL*
November 13	Muhlenberg	at Moravian

November 12, 2005, Moravian at Muhlenberg

On November 12, 2005, Dapp and the members of the Moravian 2005 football team traveled from Bethlehem to Allentown. There they met Donnelly and the Muhlenberg 2005 team members. Together, Dapp and Donnelly and their respective team members played to a 24-19 Moravian win and Muhlenberg loss. Together, they traversed a boundary between leagues and circles of competitors.

Moravian belonged to the MAC for the 2005 season. Muhlenberg belonged to the Centennial league for the 2005 season. The capitalized entries in the Moravian schedule are other MAC teams. The capitalized entries marked with an asterisk in the Muhlenberg schedule indicate the other members of the Centennial. These schedules are shown in Table 2.48.

Table 2.48.   Football Schedules for 2005

	Moravian 2005	*Muhlenberg 2005*
September 2		at College of New Jersey
September 3	DELAWARE VALLEY	
September 10	SUSQUEHANNA	
September 17	at KING'S	Union (NY)
September 24	JUNIATA	at Grove City
October 1	at WIDENER	at FRANKLIN & MARSHALL*
October 8		DICKINSON*
October 15	at FDUC-FLORHAM	at URSINUS*
October 22	WILKES	JOHNS HOPKINS*
October 29	at LYCOMING	at GETTYSBURG*
November 5	LEBANON VALLEY	MCDANIEL*
November 12	at Muhlenberg	Moravian

Table 2.49.   Football Schedules for 2006

	Moravian 2006	*Muhlenberg 2006*
September 2		College of New Jersey
September 9	at SUSQUEHANNA	William Paterson
September 16	KING'S	at Union (NY)
September 23	at JUNIATA	
September 30	WIDENER	FRANKLIN & MARSHALL*
October 7	at DELAWARE VALLEY	at DICKINSON*
October 14	FDU-FLORHAM	URSINUS*
October 21	at WILKES	at JOHNS HOPKINS*
October 28	LYCOMING	GETTYSBURG*
November 4	at LEBANON VALLEY	at MCDANIEL*
November 11	Muhlenberg	at Moravian

Scheduling this game enabled Dapp, Donnelly, and their respective team members to span jointly a boundary between the MAC and Centennial and a boundary between the MAC and a Muhlenberg circle (with College of New Jersey, Union, and Grove City).

November 11, 2006, Muhlenberg at Moravian

On November 11, 2006, Donnelly and the members of the Muhlenberg 2006 football team traveled from Allentown to Bethlehem. There they met Dapp and the Moravian 2006 team members. Together, Donnelly and Dapp and their respective team members played to a 24-10 Muhlenberg win and Moravian loss. Together, they traversed a boundary between leagues and circles of competitors.

Moravian belonged to the MAC for the 2006 season. Muhlenberg belonged to the Centennial league for the 2006 season. The capitalized entries in the Moravian schedule are other MAC teams. The capitalized entries marked with an asterisk in the Muhlenberg schedule indicate the other members of the Centennial. These schedules are shown in Table 2.49.

Scheduling this game enabled Dapp, Donnelly, and their respective team members to span jointly a boundary between the MAC and Centennial and a boundary between the MAC and a Muhlenberg circle (with College of New Jersey, William Paterson, and Union).

NEXT EPISODE

The 2007 season marks the fiftieth year in the modern Moravian-and-Muhlenberg football relationship. There is more to the 2007 scheduled game than the recognition customarily accorded fifty years in any relationship. The year 2007 is the beginning of one more new chapter in the Moravian-and-Muhlenberg football relationship. In 2005, representatives of Moravian College and the other members of the Centennial Conference announced that Moravian (along with Juniata College) will join the Centennial Conference for football competition in 2007.

Once again in 2007, members of the Moravian and Muhlenberg football teams are scheduled to meet on the field of play. For the first time since 1982, their engagement counts in the same league standings. A new chapter dawns in the Moravian-and-Muhlenberg relationship, in part because decision makers in years past found ways to sustain the relationship. To those human beings, some of whom are no longer around to hear it, go a full measure of ethical praise.

CONCLUSION

The subject of this chapter is a voluntary human activity undertaken across several generations. For much of this forty-nine-year historical record of the Moravian-and-Muhlenberg football relationship (thirty-five years, to be exact), these human beings found ways and reasons to reach across multiple customary boundaries and to collaborate with one another. Many of these collaborators sustained the Moravian-and-Muhlenberg football playing relationship long after their predecessors in the relationship had departed, or had passed away.

This is a story of human beings accepting an obligation of their own making to inherit and sustain a playing relationship. They did this without being ordered, or led, to do so.[22] It is a story of citizens taking steps to solidify civil society through their civil acts.

This is a story about ethics and athletic competition that rarely gets told. The ethical accomplishment is not glamorous. It is not the typical stuff of sports headlines. By conventional wisdom about athletics and ethics, competition is a breeding ground for excess, hypocrisy, and scandal. There is not one whiff of any of this in the historical record that I interpret.

Furthermore, in a departure from conventional wisdom about athletic competition, the story in this chapter is not dominated by wins and losses. Some readers might be stunned to learn about a football relationship in which there have been five winning (and losing) streaks that each lasted at least five years. In one ten-year span, during which Moravian and Muhlenberg belonged to different leagues, one of the teams won every game. By the win-oriented thinking of modern sports, it makes no sense that the losing team (and perhaps the winning team, too) elected to remain in such a lopsided series. Moreover, it was at least conceivable that a representative of one of these colleges, looking at winning and losing trends, might have lost patience with an optional playing relationship and might thereby have begun to push for its abandonment. Still, the playing relationship continued uninterrupted. In the ongoing construction of the Moravian-and-Muhlenberg football partnership, wins and losses have been historical byproducts.

Two more chapters follow in the ethical, historical interpretation of this remarkable relationship among intercollegiate athletic competitors.

NOTES

1. *Competitor* refers to a collective here, a college's football team (or, program).

2. To the economist, this benefit is recognizable as minimized "transaction costs."

3. Michael Porter discusses how a "good competitor" provides this benefit. Michael E. Porter, *Competitive Advantage* (New York: Free Press, 1985), 212–28.

4. This happens when league membership is small. The members of larger leagues can cap the size of the round robin and agree to a rotating round robin. Football in the Big Ten Conference is a prime example. The New England Small College Athletic Conference (NESCAC) schedules a round robin in this way. The teams from Colby and Williams, for example, do not meet every season in the NESCAC football round robin.

5. The member institutions of the National Collegiate Athletic Association (NCAA) agree to a maximum number of competitions in a "regular season." The Moravian and Muhlenberg football teams are now permitted ten games annually.

6. The principal source of schedules and league affiliations is an annual NCAA football guide (see Bibliography). Through 1978, the Moravian schedules were also drawn from my private collection of annual Moravian intercollegiate athletic schedules.

7. A sports historian could investigate the particular challenges of maintaining this relationship. For my purposes here, the decision making process is unimportant. I start from the fact that representatives of the two colleges agreed to schedule a football game.

8. "Mules Whip Moravian, 47-0," *Sunday Call-Chronicle*, 17 November 1946, 17.

9. This journalistic format has long been used when space is limited.

10. I coin *competition circle* to show that a team moves in the company of other competitors, company that sometimes extends outside league membership. With the term, I highlight the uniqueness of an athletic schedule. Since Albright appears on both the Moravian and Muhlenberg 1959 schedules, I do not include Albright in either "circle."

11. "Circle" seems an overstated way to describe the continuing bilateral Moravian-and-Pennsylvania Military playing relationship. "Relationship" is sufficient.

12. The cancellation was listed in the *Washington Post*, 23 November 1963, D1.

13. I omit Pennsylvania Military College and Lebanon Valley from the list of Muhlenberg competitors, because I want to call attention to Moravian seeking a place in the MAC South. As new entrant, Moravian's league schedule consisted of three games.

14. Pennsylvania Military College became Widener College in this year.

15. The Haverford College football program was discontinued after this season.

16. When NCAA Division III members approved a 10-game maximum regular season, a schedule slot opened. Still, Moravian had scheduling options other than their "neighbor" in Allentown. Football programs were added at King's, Fairleigh Dickinson-Madison (later FDU-Florham, then FDUC-Florham), and Wesley.

17. The Centennial scheduled a full round robin right from the beginning.

18. Upsala College ceased operation several years later.

19. The division of the MAC into the Commonwealth League and the Freedom League came at a time when the field of qualifiers for the NCAA Division III football playoffs was expanding. Two MAC leagues might translate into two qualifiers. This happened, for example, in 1995.

20. The Swarthmore football program was discontinued after the 2000 season.

21. Western Maryland College was renamed McDaniel College.

22. That is, we can explain human collaboration without appealing to *leadership*.

Chapter Three

They Passed through the Weather

The intercollegiate football field might seem an odd place to make a point about competition, ethics, and the natural world. The field is a rectangular pattern of straight lines and right angles. At precise intervals, twenty-three parallel lines connect the long sides of the rectangle. This two-dimensional geometry is a picture of human will imposed on a natural space. Gridiron is the name commonly given to this design. The gridiron design is a master-stroke of convenience. Football players, coaches, and commentators alike use the design to locate precisely the action on the field. With the gridiron, they can communicate with statements like, "He ran the ball from his own 40-yard line to the far hash mark at the other 42-yard line, a gain of 18 yards." Convenience aside, the gridiron looks out of touch with the natural world. *Gridiron* even sounds discordant with nature.

A generation ago, some organizers of intercollegiate football competition decided to take this unnatural conception of football field one step further. They replaced a grass-and-dirt playing surface with a carpet of plastic "grass" that was glued to a foundation of concrete and asphalt. On those football fields, players no longer ran and tumbled on grass and dirt. They ran and tumbled on the equivalent of a paved parking lot. The double artificiality of gridiron and plastic grass serves to distance human beings from football competition as a natural experience.

This distancing is optional. In many places, the football field was never converted to artificial grass. Furthermore, whether the playing surface is natural grass or plastic, we need not limit our perspective on football playing fields to two dimensions. We can lift our eyes from the gridiron to take in the sky, wind, clouds, fog, sunshine, precipitation, and haze. When we open our senses to the natural surroundings, we are ready to ponder a new connection between the natural space that is a football field and human efforts to play the game of football there.

THE FORWARD PASS AND AN ETHICAL PROPOSITION

My football focus in this chapter is the forward pass. The forward pass is an attempt to cover considerable distance on the football field in a single play. The forward pass is an endeavor in which passer, receiver, and defender are joined. Sometimes the result is artistic, and sometimes it is not.[1] Passes are caught, deflected, dropped, intercepted, and overthrown.

Every pass play is a new event. Participants in the passing game are students learning together in one another's company, striving to improve.[2] They take turns, many times each game, refining their proficiency in the passing offense. They do this under a variety of atmospheric conditions that they can neither predict nor control.

Passers, receivers, and defenders on both teams thus join in an intriguing ethical endeavor. The forward pass is one part imagination and one part humility. Passers and defenders venture together on each new play, and publicly court failure each time. Embedded in the natural world, the forward pass is an imaginative and humbling act that is connective. Every time football players join in a pass play, they claim their places together in the natural world. Passers and receivers, in the company of pass defenders, embark on a journey through air and sky. Joined in the forward pass, these players affirm with every pass play that this is where they choose to belong together. This chapter contains an ethical, meteorological, historical narrative about the forward pass in the modern Moravian-and-Muhlenberg football playing relationship.

MID-NOVEMBER WEATHER CONDITIONS

The Moravian-and-Muhlenberg football game has been scheduled every football season since 1958 as the final regular-season game for both teams.[3] This means that each game was scheduled for a Saturday afternoon in the middle one-third of November, and sometimes in the latter half of the month.[4] Transition toward winter is in full swing then in eastern Pennsylvania. Past mid-autumn, a warm and humid air mass can linger for a week, or the first icy blast can arrive from Canada. The soggy remnants of a hurricane can pay a visit. A pattern of clear days, cool nights, and wisps of morning fog hanging over a creek can last for days. The modern Moravian-and-Muhlenberg football playing relationship has been scheduled and played under all these conditions, although nothing as meteorologically exciting as a hurricane has ever been recorded on a game day.

The meteorological vitality of this natural setting can be linked to the Moravian-and-Muhlenberg playing relationship with statistics that meteorologists like to record and report. The highest temperature recorded during a Moravian-and-Muhlenberg football game since 1958 was 67 degrees Fahrenheit on November 10, 2006. The coldest temperature was 32 degrees on November 16, 1985, as freezing rain fell. Over the forty-nine-year span of the modern Moravian-and-Muhlenberg football relationship, temperatures above 60 degrees were recorded on eight game days and in the 30s on ten others. On four of those eight balmy occasions, the temperature did not drop below 60 degrees during a game. On six of the ten cold days, the temperature remained in the 30s. Bright sunshine did little to offset the bone-chilling cold (upper 30s) and wind chill (sustained northwest winds exceeding 20 miles per hour) that passers and receivers (and spectators, including the author) endured on November 21, 1964. During the six-year period beginning in 1982, the high temperatures recorded during the game were 46, 37, 64, 34, 43, and 61 degrees.

The wind is a telltale indicator of sharp air pressure differences in mid-November in eastern Pennsylvania. Throughout twenty-five of the forty-nine game days, winds blew steadily in excess of ten knots. The peak wind gust was recorded at 37 miles per hour on November 11, 1995.[5] The highest barometric pressure recorded was 30.73 inches on November 16, 1996; the lowest was 29.37 inches on November 10. 1990.[6] That 1990 afternoon was the wettest in the modern Moravian-and-Muhlenberg football relationship. One inch of rain fell during that game.

THREE PLAYING FIELDS

These weather conditions have enveloped three natural settings in the modern Moravian-and-Muhlenberg football relationship. Games were played on Moravian Field in Bethlehem in 1958, 1960, 1962, 1964, and 1966. Moravian home games were then moved six blocks to Steel Field (renamed Rocco Calvo Field), where the Moravian-and Muhlenberg football game has been played in every even-numbered year since 1968. In Allentown, Muhlenberg Field (renamed Scotty Wood Stadium) has been the site of every Moravian-and-Muhlenberg football game scheduled for odd-numbered years since 1959.[7]

All three locations are inviting places for players, coaches, and spectators to link football with the air and the sky. Moravian Field stretched north to south in a residential neighborhood. The sky enveloped the field. Looking west across the Monocacy Creek valley, one could follow the paths of aircraft bound for the Allentown-Bethlehem-Easton (ABE) Airport. Steel Field is bordered by neighborhood, office buildings, tennis courts, and ball fields. Three miles to the south, the hill called South Mountain comes into view. ABE-bound aircraft move from left to right across this vista. Muhlenberg Field sits amidst a tree-shaded neighborhood, soccer field, the Muhlenberg campus grounds, and a gymnasium.[8] The open sky arcs from east to west. Along Liberty Street behind the main grandstand, deciduous trees are indicators of wind speed and the march of autumn.

The east-west orientation of Muhlenberg Field brings the setting sun into play. In 1971, an observer linked the sun and the forward pass in his game account:[9]

> The sun could have very well had something to do with a number of dropped passes. The field lies from east to west and at this time of year the brilliant sunshine goes down early. It was especially hard to see the yard lines toward the west from the press box late in the game. The sun obviously had to be rough at times on the quarterback when moving westward and on the receivers when rolling toward the east and having to look back into it.

At Rocco Calvo Field, the setting sun is obscured behind the houses along New Street.

TELLING AN ETHICAL, METEOROLOGICAL STORY THROUGH THE RAIN

In the modern Moravian-and-Muhlenberg football relationship, measurable precipitation fell on ten afternoons. Five times, it rained throughout the game. In this chapter, each of these rainy days marks the end of a meteorological era in the Moravian-and-Muhlenberg football relationship. A sixth era began in 2003. Not a drop of rain has fallen during the four most recent games. Indeed, no clouds have been seen in this period.

Data and Methodology

I draw on two data sources for this chapter. One is meteorological data for each day of a scheduled Moravian-and-Muhlenberg game. These data are the official weather observations recorded at the Allentown-Bethlehem-Easton Airport station (renamed as Lehigh Valley International Airport).[10] This station is located 3.5 driving miles from Moravian Field, 3.8 miles from Steel

Field, and 9 miles from the Muhlenberg home field.[11] The other data consists of the passing offense statistics, individual and team, for each of the Moravian-and-Muhlenberg football games since 1958.

I weave these two sets of data into a game-by-game narrative in which I translate the passing game into a collaborative, hopeful, and humbling venture embedded in the weather. This ethical act has been witnessed by thousands of spectators. We all can take inspiration. Whether Moravian-and-Muhlenberg passers fill the air with 79 passes, as they did on November 13, 1993, or with 20 passes on that cold 1964 day, this proposition about human beings belonging to the natural world is as breathtaking as a mid-November wind in eastern Pennsylvania.

A Word to Readers

There is repetition and redundancy in the narrative that follows. This is necessary. This chapter is an introduction to a different way of talking about athletic competition. In this chapter, there are forty-nine opportunities—the forty-nine games scheduled in the modern Moravian-and-Muhlenberg football relationship—to connect intercollegiate athletics and ethics through the acts of competitors jointly claiming their place in the natural world. Be patient. Immerse yourself in this new way of talking. Midway through the chapter, I streamline the narrative. Subheadings disappear, for example. By then, you likely will not even notice.

IN THE EARLY YEARS, A SEVEN-YEAR WEATHER CYCLE

The story starts with passers and receivers playing catch over a seven-year period that concludes with clouds, rain, and icy winds. In this meteorological era, the passing results were spotty. The 1962 Moravian-and-Muhlenberg game was an exception.

Changeable on November 22, 1958

By the hour before the 4:40 p.m. sundown in Bethlehem on Saturday afternoon, November 22, 1958, skies were clearing to 40% cloud cover. The dew point had dropped into the upper 20s. Air pressure rose steadily. The temperature was 45 degrees. Visibility had been 15 miles throughout the afternoon. Sunshine had been variable.[12]

Through periods of sun and overcast, Muhlenberg passers completed 11 of 17 passes for 160 yards gained. Moravian passers completed 2 of 8 passes for

34 yards. Ralph Borneman, the Muhlenberg Quarterback (QB, hereafter), and his receivers accomplished a precise passing game. Moravian QBs Tony Matz and Russ DeVore mostly handed the ball to Moravian rushers.

Borneman completed 8 of the 10 passes for 113 yards. In mid-afternoon, he connected with receiver Bob Pearsons on a 10-yard touchdown pass. At the time, a cloud layer at 6,000 feet covered 60% of the sky. A northwest wind was measured at 17 knots.[13] The temperature and the dew point were 44 and 28 degrees, respectively. Pearsons caught a two-point conversion pass thrown by halfback Herb Owens after Moravian took the lead on an 8-yard pass completion from Matz to Johnny Olson and a rushing touchdown. At the time of Olson's reception, clouds covered 70% of the sky at 6,000 feet. A west-northwest wind blew at 14 knots. The temperature was 45 degrees, en route to the daily high of 47.

In the third quarter, Matz and receiver Dave Coe connected on a 26-yard pass play. The receptions by Olson and Coe were the only two for the Moravian passing offense. (Coe also caught a conversion pass from Matz. It did not count in the passing statistics.)

Shortly after sundown, scattered cumulus covered 20% of the sky over Moravian Field. The wind had eased to 10 knots. The temperature fell to 41, en route to a low of 27. High pressure continued to build on a tranquil evening, to 30.30 inches by midnight.

Clearing on November 21, 1959

By the hour before sundown in Allentown on Saturday afternoon, November 21, 1959, clearing had begun. The air had warmed to a daily high of 46 degrees. A 6-knot breeze blew from the southeast. The light, trace rainfall had ended. Visibility was 6 miles.

Moravian passers completed 10 of 19 attempts for 111 yards. Muhlenberg passers completed 3 of 12 passes for 90 yards.

The forward pass was consequential in the second quarter. After a Muhlenberg touchdown, Moravian QB John Williams led an 83-yard touchdown drive on which he completed passes for 67 yards. Bill Hershey was his favorite receiver. As the light rainfall continued in the 45-degree air, Moravian's Jeff Gannon, from a single-wing formation, completed a two-point conversion pass to Dave Coe. In a 6-knot southeast breeze, with clouds covering 90% of the sky, one pass thrown by Muhlenberg QB Rollie Houseknecht restored the Muhlenberg lead. On the first play from scrimmage after Moravian scored the 8 points, Herb Owens caught a Houseknecht pass for a 71-yard touchdown play.

Neither team used the forward pass much after halftime. As the air warmed to the daily high temperature at 46 degrees by 4:00 p.m., Muhlenberg QBs

Houseknecht and Ralph Borneman attempted few passes under clearing skies (to 20% cloud cover). Their passing offense produced only 19 yards besides the Houseknecht-to-Owens completion.

Shortly after sundown, skies were 80% clear over Muhlenberg Field. The windless air cooled to 42 degrees, en route to a low of 29. Low air pressure held steady.

Sunny on November 19, 1960

By the hour before sundown in Bethlehem on Saturday afternoon, November 19, 1960, skies were clear. The 30-degree dew point indicated dry air. Air pressure was rising. The temperature was 54 degrees. Visibility was 15 miles. The afternoon had been sunny, with a few clouds early.[14] In steady northwest winds of 15 knots, Muhlenberg QB Rollie Houseknecht completed 6 of 17 passes for 87 yards. Moravian QB Andy Semmel completed 4 of 13 passes for 32 yards.

Houseknecht completed a 10-yard touchdown pass to Charlie Kuntzleman in the second quarter, before the temperature rose to a daily high of 56. Under the clear skies of mid-afternoon, Houseknecht completed a 20-yard pass to Bob Butz to set up the final Muhlenberg touchdown. Just before halftime, on a fourth-down play, Semmel completed a short pass that receiver Jim Insinga turned into a 33-yard touchdown play. The play covered one yard more than Moravian's net passing yardage (32). Semmel then completed a two-point conversion pass to Jim Kritis.

Two other pass completions in the third quarter resulted in points. After a Muhlenberg touchdown, Butz caught a two-point conversion pass from Houseknecht. After the second Moravian touchdown, receiver Jim Kelyman caught a two-point conversion pass from Moravian back Dick Ritter. In mid-50s temperatures, the two teams played a scoreless fourth quarter.

Shortly after sundown, the air cooled into the upper 40s. The wind was 8 knots.

Cool on November 18, 1961

By the hour before sundown in Allentown on Saturday afternoon, November 18, 1961, clouds covered 40% of the sky. The dew point was in the low-20s. Air pressure held steady. The temperature was 42. Visibility was 15 miles. It was sunny.

Sunshine and west winds had been plentiful all afternoon. A wind speed of 22 knots was recorded at 2:00 p.m. Muhlenberg QB Rollie Houseknecht and his receivers connected on 12 of 20 passes for 141 yards. One was a 26-yard touchdown pass to Dean Lowe in the second quarter. Moravian passers completed only 2 of 12 pass attempts for 22 yards. In the final minute of play, Moravian QB Andy Semmel threw a 13-yard touchdown pass to Paul Riccardi.

Shortly after sundown, skies were mostly clear over Muhlenberg Field. The wind persisted at 14 knots. The air was crisp at 40 degrees. Air pressure was building toward 30.12 inches by midnight.

Light Rain on November 17, 1962

By the hour before sundown in Bethlehem on Saturday afternoon, November 17, 1962, light rain fell from a cloud ceiling at 2,700 feet. The air was cool (41 degrees) and calm. Air pressure was low and steady. Visibility had dropped to 10 miles.

Muhlenberg QB Terry Haney and his receivers staged a passing clinic. Moravian QBs Andy Semmel, Russ DeVore, Bob Mushrush, and their receivers struggled. Haney completed 13 of 24 passes for 233 yards, the most productive passing since the Moravian-and-Muhlenberg relationship resumed. Haney and receiver Charlie Woginrich combined on 7 completions. Moravian passers completed 7 of 19 passes for 83 yards.

By the time rain began in mid-afternoon, Haney had completed touchdown passes to Dave Brown, Woginrich, and Dean Lowe, covering 40, 17, and 37 yards, respectively. Early in the fourth quarter, DeVore and his receivers connected on four consecutive plays for 35 yards. With light rain continuing in the fourth quarter, each team scored on a two-point conversion pass. Haney and Woginrich connected for Muhlenberg. Mushrush and Pat Mazza then connected for the Moravian points.

Shortly after sundown, clouds lowered to 2,000 feet. Light rain continued; 0.07 more inches fell by 8:00 p.m. The temperature was 37 degrees by 10:00 p.m.

Fittingly, Rain in 1963

Rain fell steadily on Muhlenberg Field on Saturday, November 23, 1963. One-half inch was recorded between 1:00 and 5:00 p.m. Clouds lowered to 700 feet by 4:00 p.m. Southwest winds, peaking at 17 knots at 2:00 p.m., ushered in balmy 60-degree air.

No one got the chance to throw and catch a wet football on this day. The Moravian-and-Muhlenberg football game was cancelled. It rained in the evening, too.

Bone-Chilling on November 21, 1964

By the hour before sundown in Bethlehem on Saturday afternoon, November 21, 1964, skies were clear over Moravian Field. The air was dry and cold. The dew point had fallen into the upper teens, and the temperature was 35 degrees. Visibility was 15 miles.

The afternoon was windy and cold. Muhlenberg QBs Terry Haney and Ron Henry and Moravian QBs Jerry Transue and Warren Hall, and their receivers, staged a forgettable passing game.[15] Northwest winds gusted to 23 knots early in the game. Muhlenberg passers completed 2 of 9 attempts for 9 yards. The Moravian passing offense consisted of one completion for 21 yards and 10 incomplete attempts. The only points scored directly with a pass came in the fourth quarter. In a 17-knot wind, Henry threw a two-point conversion pass to Dave Binder.

Shortly after sundown, skies remained clear over Moravian Field. The wind continued at 15 knots. Air temperature had fallen to 33 degrees, en route to a daily low of 23 by midnight. High pressure had risen to 30.24 inches.

FIFTEEN YEARS, BREEZY AND VARIABLY CLOUDY

It would be fifteen years before the next Moravian-and-Muhlenberg game was played in the rain. The playing relationship entered an era notable for wind and clouds. The relationship also entered an era when different histories unfolded for the Moravian and Muhlenberg passing offenses. In the fifteen Moravian-and-Muhlenberg football games from 1965 through 1979, the Moravian passing offense exceeded 100 yards three times, and the Muhlenberg passing offense fell short of 100 yards on only five occasions. Only twice (1974 and 1977) did one team's passing offense (Muhlenberg, both times) exceed 200 yards. In these years of normal November weather for eastern Pennsylvania, the Moravian-and-Muhlenberg football game was primarily a rushing game.

By the hour before sundown in Allentown on Saturday, November 20, 1965, skies were clear. The dew point held steady at 30 degrees. The temperature remained at 47. Air pressure was steady. Visibility was 13 miles. A "sun dog" was noted at 3:53 p.m.

As high clouds filtered the sunshine, Muhlenberg QB Ron Henry and Moravian QB John Petley used the pass differently. Henry filled the breezy (12 knots) air with 36 passes, completing 16 for 170 yards. Petley threw 13 passes, completing 5 for 70 yards. In the fourth quarter, Henry connected with Charlie Woginrich on a 41-yard touchdown pass. On a subsequent touchdown drive, John Shipley caught a 28-yard Petley pass.

Shortly after sundown on November 20, 1965, skies were clear over Muhlenberg Field. The south wind eased to 8 knots. Air pressure fell to 29.88 inches in the evening.

By the hour before sundown in Bethlehem on Saturday, November 19, 1966, skies were clear. The temperature fell into the upper 30s. The air was very dry; the dew point was 17. Air pressure was high at 30.36 inches and rising. Visibility remained 15 miles. It had been a sunny afternoon.

Sunshine broke through the overcast at 10:00 a.m. On this windy afternoon, neither Muhlenberg QB Paul Fischer nor Moravian QBs Greg Seifert and Jim Dietz threw the ball very often. In a 16-knot northwest wind, Dietz and receiver Ralph Eltringham combined on a 37-yard touchdown pass in the first quarter. The completion was one of 2 (in 9 attempts) for the Moravian passing offense. The other completion covered 25 yards. With 1965 Muhlenberg QB Ron Henry playing defensive back a year later, Fischer completed 4 of 15 passes for 57 yards.

Shortly after sundown on November 19, 1966, skies were clear over Moravian Field. The northwest wind eased to 11 knots. The temperature had fallen to 34 degrees, en route to a daily low of 24 by midnight. High pressure had risen to 30.39 inches.

By the hour before sundown in Allentown on Saturday, November 18, 1967, skies were partly cloudy. The air was drying, as the dew point fell to 34 degrees. Air pressure remained low at 29.54 inches. The temperature had fallen to 42 degrees. Visibility was 15 miles. The northwest wind gusted to 36 knots.

The day dawned with a two-inch snow cover. A rain shower fell between 12:30 and 1:15 p.m., totaling 0.06 inches. Sunshine broke through the clouds by 2:00 p.m. Then the northwest wind increased to 10 knots and more.

On a muddy field, Moravian QBs Jim Dietz and Greg Seifert used the forward pass sparingly yet productively. Dietz attempted 5 passes and completed 3 for 119 yards. A touchdown pass from Dietz to Paul Martinelli in the third quarter covered 65 yards. Seifert completed 2 of 6 passes for 12 yards. Muhlenberg QBs Ron Henry and Bill Evans attempted 32 passes, but completed only 10. One of those completions was a 32-yard touchdown pass in the fourth quarter from Evans to Tom Saeger. The Muhlenberg passing offense totaled 120 yards.

Shortly after sundown on November 18, 1967, skies were mostly clear over Muhlenberg Field. The wind increased to 15 knots with higher gusts. The temperature had fallen to 39 degrees. High pressure began to rise slowly to 29.67 inches.

By the hour before sundown in Bethlehem on Saturday, November 23, 1968, clouds covered 90% of the sky. The air was dry. The dew point was 31 degrees. High pressure was steady. The temperature was 50 degrees. Visibility dropped to 10 miles. The afternoon had been cloudy, with a 12,000-foot ceiling. The sun shone briefly early.

With the sun dimmed by high clouds, the Muhlenberg passing unit struggled, and the Moravian passing game was sharp. Muhlenberg QB Randy Uhrich completed 8 of 19 passes for 65 yards. Moravian QB Jim Dietz completed 9 of 11 passes for 140 yards. Dietz threw an 11-yard touchdown pass to Hugh Gratz and a 24-yard touchdown pass to Paul Martinelli. In the time between the touchdowns, the temperature had risen to the daily high of 53 degrees. In the fourth quarter, Uhrich completed a two-point conversion pass to John Harding. Gratz and Martinelli each caught 3 passes, for 40 and 57 yards, respectively.

Shortly after sundown on November 23, 1968, skies remained cloudy over Steel Field, Moravian's new home football field. A southeast wind continued at 8 knots. The temperature had fallen into the upper 40s. Air pressure held steady at 30.13 inches.

By the hour before sundown in Allentown on Saturday, November 22, 1969, high clouds covered 70% of the sky. The air was cold (37 degrees) and dry (dew point at 19). Air pressure was high at 30.28 inches. Visibility had been 15 miles all day.

Under a cirrus-filled sky, in an 11-knot south wind, the Muhlenberg passing game struggled, while Moravian rarely passed. Muhlenberg QBs Randy Uhrich and Ed DiYanni attempted 26 passes, completing only 7 for 79 yards. One of Uhrich's passes was caught by Carl Evans for 10 yards. Of the 62 Moravian offense plays, 52 were rushes. On their combined 10 pass attempts, Moravian QBs Gary Martell, Joe Dowling, and Steve Markovich completed 5 for 83 yards. This was the first game in the modern Moravian-and-Muhlenberg relationship where no points were scored on pass plays.

Shortly after sundown on November 22, 1969, skies remained cirrus-filled over Muhlenberg Field. The wind eased to 8 knots. The temperature had fallen to 34 degrees. A lunar halo was observed at 9:00 p.m. on a tranquil evening.

By the hour before sundown in Bethlehem on Saturday, November 19, 1970, cirrus clouds had appeared. The air was dry (dew point at 28). Air pressure was rising. The temperature was 48 degrees. Visibility was 15 miles. The afternoon had been sunny with scattered cumulus.

A west wind gusted to 22 knots in the first half. By halftime, a familiar story was unfolding. The Muhlenberg passing game struggled, while Moravian passed infrequently. For the game, Muhlenberg QB Randy Uhrich completed 8 of 21 passes for 125 yards. One completion to Carl Evans covered 35 yards late in the first half, as an 18-knot wind cooled the 51-degree air, the daily high. Moravian QBs Joe Dowling and Gary Martell completed 10 of 16 attempts for 94 yards. Dowling completed 6 passes for 44 yards. Danny Joseph caught 5 passes for 52 yards, including an 11-yard touchdown from Dowling in the third quarter. By that time, the air temperature had settled at 50 degrees.

Shortly after sundown on November 19, 1970, cirrus clouds lingered over Steel Field. The west wind continued at 12 knots. The temperature had fallen to 45 degrees, en route to a daily low of 34 by mid-evening. High pressure had risen to 30.11 inches.

By the hour before sundown in Allentown on Saturday, November 20, 1971, clouds covered 70% of the sky. The air was dry (dew point at 29). Air pressure was 29.55 inches and falling. The temperature was 43 degrees. Visibility remained 15 miles.

In clouds and sun, the Moravian and Muhlenberg passing offenses both struggled. Of the 47 passing attempts combined, 38 fell incomplete. Moravian passers completed 4 of 19 attempts for 91 yards. Muhlenberg QB Ed DiYanni completed 5 of 28 attempts for 62 yards.

DiYanni and receiver Carl Evans connected on 3 passes for 32 yards. By mid-afternoon, as the wind shifted to the southwest at 9 knots, Moravian QB Joe Dowling completed two passes that led directly to touchdowns. A 31-yard completion to Keith Lambie preceded Moravian's first score. Later in the third quarter, Dowling and Danny Joseph connected on a 39-yard play. Four plays later, Moravian scored. In the closing minutes, a DiYanni-to-Evans pass moved the ball on the Moravian 22-yard line. Muhlenberg did not score on that drive.

Shortly after sundown on November 20, 1971, skies remained mostly cloudy over Muhlenberg Field. The southwest wind continued at 9 knots. The air had cooled to 41 degrees. Air pressure was falling. Trace rainfall was measured before midnight.

By the hour before sundown in Bethlehem on Saturday, November 18, 1972, mostly cloudy skies had returned. The air was dry (dew point at 25 degrees). Air pressure had risen to 30.23 inches. The temperature was 41 degrees. Visibility was 12 miles.

The afternoon had been mostly cloudy with sunny breaks. Muhlenberg QBs Mike Reid and Bob Shirvanian and Moravian QBs Gary Martell and Fred Ferratti used the forward pass quite differently. Moravian built an early lead. Reid and Shirvanian attempted 26 passes in an effort to catch up. They completed 7 passes for 144 yards. Martell, then Ferratti, directed an offense unit that rushed for 326 yards. Martell and Ferratti completed 8 of 19 passes for 80 yards.

As the wind moved to the northwest at 9 knots late in the first half, Reid and Randy Boll teamed on a 53-yard touchdown pass. Martell ran for more yards (75) than he gained (68) on 7 pass completions. With less cloud cover (30%) in the fourth quarter, Shirvanian threw a screen pass to Ken Hedden, who ran for a 55-yard touchdown. The two Muhlenberg touchdown passes accounted for 118 of the 144 passing yards.

Shortly after sundown on November 18, 1972, skies remained mostly cloudy over Steel Field. The northwest wind subsided to 7 knots. The temperature had fallen to 37 degrees. High pressure held steady.

By the hour before sundown in Allentown on Saturday, November 17, 1973, stratocumulus clouds covered 80% of the sky. The air was dry, with dew point at 20 degrees. Air pressure was high and steady. The temperature was 42 degrees. Visibility had been more than 25 miles all afternoon.

Throughout this mostly cloudy and windy afternoon, the Muhlenberg passing offense was uncharacteristically quiet. The 8 passing attempts by Muhlenberg QB Bob Shirvanian were the fewest for Muhlenberg since the Moravian-and-Muhlenberg football relationship resumed in 1958. But, it only took one pass completion in 16-knot northwest air to change the flow of the game. Seven seconds before halftime, as the air warmed to the daily high temperature of 44 degrees, Shirvanian and receiver Eric Butler combined on a 73-yard touchdown pass. For the rest of the game, Shirvanian and his receivers teamed on 3 of 7 pass attempts for 27 yards.

After halftime, as the west wind eased from 16 knots to 10 knots, Moravian backup QB Fred Ferratti connected with Charlie Kasky on a 54-yard touchdown pass. Under continuing cloudy skies and cool westerly winds, Ferratti led a fourth-quarter touchdown drive by completing passes to Larry Claudia, Vince Pantalone, and Dale Conicella, covering 35 yards in all. Ferratti and starting QB Jon Van Valkenburg combined for 10 completions in 27 attempts for 131 yards.

Shortly after sundown on November 17, 1973, skies remained mostly cloudy over Muhlenberg Field. The west wind continued at 11 knots. The temperature remained at 42 degrees, en route to a daily low of 30 by midnight. Skies cleared by 9:00 p.m. Air pressure rose to 30.20 inches.

By the hour before sundown in Bethlehem on Saturday, November 23, 1974, skies were clear. The air was dry, with dew point at 30 degrees. Air pressure was high and steady at 30.28 inches. The temperature was 45 degrees, the daily high. Visibility was 13 miles. The air was calm. Dawn had been calm, frosty, and cold (20 degrees).

On this cloudless, cool afternoon, Muhlenberg QB Mike Reid and Moravian QB Jon Van Valkenburg gave everyone more than 40 opportunities (30 generated by Reid) to scan the clear air for balls in flight. For the first time in the modern Moravian-and-Muhlenberg football relationship, five touchdowns were scored on pass plays.

By the time the light breeze backed into the southwest, Van Valkenburg had completed two touchdown passes to Larry Claudia, and Reid had connected with Randy Boll on a 36-yard scoring play. As the daily high reached 45 degrees and wind eased to 5 knots, Reid threw touchdown passes to John Mill (20 yards) and Boll again (14 yards) to bring Muhlenberg within one point at the end of the third quarter.

In calm air, Van Valkenburg led two fourth-quarter touchdown drives, the second marked by a 32-yard completion to Don DaVanzo. Reid's passing carried Muhlenberg to the Moravian 8-yard line as time expired. Boll's 8 receptions accounted for 151 of Reid's 270 passing yards in 17 completions. Jim Stampfle caught 4 passes from Reid for 62 more yards. On the day, Van Valkenburg completed 5 of 11 attempts for 86 yards.

Shortly after sundown on November 23, 1974, skies remained clear over Steel Field. The south wind returned at 6 knots. The temperature had fallen quickly to 40 degrees. High pressure held steady.

By the hour before sundown in Allentown on Saturday, November 22, 1975, skies were partly cloudy. The dew point was 30. Air pressure had risen to 30.13 inches. The temperature was 45 degrees. Visibility was 30 miles. A northwest wind blew at 11 knots.

As the west wind blew at 13 knots, and sometimes more, throughout the game, the passing game created by Moravian QB Jon Van Valkenburg and Muhlenberg QB Mike Reid and their receivers was most prominent in the fourth quarter. Van Valkenburg's 16-yard touchdown pass to Gregg Feinberg stretched a Moravian lead. As the clouds became more scattered, Reid's pass to Eric Butler put the ball on the Moravian 5-yard line as time expired. Reid was successful on 9 of 23 pass attempts for 117 yards. Van Valkenburg's 7 completions in 13 attempts gained 70 yards, less than one-quarter of Moravian's total offense.

Shortly after sundown on November 22, 1975, skies cleared over Muhlenberg Field. The wind eased to 9 knots. The temperature had fallen to 42 degrees, en route to a daily low of 33 by midnight. High pressure had risen to 30.16 inches.

By the hour before sundown in Bethlehem on Saturday, November 20, 1976, occasional breaks were visible in the stratocumulus clouds. The air was dry, with the dew point at 23 degrees. Air pressure was low and steady at 29.68 inches. The temperature was 43 degrees. Visibility was 25 miles. The west wind had increased to 18 knots.

Throughout this blustery and cloudy afternoon, Muhlenberg QB John Schlechter attempted 33 passes. (There were 2 other Muhlenberg pass attempts.) When Moravian had the ball, spectators had fewer opportunities to peer high into the autumn sky. Moravian QB Jon Van Valkenburg attempted only 7 passes, completing 3 for 43 yards. Late in the first half, with the temperature in the mid-40s, substitute Muhlenberg QB Don Sommerville completed a 9-yard touchdown pass to John Sartori. After halftime, as the air warmed to the daily high of 46 degrees and the sun occasionally broke through the overcast, Sartori was on the receiving end of a second touchdown pass. This time, it was an 8-yard play with Schlechter. The west wind gusted to 24 knots in that hour. Schlechter's 16 completions gained 164 of the 180 Muhlenberg passing yards.

Shortly after sundown on November 20, 1976, skies over Steel Field remained mostly cloudy with some breaks. The northwest wind eased to 7 knots. Air pressure held steady. The temperature was 42 degrees. A clear evening was ahead, with the daily low of 31 recorded at 11:00 p.m.

By the hour before sundown in Allentown on Saturday, November 19, 1977, scattered clouds covered 20% of the sky. The air was dry, with the dew point at 24. Air pressure had risen to 30.30 inches. The temperature was 45 degrees, the high for the day. Visibility was 25 miles. The west wind blew at 10 knots.

Under increasing sunshine, Moravian QB Jack Bradley and Muhlenberg QB Don Sommerville and their receivers accomplished two different performances. Bradley completed 4 of 10 attempts for 36 yards. After a gusty northwest wind subsided to 14 knots in the second quarter, Ed McGettigan and Gregg Feinberg caught two of Bradley's passes during the second Moravian touchdown drive. Later in the quarter, Feinberg caught a 10-yard touchdown pass from Bradley. It was the last time Moravian scored.

As cloud cover decreased to 40% and the wind shifted to the west at 11 knots, Sommerville and Ted Nivison teamed on an 82-yard touchdown that began a Muhlenberg comeback in the third quarter. Catches by Nivison (5 for 179 yards) and John Sartori (6 for 49 yards) accounted for the bulk of Sommerville's 14 completions in 23 attempts for 269 yards. (One other Muhlenberg completion gained 3 yards.)

Shortly after sundown on November 19, 1977, skies remained mostly clear over Muhlenberg Field. The wind eased to 6 knots. The temperature had fallen to 41 degrees. High pressure continued to build to 30.32 inches. A clear evening followed.

By the hour before sundown in Bethlehem on Saturday, November 11, 1978, skies were partly cloudy. Visibility was 4 miles in haze. Southwest winds of 7 knots delivered balmy air. The temperature was 58 degrees, and the dew point was 48. Air pressure was high and steady at 30.20 inches.

Muhlenberg QB John Schlechter and Moravian QBs Jack Bradley and Daryl Eppley filled the warm air with 45 passes, 23 by the Moravian passers. By the time the temperature reached a daily high of 61 degrees, Schlechter had completed a 21-yard pass play to Ted Nivison to set up the first Muhlenberg touchdown.

Under scattered cumulus clouds that filled half the sky, Bradley and Eppley and their receivers struggled. They completed 6 of 23 pass attempts for 60 yards. Gregg Feinberg caught 3 of those passes for 38 yards. In the hazy air (4-mile visibility after halftime), John Sartori caught 2 passes for 21 of the Muhlenberg 116 passing yards. In all, Schlechter completed 12 of 22.

Shortly after sundown at 4:48 p.m. on November 11, 1978, skies remained partly cloudy and hazy over Steel Field. The southwest wind continued at 8 knots. The temperature remained 55 degrees. High pressure held steady.

By the hour before sundown in Allentown on Saturday, November 10, 1979, light rain had ended. The sky was 100% overcast. Fog reduced visibility to 5 miles. The air was saturated. The temperature and dew point were 59 and 58 degrees, respectively. A southwest wind blew at 6 knots. The air pressure had risen to 29.90 inches. In the saturated air (relative humidity near 100% for the entire game), Moravian QBs Jack Bradley and Ed Stange and Muhlenberg QB Brian Schulte (subbing for injured Don Sommerville) attempted more than a pass a minute, 66 attempts in all.

The field was soaked by the time of the opening kickoff. Rainfall through 11:00 a.m. totaled 0.35 inches. Another 0.05 inches was recorded through halftime. By then, Schulte had completed two touchdown passes to John Sartori. In a light southwest wind and balmy air (60 degrees through 2:00 p.m., upper 50s thereafter), Schulte and Sartori combined on 7 completions for 84 yards. Schulte and Ted Nivison connected on 3 more pass plays for 54 yards. This accounted for the bulk of Schulte's 14 completions (in 29 attempts) for 174 passing yards.

For the sixth straight year, the Moravian passing offense did not gain 100 yards. Bradley and Stange completed 14 of 37 attempts for 99 yards.

Shortly after sundown on November 10, 1979, skies remained cloudy and foggy over Muhlenberg Field. The wind continued at 6 knots. The air was balmy (58 degrees) and humid (dew point at 57). Air pressure continued rising to 29.95 inches.

WIDE WEATHER SWINGS IN A SIX-YEAR SPAN

A daylong rainstorm, at times freezing on contact, concluded the ensuing six-year period of weather variation in the Moravian-and-Muhlenberg football relationship. The period was marked by a typical variety in November weather in eastern Pennsylvania. In this stretch, the forward pass played a diminished role. The exceptions were the 1980 Moravian passing offense and the 1984 Muhlenberg passing offense.

By the hour before sundown in Bethlehem on Saturday, November 15, 1980, skies were overcast at 22,000 feet. The air was dry, with the dew point at 29 degrees. Visibility was 15 miles. A northwest wind continued at 9 knots. The temperature was 45 degrees. Air pressure was high and steady.

A trace rain shower was recorded in the first hour after noon. The temperature held steady at 46 (and the dew point at 31) until 4:00 p.m. By then, Moravian QB Jack Bradley and his receivers had filled the air with passes. Paul Tuttle (8 for 73 yards) and D. J. Nimphius (7 for 99 yards) caught the majority of Bradley's 22 completions in 49 attempts. Bradley passed for 232 yards. One other Moravian pass fell incomplete.

Muhlenberg QB Gary Greb completed 8 of 23 passes for 54 yards. Under gray skies and a 9,000-foot cloud layer, Greb and receiver Marc Spatidol combined on a 10-yard scoring play to open the scoring in the third quarter. The scoring play broke a halftime tie.

Shortly after sundown on November 15, 1980, skies remained overcast over Steel Field. The north wind eased to 6 knots. The air temperature, dew point, and air pressure all held steady. The air cooled to 40 degrees, the daily low, by 8:00 p.m.

By the hour before sundown in Allentown on Saturday, November 14, 1981, high clouds covered the sky at 23,000 feet. Visibility was 30 miles. The dew point was a dry 30 degrees. An east wind blew at 5 knots. The temperature was 53 degrees. Air pressure fell slowly to 30.09 inches. Throughout the mild and cloudy afternoon, Moravian QBs Dave Kaercher and Tim Williams and Muhlenberg QB Gary Greb and their receivers accomplished little with the forward pass until the fourth quarter.

One of Greb's 8 completions (in 24 attempts) resulted in a 5-yard touchdown reception by Mike Hiller. Hiller caught 4 passes for 46 yards. After the midpoint of the fourth quarter, with the temperature lingering at 53 degrees, Kaercher and receiver Jim Laverty connected on a 19-yard pass play that set up the lone Moravian touchdown. Entering the game in the second quarter, Kaercher completed 4 of 14 passes. Williams completed 2 of 3 attempts. Neither the Moravian passing offense (73 yards) nor the Muhlenberg passing offense (99 yards) could move the ball the length of a football field.

Shortly after sundown on November 14, 1981, the overcast lowered to 8,000 feet over Muhlenberg Field. The east wind continued at 5 knots. The temperature fell to 51 degrees, while the dew point held steady at 30. The air pressure continued a slow fall.

By the hour before sundown in Bethlehem on Saturday, November 13, 1982, scattered clouds covered 30% of the sky. Visibility was 30 miles. The northwest wind had eased to 15 knots. The air temperature was 44 degrees, and the dew point was 24 degrees. Rising air pressure signaled a clearing trend. The reading was 30.12 inches, up from 29.71 inches at midnight.

More than one-half inch (0.56 inches) of rain fell in the pre-dawn hours. By 3:00 p.m., skies had cleared to 20% cloud cover, and the air had dried to a 23-degree dew point. By then, Muhlenberg QB Gary Greb and Moravian QB Scott Rhinehart and their receivers had used the forward pass differently.

As northwest winds howled at more than 20 knots, gusting to 28 knots, for much of the afternoon, Greb completed 9 of 28 passes for 111 yards. One completion was a 14-yard play with Todd Langdon that set up the game-tying Muhlenberg touchdown in the fourth quarter. By then, winds had eased to 15 knots. Rhinehart passed little, completing 2 of 5 attempts for 28 yards.

Shortly after sundown on November 13, 1982, scattered clouds remained over Steel Field. The 12-knot northwest wind gusted to 28 knots. The temperature was 42 degrees, and the dew point was 23. Air pressure had risen to 30.15 inches, en route to 30.31 inches at midnight. The daily low of 40 degrees was recorded in early evening.

By the hour before sundown in Allentown on Saturday, November 12, 1983, thick clouds hovered at 3,300 feet. Visibility was 30 miles. A 19-knot northwest wind gusted to 24 knots. The temperature and dew point held steady all afternoon at 37 and 24 degrees, respectively.[16] Low pressure had risen to 29.74 inches, up from 29.40 inches at midnight.

Before sunrise, several hours of rain and show showers (trace amounts) were observed. Wind gusts of 28 knots were recorded just before kickoff and again in mid-afternoon. The *lowest* recorded wind speed during the game was 19 knots. Under gray skies (3,300-foot cloud ceiling), Moravian QB Frank Godshall and Muhlenberg QBs Pete Broas, John Hobby, and Brad Fischer and their receivers used the forward pass sparingly. Godshall completed 6 of 16 passes for 61 yards. Dave Salter caught two passes for 28 yards to set up a Moravian field goal near the end of the first half.

With the temperature holding steady at 37 degrees for the entire game, three Muhlenberg passers attempted 14 passes, completing 6 for 57 yards. The combined 118 passing yardage was the lowest game total in the playing relationship since the frigid November afternoon in 1964.

Shortly after sundown on November 12, 1983, conditions were largely unchanged from an hour earlier. A brief break in the clouds was visible over Muhlenberg Field. The wind still gusted to 23 knots. Air pressure continued to rise, to 29.77 inches, en route to 29.93 inches by midnight. There was a nip to the November air.

By the hour before sundown in Bethlehem on Saturday, November 10, 1984, skies were 90% overcast at 12,000 feet. Visibility was 15 miles. Southwest winds of 12 knots ushered in unseasonably mild air. The temperature was 63 degrees, and the dew point was 32 degrees. Air pressure held steady. Overnight and into the pre-dawn hours, rainfall totaled 0.04 inches.

As the sun periodically broke through the 25,000-foot cloud layer, Muhlenberg QB Pete Broas and Moravian QB Scott Rhinehart and their receivers achieved their most notable passing accomplishments after halftime. As the daily high of 64 degrees was reached and as the 11-knot south wind persisted, Broas completed a screen pass that receiver Chris Pelschi turned into a 71-yard touchdown. Under continuing balmy conditions, Broas connected with Tom Neumann on pass plays covering 18 and 16 yards, to set up the game-tying Muhlenberg touchdown in the fourth quarter. These three pass plays were among Broas's 15 completions (in 25 attempts) that resulted in 237 yards gained.

Rhinehart and receivers Dave Bianco and Jimmy Lasko saved the Moravian passing highlights until the game-winning drive. Completions of 15 yards to Bianco and 6 yards to Lasko set up a Moravian field goal kick. Rhinehart completed 9 of 18 attempts for 131 yards in all. With the air drier than it had been all day (dew point at 32 degrees), one more Broas completion, 14 yards to Jeff Andrews, moved the ball deep into Moravian territory as time expired.

Shortly after sundown on November 10, 1984, skies remained cloudy over Steel Field. The southwest wind had dropped to 3 knots. The temperature was still in the lower 60s, and the air pressure held steady at 29.90 inches.

By the hour before sundown in Allentown on Saturday, November 16, 1985, low clouds and fog reduced visibility to 2½ miles. The temperature remained at 34 degrees all afternoon. The dew point held steady at 30 degrees. An east wind blew at 6 knots. Air pressure was high and steady. Rain fell throughout the game, totaling 0.63 inches. Freezing rain was observed until 2:00 p.m. Moravian QB Frank Godshall and Muhlenberg QB Chris Giordano threw 57 passes.

Giordano attempted 35 passes, completing 15 for 166 yards. Jeff Andrews caught 8 passes, matching the number of completions by the Moravian offense. The 121 yards gained on Giordano-to-Andrews passes exceeded the Moravian passing offense (87 yards) for the day. In the hour when 0.16 inches of rain fell, a 9-yard pass from Godshall to Tim McLaughlin resulted in the game-winning touchdown. With the temperature at 34 degrees, and steady rain continuing, Giordano and Andrews teamed on their final completion, before two Muhlenberg incomplete passes ended the game.

Shortly after sundown on November 16, 1985, the rain intensified. Another 1.75 inches fell between 5:00 p.m. and midnight. The 24-hour rainfall total was 2.55 inches. A light east wind continued. Fog reduced visibility below 2 miles. The temperature rose into the low 40s.

THE NEXT NORMAL PRECIPITATION CYCLE

At this point in the Moravian-and-Muhlenberg football playing relationship, rainfall had fallen on the playing field every five years. The pattern continued into 1990, as four relatively tranquil game days preceded a daylong rainfall. There was more daylight for passers and receivers by this time in the relationship. The November 10, 1990, game was scheduled thirteen days earlier than several game dates in prior decades.

The years 1986–1990 were notable for performances by two of the most prolific passing offenses in the modern Moravian-and-Muhlenberg football relationship. Moravian QB Rob Light and Muhlenberg QB Chris Elser and their receivers filled the air with footballs for four and three years, respectively.

By the hour before sundown in Bethlehem on Saturday, November 15, 1986, skies were overcast at 5,500 feet. The temperature and dew point had been steady at 42 and 18 degrees, respectively, since 2:00 p.m. Visibility was 12 miles. A west wind blew at 7 knots. Air pressure was 30.15 inches and declining gradually.

By the end of the first half, with the air warmed to 42 degrees, Muhlenberg QB Chris Elser and Moravian QB Rob Light and their receivers had been unable to put any points on the scoreboard. In the dry air (dew point at 18) and light wind (7 knots from the southwest), Elser completed 4 passes for 33 yards on a Muhlenberg drive late in the first half.

With clouds hovering a mile above the ground, and in good visibility, Light completed 9 of his 24 passes for 92 yards on the afternoon. After a daily high of 43 was reached, Muhlenberg QB John Donley replaced Elser and completed 3 passes for 60 yards in light westerly winds in the fourth quarter. Elser and Donley combined to complete 13 of 34 passes for 176 yards.

Shortly after sundown on November 15, 1986, skies remained cloudy over Steel Field. The air was calm. The air was dry (dew point at 19). The temperature was 40 degrees, and the air pressure was 30.13 inches.

By the hour before sundown in Allentown on November 14, 1987, a cloud layer at 20,000 feet covered the sky. The air was mild (55 degrees) and dry (dew point at 31). Visibility was 15 miles. A northwest wind had eased to 10 knots. Air pressure continued rising to 30.12 inches.

When the first of 55 forward passes was hurled into the air, high pressure was in place over eastern Pennsylvania. The air was clear. Throughout the afternoon, cirrus clouds at 20,000 feet covered at least 80% of the sky. The clouds did nothing to diminish the warmth of the afternoon. After a pre-dawn low temperature of 30 degrees, the air warmed to 60 degrees by 1:00 p.m. and reached the daily maximum of 61 degrees an hour later. The air was dry. The dew point held steady at 31 degrees.

As a northwest wind blew at 13 knots into mid-afternoon, Moravian QB Rob Light attempted half (18) the number of passes (37) attempted by Muhlenberg QB Chris Elser. Light and his receivers gained 108 passing yards on 9 completions, less than half of the total Moravian offense yardage. By contrast, Elser and his receivers connected on 22 completions, gaining 214 of the 329 total yards gained by the Muhlenberg offense.

As a 15-knot wind blew 59-degree air over Muhlenberg Field at 3:00 p.m., Elser led a scoring drive in the third quarter. He completed passes to Tony Concordia, Andy Schlecter, Jeff Potkul, and Concordia again (9-yard touchdown). On the Muhlenberg scoring drive in the fourth quarter, Elser completed passes to Tom Papa, Bobby Mann, Jim Aniello, and Potkul (3 yards for the touchdown). In the balmy (55 degrees) and dry (dew point at 31) air, the Moravian passing offense could not rally.

Shortly after sundown on November 14, 1987, the overcast sky persisted over Muhlenberg Field. The northwest wind eased to 7 knots. The temperature had dropped to 52 degrees, and the dew point was down to 29. Air pressure was rising gradually.

By the hour before sundown in Bethlehem on November 12, 1988, cirrus clouds appeared. The temperature was 47 degrees, and the dew point was 26. A south breeze blew at 6 knots. High pressure was steady at 30.40 inches. Visibility remained 25 miles.

As the air warmed to the high of 49 degrees in a light south breeze (5 knots), Muhlenberg QB Chris Elser and Moravian QB Rob Light, and their respective receivers, were on their way toward two accomplishments. This was the first modern Moravian-and-Muhlenberg football game in which each passing offense totaled more than 200 yards and each passing offense completed more than 50% of its attempts.

Under increasing mid-afternoon sunshine, Elser connected on touchdown passes to Jim Aniello (twice) and Nick DiGiorgio. The Muhlenberg passing statistics included a 34-yard touchdown pass from running back Jeff Potkul to Tony Concordia. On 3 catches, Concordia accounted for 100 of Muhlenberg's 238 passing yards (on 16-for-27 passing). Aniello gained 62 yards with his 5 catches.

Under tranquil and dry (dew point at 26) conditions in the third quarter, Light threw touchdown passes to Mike Cara covering 48 yards and 35 yards. Light's 13 completions in 22 attempts for 218 yards included Cara's 3 receptions for 86 yards.

Shortly after sundown on November 12, 1988, skies were mostly clear over Steel Field. The air had cooled to 42 degrees, and the dew point held at 26 degrees. The wind had shifted to the southeast at 7 knots. High pressure held steady.

By the hour before sundown in Allentown on November 11, 1989, breaks were visible in the high overcast (25,000 feet). The temperature had risen a degree to 53. The air was dry, with the dew point measured at 31. Visibility was 20 miles. The southwest wind has eased to 11 knots. Air pressure was 29.85 inches and falling gradually.

In mild (low 50s) and windy (18-knot west winds early) conditions, Moravian QB Rob Light and his receivers used the forward pass on one-third (21) of Moravian's 62 plays from scrimmage. Of Light's 13 completions, a 40-yard screen pass play with Mike Howey figured significantly in the outcome. Completed in a 12-knot southwest wind and 52-degree air, the play set up a third-quarter Moravian touchdown, the last scoring play in the game. Mike Cara caught a 55-yard pass from Light late in the first half. Light passed for 213 yards in all.

Mickey Rowe was the Muhlenberg QB. His 19 attempts resulted in 7 completions for 109 yards. With occasional breaks in the overcast visible in the northwest sky, Nick DiGiorgio caught a Rowe pass for 46 yards. The play preceded the lone Muhlenberg touchdown in the game. DiGiorgio caught two other passes from Rowe for 25 yards.

Shortly after sundown on November 11, 1989, skies were mostly (80%) cloudy over Muhlenberg Field. The southwest wind continued at 10 knots. The temperature had dropped to 51, while the dew point held at 31. Air pressure continued to fall. Just before midnight, a trace of rainfall was recorded.

By the hour before sundown in Bethlehem on November 10, 1990, low clouds and fog skies reduced the visibility to 5 miles. It was cool and humid. The temperature and dew point were 47 and 44 degrees, respectively. The northwest wind had increased to 15 knots, with gusts to 23. Low pressure held steady at 29.37 inches. Light rain had fallen (0.03 inches) in the previous hour.

Heavy rain fell throughout the game. Rainfall of 1.66 inches soaked the field from midnight until noon. Nearly one-half inch more fell between noon and 1:00 p.m. Another 0.90 inches of rain fell between noon and 3:00 p.m.[17] Low clouds hung over Steel Field. A damp north wind blew at 10 knots during the first half. As the storm deepened, air pressure fell to 29.37 inches by 3:00 p.m. The wind increased to 15 knots by 4:00 p.m., with gusts to 23 knots. The temperature held steady at 49. North winds brought some drier air. The dew point at noon was 50 degrees. At 4:00 p.m., it had dropped to 44.

Muhlenberg QB Doug Donovan and Moravian QB Mike Harth combined to attempt 42 passes. Only 12 were caught. Donovan completed 10 of his 27 attempts for 112 yards, the bulk of Muhlenberg total offense (132 yards). Harth and his receivers could do little with the pass. Harth completed 2 of 15 attempts for 19 yards.

In the closing minutes of the fourth quarter, as northwest winds gusted past 20 knots, Donovan completed a pass to Eric Slaton for 43 yards. A dropped pass with 19 seconds remaining ended the Muhlenberg drive.

Shortly after sundown on November 10, 1990, skies remained cloudy over Steel Field. A break in the clouds was visible in the west. Visibility had improved to 20 miles. The northwest wind was 18 knots, gusting to 24. Air pressure had begun to rise. Skies were clear by midnight.

PASSING PEAKS IN A LONG DRY SPELL

It would be twelve more years before the next rainy day in the Moravian-and-Muhlenberg football relationship. Temperatures exceeded 50 degrees for more than half of the game days in this stretch. Nine of the twelve games were played in sunshine. The era ended with three windy game days. The 2002 game was played in a steady, cold rain.

Quarterbacks and receivers took the passing game to a new level in these years. Moravian QBs Sean Keville and Rob Petrosky and Muhlenberg QBs Sean McCullough and Mike McCabe, and their respective receivers, posted unprecedented passing gains. In each game from 1991 through 1994, passes were attempted at a rate greater than one per minute of playing time. The combined passing yardage (593) in the 1999 game exceeded the total for both teams in the 1958, 1959, and 1960 games combined.

Then things changed. Passing gains dropped quickly after the 2000 game.

By the hour before sundown in Allentown on November 16, 1991, skies were clear, and visibility was 20 miles. The temperature was 53 degrees. The air was drying rapidly. The dew point had fallen from 42 to 34 in the most recent hour. Air pressure was 30.02 inches and gradually rising. A northwest wind continued at 10 knots.

Throughout this sunny and mild afternoon, Muhlenberg QB Sean McCullough and Moravian QBs Mike Harth and Sean Keville, and their respective pass receivers, used the forward pass to create two different football games. By halftime, as cumulus clouds covered less than half of the sky, McCullough had completed three touchdown passes, two caught by Steve Callahan. The air had cooled to 55 degrees on 10-knot northwest winds. Clearing was less than an hour away when McCullough connected with Eric Slaton on a 56-yard touchdown pass that extended the Muhlenberg lead.

Soon thereafter, Keville entered the game. By the time skies cleared and drier air (dew point dropping from 42 to 34) arrived, Keville had completed touchdown passes to Doug Durepo and Tim Hahn. Four Keville completions preceded the pass to Hahn. After Hahn scored with 1:21 remaining in the game,

Keville's two-point conversion pass attempt was caught by Durepo. It was the second completed two-point conversion pass in the Moravian-and-Muhlenberg relationship since 1968. The other one occurred one quarter earlier when Harth connected with Vince Bagnaturo. Harth and Keville combined to complete 19 of 32 passes for 219 yards. McCullough's 11 pass completions in 36 attempts gained 193 yards. Slaton caught 4 passes for 104 yards.

Shortly after sundown on November 16, 1991, skies remained clear over Muhlenberg Field. The air had cooled to 49 degrees, while the dew point held at 34 degrees. The northwest wind eased to 7 knots. Air pressure continued a gradual rise. By 11:00 p.m., the temperature had fallen to a daily low of 40 degrees.

By the hour before sundown in Bethlehem on November 14, 1992, scattered altostratus clouds had appeared. Visibility was 25 miles. The air was cool (41 degrees) and quite dry (dew point at 16). West winds held at 9 knots. Air pressure was 30.11 inches and rising gradually.

Muhlenberg QBs Sean McCullough and Doug Donovan and Moravian QBs John Mattes and Sean Keville filled the cold air with more than a pass per minute of playing time. In this setting of crystal clear (30-mile visibility) and very dry air (mid-teen dew points), McCullough and Mattes were in the sunny spotlight. McCullough launched 30 passes, completing 13 for 235 yards. Other Muhlenberg passers connected on 2 of 4 attempts for 3 yards. Mattes threw 31 passes and completed 22 for 319 yards.

Moravian running back Craig Cubbin completed a second-quarter touchdown pass. In all, Moravian passers completed 26 of 38 attempts for 349 yards. The passing 349 yards remains the most prolific single-game Moravian performance in the playing relationship.

Under clear skies in a 9-knot west wind, McCullough and receiver Rob Lokerson connected on a 60-yard touchdown pass in the fourth quarter. The play was the last score of the game. Lokerson caught 8 passes for 151 yards. Among eight Moravian pass catchers, Doug Durepo caught 6 to account for 90 yards.

Shortly after sundown on November 14, 1992, high clouds covered 20% of the sky over Steel Field. The temperature had fallen to 37 degrees, en route to a daily low of 29 at 10:00 p.m. The dew point held at 16. Air pressure continued a gradual rise. The west wind had eased to 7 knots. Skies were overcast by midnight.

By the hour before sundown in Allentown on November 13, 1993, low clouds at 2,600 feet covered the sky. Visibility had been 6 miles all afternoon. The 48-degree air was saturated; the dew point had risen to 47 degrees. A northeast wind blew at 6 knots. High pressure had fallen to 30.17 inches. The rain had ended.

Clouds hovered at or below 2,600 feet all afternoon, as Moravian QB Sean Keville and Muhlenberg QB Sean McCullough once again filled the air with footballs. In a light northeast breeze, Keville completed 15 of 25 passes for 281 yards. By the time the trace rainfall ended late in the first half, Keville had thrown touchdown passes covering 72 yards to Jud Frank and 25 yards to Kevin Anderko. The catch was one of 4 by Anderko for 88 yards.

Under gray skies, McCullough connected with Craig Bokus on touchdown passes of 3 yards and 37 yards. McCullough completed 18 passes to three receivers: Bokus (6 for 90 yards); Bill Van Dyke (7 for 71 yards); and Rob Lokerson (5 for 92 yards). As the temperature rose a degree to 48 by game's end, McCullough had attempted more passes (54) than anyone in the modern playing relationship, before or since. His 22 completions accounted for 287 yards.

Shortly after sundown on November 13, 1993, skies remained overcast over Muhlenberg Field. Light rain had resumed; 0.14 inches would fall between 5:00 p.m. and midnight (when the daily high reached 50 degrees). Temperature and dew point held constant. The northeast wind was 7 knots. Air pressure had risen slightly.

By the hour before sundown in Bethlehem on November 12, 1994, cirrus clouds filled the sky. Visibility was 20 miles, and a light west wind blew at 8 knots. The air had cooled to 49 degrees, and the dew point was up to 32 degrees. High pressure was 30.30 inches. For the day, 63% of possible sunshine was measured.

In bright sunshine and a sky filled with cirrus clouds, Muhlenberg QB Jason Jack and Moravian QB Sean Keville and their receivers put the ball in the air often. The statistical results were nearly identical. Jack's 17 completions in 37 attempts gained 278 yards. Keville's 17 completions in 32 attempts gained 283 yards. Another Moravian attempt was completed for 12 yards.

In the second quarter, as the air warmed to the daily high of 52 degrees, Jack and Mike Kern teamed on a 10-yard touchdown in a 10-knot, west-southwest wind. It was the last time Muhlenberg led in the game. In the next thirteen minutes of play, Keville threw touchdown passes to Jeff Roy and Kevin Anderko in dry (dew point at 31) and mild (51 degrees) air.

The tranquil afternoon was the scene of numerous long pass plays. Three pass receivers amassed over 100 yards each. Muhlenberg's Jack completed 6 passes to Rob Lokerson for 110 yards and 4 passes to Bill Van Dyke for 102 yards. Seven Keville passes were caught by Anderko for 124 yards.

Shortly after sundown on November 12, 1994, skies over Steel Field remained cirrus-filled. A low overcast (6,300 feet) arrived by 11:00 p.m. The air had cooled to 47. Air pressure and the dew point both held steady. A light west wind continued at 6 knots.

By the hour before sundown in Allentown on November 11, 1995, clouds were lowering and thickening. Visibility remained 10 miles. Balmy, humid air arrived on a southeast wind of 16 miles per hour, gusting to 23 miles per hour. The temperature was 63 degrees, and the dew point was 55 degrees. Air pressure was low and falling rapidly.

On this warm and windy afternoon, Moravian QB Joe Schroeder and Muhlenberg QBs Ryan Simunovich and George Fosdick used the forward pass less frequently and less effectively than had their immediate predecessors. In the warm air of the first half (reaching 67 degrees), borne on a south wind reaching 25 miles per hour, no touchdown passes were thrown. As clouds lowered to 3,600 feet by late afternoon, no touchdown passes were thrown in the second half either.

Nine of 23 Moravian attempts were completed for 112 yards. Eleven of 31 Muhlenberg attempts were completed for 81 yards. Schroeder and Mike Folcher joined on passes covering 77 yards for Moravian. Muhlenberg receiver Bill Van Dyke caught 7 passes for 41 yards.

Shortly after sundown on November 11, 1995, clouds had lowered to 3,500 feet over Muhlenberg Field, and rain was imminent. The southeast wind continued at 15 miles per hour, with gusts to 26. The temperature was 62, and the dew point rose to 57. Rain began by 6:00 p.m., and fell heavily at times in late-evening. Rainfall totaled 1.30 inches by midnight.

By the hour before sundown in Bethlehem on November 16, 1996, skies were clear. Visibility was 10 miles. The air was cool (41 degrees, the daily high). It was also very dry; the dew point was 9 degrees. A light west wind blew at 4 knots. Air pressure was high and steady at 30.69 inches.

In cold and dry conditions, with a light west wind, Muhlenberg and Moravian passers attempted 37 passes combined, 19 by Muhlenberg. By the time the air had warmed to the daily high of 41 degrees past halftime, Moravian QB Mike Harrison and Mike Szabo had teamed on a 30-yard touchdown pass. Harrison's 11 completions in 16 attempts accounted for 170 yards. Two other Moravian passes fell incomplete.

Muhlenberg QB George Fosdick completed 7 of 16 passes for 115 yards. In the first half, he completed passes for 38, 31, and 17 yards. Two other Muhlenberg passes were completed, in 3 attempts, for 13 additional yards.

Shortly after sundown on November 16, 1996, skies remained clear over Steel Field. The evening began cool (36), dry (dew point at 10 degrees), and almost calm (southwest breeze at 3 knots). High pressure held steady at 30.68 inches.

By the hour before sundown in Allentown on November 15, 1997, occasional breaks were visible in the 3,600-foot cloud deck. Visibility was 10 miles. Winds were light and variable. Air pressure was steady at 29.86 inches. The temperature reached the daily high of 35 degrees. The dew point held at 29 since early afternoon.

The air never warmed past 35 degrees for the afternoon. Moravian QB Rob Petrosky and Muhlenberg QB George Fosdick passed the ball in light and diminishing winds. By the time conditions grew calm near halftime, Fosdick and fullback Matt Lunn had teamed on two short touchdown passes, covering 2 yards and 3 yards. The first scoring drive was extended by a 12-yard, fourth-down completion from Fosdick to Kevin Cannon. As the Moravian offense began to cut into the Muhlenberg lead, Petrosky passed sparingly. On the day, he completed half his passes (9 for 18) for 137 yards. Vince Szabo, Mike Folcher, and Colin O'Hara caught two passes each.

Under occasional breaks in the overcast, Fosdick and receivers Cannon (7 catches for 98 yards) and Lunn (6 for 54 yards) were frustrated in their attempts to cross the Moravian goal line. Fosdick completed 19 of 41 passes for 213 yards.

Shortly after sundown on November 15, 1997, clouds lowered over Muhlenberg Field. The temperature was 34 degrees, and the dew point was 29. Air pressure had risen slightly. A west wind blew at 3 knots. Between 9:00 and 11:00 p.m., a snow shower left a trace.

By the hour before sundown in Bethlehem on November 14, 1998, a few scattered clouds were visible at 18,000 feet. The daily high temperature held at 57 degrees, with a dew point of 39. A light south wind blew at 4 knots. Air pressure held at 29.85 inches. Visibility had been 10 miles all afternoon.

On this sunny, mild afternoon, passing by Muhlenberg QB Mike McCabe and Moravian QBs Rob Petrosky and Jed Moyer complemented two productive rushing offenses. Muhlenberg rushers gained 210 yards, and Moravian rushers gained 155 yards. As the air warmed to the daily high of 57 degrees near halftime, McCabe and Petrosky had each thrown a touchdown pass. McCabe connected with freshman Joshua Carter on a 40-yard scoring pass. Petrosky connected with Scott Farkas on a 21-yard scoring play.

Under scattered clouds at 18,000 feet, with visibility at 10 miles, the two offenses completed fewer than half of 57 pass attempts. Petrosky completed 9 of 22 passes for 96 yards. Moravian passing totals included 3 other completions in 5 attempts for 31 yards. McCabe completed 11 of 30 attempts for 199 yards. In light and variable winds, neither passing offense produced a second-half score.

Shortly after sundown on November 14, 1998, skies remained mostly clear over Steel Field. The air had cooled to 52 degrees. The light south wind continued at 4 knots. Slightly drier air (dew point at 37) was in place as the air pressure fell to 29.82 inches.

By the hour before sundown in Allentown on November 13, 1999, breaks were visible in the 18,000-foot cloud layer. The temperature remained at the daily high of 54 degrees. The dew point had risen slightly to 39. The air was calm. Air pressure held steady at 30.06 inches.

There was something different about the setting on this afternoon. Moravian QB Rob Petrosky and Muhlenberg QBs Mike McCabe and Justin Jones combined to attempt 67 passes on and above the green field. But, it was not natural grass under their feet. An artificial surface had been installed at the playing field now called Scotty Wood Stadium.

By the time a light northwest breeze went calm, McCabe had thrown first-half touchdown passes to Joshua Carter (2), Kenyamo McFarlane, and Anthony Wolfsohn. Petrosky connected with Mike Buscio on a 29-yard touchdown pass in the 54-degree air.

Chuck Draper of Muhlenberg caught 4 passes for 52 yards and completed a pass for another 47 yards. Muhlenberg's Wolfsohn (47 yards) joined Draper with 4 catches.

Under breaks in the 18,000-foot cloud layer, McCabe completed 17 of 31 passes for 261 yards. He threw a fifth touchdown pass after halftime. In all, Muhlenberg passers completed 21 of 37 attempts for 352 yards. Petrosky completed 13 passes (in 30 attempts), four each to Jarod Rhinehart (98 yards) and Mike Abbate (67 yards).

Shortly after sundown on November 13, 1999, skies were clear over the artificial turf at Scotty Wood Stadium. The air had cooled to 50, en route to a daily low of 37 at 10:00 p.m. There was a 3-knot east wind. Air pressure and dew point were unchanged.

By the hour before sundown in Bethlehem on November 11, 2000, low clouds covered the sky at 2,600 feet. Visibility was 10 miles. A northwest wind continued at 14 knots. The temperature and dew point held at 48 and 39, respectively. The air pressure had risen slightly to 29.99 inches. There was a chill in the air.

Occasional glimpses of the sun were gone by 2:00 p.m. A 15-knot west-northwest wind gusted to 22 knots by halftime. Muhlenberg QB Mike McCabe and Moravian QB Charlie Bowden pressed ahead on the gray day. Each threw a touchdown pass in the first half. McCabe's passing accounted for 159 yards, one-third of the Muhlenberg offense. His 11 completions in 24 attempts included 4 passes caught by Alfredo Mercuri for 49 yards. In the third quarter, as the air cooled (to 48 degrees) and a stiff wind persisted, Bowden completed a two-point conversion pass to Jarod Rhinehart. Moravian got no closer. Bowden completed 16 of 33 passes for 250 yards. Rhinehart caught 4 passes for 39 yards.

Shortly after sundown on November 11, 2000, a few breaks appeared in the low clouds over Steel Field. Temperature and dew point were unchanged from the previous hour. The wind eased to 8 knots. The air pressure continued a slow rise to 30.01 inches.

By the hour before sundown in Allentown on November 10, 2001, the sky was clear. The late afternoon was warm and dry. The daily high temperature of 61 degrees lingered for three hours. The dew point dropped to 21. Visibility was 10 miles. A west wind continued at 10 knots. Air pressure was low at 20.79 inches and slowly falling.

It had been a frosty 30 degrees at dawn. By the time Moravian QB Charlie Bowden and Muhlenberg QB Justin Jones had each completed a first-half touchdown pass, the air warmed to 61 degrees, the daily high. In the 12-knot southwest wind, Jones and backup Ryan Newman attempted 22 passes and completed 11 for 111 yards. Jones completed 8 of 17 passes for 55 yards. Joshua Carter caught 4 passes for 53 yards.

In the clear and dry air (dew point at 21), Bowden completed 9 passes for 113 yards, including a 37-yard touchdown pass to Mike Abbate. (One other Moravian completion gained 7 yards.) Neither passing offense stood out in the second half, as the temperature held steady at 61 and the dew point remained at 21 degrees. Not a cloud appeared in the sky.[18]

Shortly after sundown on November 10, 2001, skies remained clear over Scotty Wood Stadium. The air had cooled to 54. The dew point and air pressure were steady. The wind had eased to 4 knots.

By the hour before sundown in Bethlehem on November 16, 2002, low clouds had lifted to 2,200 feet. Cold rain continued in the 37-degree air. The air was saturated (dew point at 36). Visibility was 6 miles. A northeast wind blew at 14 knots. Air pressure held at 30.09 inches. Since noon, 0.44 inches of rain had fallen on the turf.[19]

Muhlenberg QB Justin Jones and Moravian QB Charlie Bowden and their respective receivers gamely attempted to move the ball through the rain. Jones threw 18 passes, and Bowden threw 16. (A teammate attempted one more.) Early in the second quarter, in 39-degree air, Jones and Kodi Shay teamed on a 29-yard touchdown. It was the only touchdown in the game. The play covered all but 15 of the 44 passing yards that Jones gained on 4 completions.

Rain fell throughout the game. A 10-knot northeast wind gusted to 17 knots after halftime. Visibility dropped to 3 miles at 3:00 p.m. as the rain intensified. More than one quarter-inch fell in the hour before 3:00 p.m. Bowden put the ball in the air 16 times. Three receivers caught one pass each. Dave Darmofal's catch covered 15 of Moravian's 27 total passing yards.

Shortly after sundown on November 16, 2002, clouds had lowered again, and the rain continued. Another 0.60 inches would fall by midnight. Temperature, dew point, and air pressure were unchanged. A raw east wind continued at 12 knots.

A RAINSTORM IS OVERDUE

A dry spell is underway in the most recent meteorological era of the Moravian-and-Muhlenberg football relationship. No rain fell on the playing field during the 2003, 2004, 2005, and 2006 games. Indeed, not one wisp of cloud has been seen overhead since midway through the 2003 game! Dew points were in the upper 20s, upper teens, and low 30s throughout the 2003, 2004, and 2005 games, respectively. The weather conditions on November 12, 2006, were the warmest ever in the modern Moravian-and-Muhlenberg football playing relationship. The weather was more typical of mid-September than mid-November in eastern Pennsylvania.

In this time of meteorological calm before the next storm, the forward pass waned in importance. In these four games, there were only five touchdown pass plays. Only once, Moravian in 2005, did a passing offense surpass 200 yards.

The natural history of the modern Moravian-and-Muhlenberg football relationship entered a new era on November 11, 2006. The game that day at Rocco Calvo Field in Bethlehem marked the first time that the annual Moravian-and-Muhlenberg game had been played on artificial surfaces in consecutive years. An artificial playing surface was installed at Moravian's home field in time for the 2006 football season. The Muhlenberg home field playing surface was converted to artificial turf in 1999. For the foreseeable future, no Moravian players and no Muhlenberg players would collect mud and grass stains on their uniforms in a Moravian-and-Muhlenberg football game.

By the hour before sundown in Allentown on November 15, 2003, skies were clear. Visibility had been 10 miles all afternoon. The air was seasonable (49 degrees) and dry (dew point at 28). The daily high of 49 degrees had lingered since 2:00 p.m. A northwest air blew at 10 knots, with gusts to 21. Air pressure was steady at 30.08 inches.

In the first quarter, with west-northwest winds gusting past 20 knots, Moravian QB Jerry Venturino and his receivers had achieved their greatest passing gains on the day. Then, one of Venturino's pass was intercepted in the Muhlenberg end zone. After that, the Moravian offense advanced no further than the Muhlenberg 41-yard line for the rest of the game.

Venturino and backup QB Will Seng completed 13 of 31 passes for 142 yards. Jeff Lowry caught 7 passes for 90 yards. Muhlenberg QB Ryan Newman completed 16 of 30 passes for 185 yards. In the fourth quarter, under clear skies as west winds continued at 12 knots, Newman connected with Kyle Douglass and Kodi Shay on passes that set up the final Muhlenberg touchdown. Douglass, Shay, and Mike Mrkobrad each caught 4 of passes.

Shortly after sundown on November 15, 2003, skies remained clear over Scotty Wood Stadium. The west wind had increased to 13 knots, holding the temperature at 48. Dry air (dew point at 29) was in place. Air pressure was steady.

By the hour before sundown in Bethlehem on November 13, 2004, skies were clear. Visibility had been 10 miles all afternoon. The air had cooled to 42 degrees. It was dry, too. The dew point was 18. A north wind continued at 13 knots, with gusts to 23. High pressure continued to build at 30.48 inches.

Not a cloud appeared in the sky on this cool afternoon. By the time the 44-degree daily high was reached, Muhlenberg QB Nick Rosetti had thrown two touchdown passes. Muhlenberg passers were 9 for 18 for 63 yards. Rosetti completed 8 of 17 passes for 46 yards. Stephen Montalto caught a touchdown pass on a play that covered 28 yards. In the second quarter, Muhlenberg half-back Matt Johnson completed a 17-yard pass.

Moravian QB Jerry Venturino completed 9 of 31 passes. Ben Hawkins, Jr., caught 5 passes for 65 of Moravian's 100 passing yards. In the cool (low 40s), dry air (dew point at 18) of late afternoon, with northwest winds gusting to 24 knots, a Venturino pass to Jed Warsager set up a Moravian touchdown.

Shortly after sundown on November 13, 2004, skies remained clear over Steel Field. The wind continued from the northwest at 12 knots. The air cooled to 39 degrees, while the dew point was 19 degrees. High pressure continued rising, to 30.55 inches by evening.

By the hour before sundown in Allentown on November 12, 2005, skies were clear. Visibility had been 10 miles all afternoon. Southwest winds continued at 5 miles per hour. Air pressure held steady at 30.25 inches. The air remained warm at 55 degrees, and the dew point was 33 degrees.

In a light southwest air (up to 7 miles per hour), Moravian QB Jerry Venturino and receiver Ben Hawkins, Jr., combined on a 64-yard touchdown pass to start the scoring in the second half. Venturino completed 12 of 21 passes for 206 yards. Shawn Martell caught 3 passes for 36 yards.

As the daily high of 57 degrees lingered past mid-afternoon, backup Muhlenberg QB Eric Santagato rallied his team for two touchdowns in the fourth quarter. Santagato teamed with Kyle Douglass on a 45-yard pass play for the second score. Santagato completed 8 of 14 passes for 137 yards. Muhlenberg starting QB David Mazzola completed 3 of 10 attempts for 19 yards. Two other Muhlenberg pass attempts were completed for 16 yards. Douglass led Muhlenberg receivers with 5 catches for 90 yards.

Shortly after sundown on November 12, 2005, skies remained clear over Scotty Wood Stadium. The dry air had cooled quickly to 48 degrees. The air was calm and remained so all evening. High pressure held steady at 30.25 inches.

By the hour before sundown in Bethlehem on November 11, 2006, skies were clear. The temperature had risen to the daily high of 67 degrees. The dew point was 54 degrees. Visibility was 8 miles in some haze. At the end of a calm afternoon, an east breeze began at 5 miles per hour. Air pressure was steady at 29.83 inches.

The day was the warmest in the history of the modern Moravian-and-Muhlenberg football relationship. The daily high was 67 degrees, shortly after Moravian backup QB Marc Braxmeier and receiver Shawn Martell improvised a 54-yard touchdown pass to tie the game. Replacing starting QB Ryan Rempe, Braxmeier completed 6 of 12 attempts for 113 yards. Rempe's 4 completions in 12 attempts gained 18 yards.

Muhlenberg QB Eric Santagato completed 14 of 20 passes for 171 yards. Not a cloud was in the sky as Santagato completed a 28-yard pass to Derek DiMattina late in the third quarter to set up the go-ahead Muhlenberg touchdown. Chris Poehls caught 5 passes from Santagato for 53 yards.

Shortly after sundown on November 11, 2006, skies remained clear over Rocco Calvo Field. The breeze had shifted to the northeast at 5 miles per hour. The air remained mild at 62 degrees. Air pressure held steady, and the dew point was 53 degrees.

CONCLUSION

Chapter by chapter, I work to expand the ethical perspective through which we can make sense of the Moravian-and-Muhlenberg football relationship, and intercollegiate football competition more widely. In this chapter, I interpret the forward pass as an act linking football strategy and the natural space of football fields. At the intersection of an historical record of forward passes and an historical record of weather conditions, I interpret one more ethical dimension of football competition.

In three natural settings on forty-eight November days, Moravian and Muhlenberg football players have enacted the football lingo that links the forward pass with the air and the sky. Passers throw aerials. Passers and receivers move the ball through the air. Passers throw spirals. They occasionally throw an inelegant pass, a wounded duck. Not long after resumption of the modern Moravian-and-Muhlenberg playing relationship, when world war was a fresh memory, sportswriters regularly described a long pass as a bomb. This chapter is the story of men joining hopefully and humbly to fill the November air, sunny and cloudy, blustery and calm, with aerials, joining to affirm their ties.

Joined in their use of the forward pass, members of Moravian and Muhlenberg football teams have long resided together in both a football playing relationship and in the natural world in which their games have been played. They have inhabited a relationship embedded in air, earth, and sky (and occasionally water). It is there that these human beings have jointly demonstrated an ethical point about humility and imagination wrapped in an ethical point about public commitment to one another in a particular place.

The human beings who incorporate the forward pass into the game of football take what comes. Passers and receivers attempt a difficult football maneuver. They do so under weather conditions, and hence field conditions, that they can neither foresee nor control. Many passes fall incomplete. This is their joint humble pursuit. Yet, this is also the site of their imaginative resilience. Passers and receivers are fallible performers who do not give up on the prospect of a completed pass play. They strive to make themselves better in dozens of attempts during a three-hour engagement on the field of play.

As they do this, football competitors claim their place together in the natural world. The passing game, I have shown, can be understood as a public, affirming act of citizenship. "We belong here together with one another in this natural space," passers and receivers affirm with each pass play.

There is a place for us spectators on this playing field, too. We who watch the forward pass are better for the engagement of passers and receivers with, and in, the natural world. We can draw inspiration from an enlarged version of a cliché that football coaches have been known to utter, "The weather was the same for both teams out there today." This ethical insight is accessible, whether we wear a football uniform or not.

NOTES

1. Regarding sports and artistry, see Hans Ulrich Gumbrecht, "They Have a Powerful Aesthetic Appeal," *Chronicle of Higher Education,* 23 June 2006, B10-11.

2. In Chapter 4, I create a place for pass interceptions and other defensive feats.

3. The season-ending game for the Moravian 2001 season came one week after the game with Muhlenberg. The Moravian-and-Fairleigh Dickinson-Madison football game, originally scheduled for September 15, 2001, was postponed until November.

4. The game dates were moved earlier as the National Collegiate Athletic Association (NCAA) Division III football playoffs became established. A common date was established for the end of the regular football season. This is why no Moravian-and-Muhlenberg game since 1977 has been scheduled for a date later than November 16.

5. For several years in the 1990s, the wind speed was reported in miles per hour.

6. Throughout, I use the altimeter readings familiarly reported in "inches."

7. The field at Scotty Wood Stadium is named Frank Marino Field, in honor of the second Muhlenberg head football coach in the modern playing relationship.

8. For a sweeping view of Muhlenberg Field, see *Ciarla 1960*, 2–3.

9. Jim Buss, "Moravian 'Fortunate at Times'," *Sunday Call-Chronicle*, 21 November 1971, C2.

10. These data were obtained from the National Climatic Data Center.

11. I consulted mapquest.com for the distances. I also drove the routes.

12. Sun and shadows are evident in game photographs in *Benigna 1959*, 144-45.

13. One knot is approximately 15% greater than one mile per hour.

14. One observer noted the "sun-drenched" scene. Don Cressman, "Mules Maul Hounds in Finale," *Bethlehem Globe-Times*, 21 November 1960, 22.

15. One observer linked the cold and the passing game. Jack Collins, "'Berg Extends Mastery over Greyhounds," *Bethlehem Globe-Times*, 23 November 1964, 24.

16. One observer noted "shivering" fans. Jack Lapos, "Joseph Scores 3 TDs as Moravian Rolls 24-7," *Sunday Call-Chronicle*, 13 November 1983, C1.

17. One observer noted Moravian "sloshing" to the win. Ernie Long, "Moravian Needs Late Stand to Down Muhlenberg 7-3," *Morning Call*, 11 November 1990, C1.

18. One observer noted "gleaming" helmets. Beth Hudson, "Greyhounds Rebound to Beat Muhlenberg, 17-7," *Morning Call*, 11 November 2001, C1.

19. One observer used "goop" to describe the playing conditions. Paul Reinhard, "For Mules' Koth, a Beautifully Muddy Day," *Morning Call*, 17 November, C11.

Chapter Four

They Wrote Their Chapter,
A Legacy for Their Successors

Intercollegiate football competition is an experience in which competitors join to create an historical record of human collaboration. The record is an artifact that they can call their own. Competitors come together, play a game of football, and sign their names to the unique episode of collaboration that they created. When this joint act is embedded in a playing relationship, the record of each game becomes a chapter in a larger narrative about the playing relationship. From 1958 through 2006, Moravian team members and Muhlenberg team members joined to write forty-eight chapters in the Moravian-and-Muhlenberg football relationship. This chapter of the book celebrates their co-authorship.

Football competition, interpreted as joint authorship in an ongoing relationship, has something in common with two ethical acts in a civil society: legacy and inheritance. Through legacy and inheritance, human beings provide knowingly for others in time.

Human beings choose to leave something valuable to others. They leave a legacy. This decision is made knowingly and formally. Recipients of legacies must decide what to do their good fortune. An inheritor chooses to cement a connection with the donor in a relationship centered on the legacy. Inheritance is partly under the recipient's control.

The historical record that football competitors create becomes available to participants, subsequent and past, in the playing relationship as their inheritance. Competitors can find meaning in an inherited historical record by looking to the record for standards and milestones with which they take measure of their own instance of collaboration on the field of play. Each game in a playing relationship thus becomes inseparable from the ethical acts of legacy and inheritance.

Table 4.1.   Team Statistics and Line Score for 1958 Game

1958		*Muhlenberg*		*Moravian*		
First downs		13		12		
Yards rushing		74		164		
Yards passing		160		34		
Passes completed-attempted		11-17		2-8		
Pass attempts intercepted		2		0		
Fumbles lost		3		2		
Punts		2		7		
Yards penalized		10		20		
Muhlenberg	0	8	6	6	—20	
Moravian	0	14	8	8	—30	

Intercollegiate football competition is well-suited for interpretation in this way. Each game is a source of ample data with which to assemble an historical record. There are over 100 separate events, called "plays," in a football game. There is a definitive end to each play. The results of each play are precisely measured. Participants and observers alike accept certain aggregate measures as useful descriptors of a football game. These descriptors are listed in the upper section of Table 4.1. This table contains the aggregate game statistics that were recorded and reported for the 1958 Moravian-and-Muhlenberg football game.

In addition, participants and observers alike are accustomed to using a shorthand method, called a line score, to record the scoring flow of a football game. A football line score contains the quarter-by-quarter scoring totals. The line score recorded and reported for the 1958 Moravian-and-Muhlenberg football game is listed in the lower section of Table 4.1. These statistical categories and the line score format have been used for every year covered in this book. With this common vocabulary, inheritors in a playing relationship can draw comparisons across their own game, recent games, and games played long ago.

AN ETHICAL PROPOSITION AND THE
NARRATIVE THAT FOLLOWS

The competing players and coaches who leave behind the historical record of a football game also leave behind an invitation for their successors and ancestors. It is an invitation to reflect on the meaningfulness of the collaboration in which those others join. The joint authors of a football game perform an act of instructional encouragement by playing their game in their own way. As authors, they are teachers.[1] They encourage others to reflect on what the latter accomplish in their own collaborations on the field of play. This act of teaching is an ethical contribution that competitors make to all who follow in their footsteps as inheritors.

The contribution is recognizable in the form of questions that competitors can ask themselves as they use the historical record to put into perspective their own game. Was our game comparatively interesting to the very end? What unusual events transpired in our game? What features of the game will players remember as they return to the playing field next year? Did we tarnish the relationship with rough play, or shoddy play? Whose involvement in the relationship ended, and what milestones endure in their wake? What under-appreciated features of this game did we make available for our descendants?

Sports journalists encourage this kind of historical reflection about intercollegiate athletic competition. Early in the modern Moravian-and-Muhlenberg relationship, one writer proposed that succeeding participants look to the 1971 game as a benchmark for accomplishment in the Moravian-and-Muhlenberg football relationship:[2]

> And one final word to rival coaches Rocco Calvo of Moravian and Frank Marino of Muhlenberg—thanks for probably one of the best games in the long history between the two schools. Give us another one next fall.

Working in this spirit, I use game statistics, line scores, and scoring summary data to interpret a legacy for each of the forty-eight games played in the modern Moravian-and-Muhlenberg football relationship. My aim is to nominate players and coaches whose actions in the playing relationship deserve gratitude from all who have followed in their footsteps, and from those who will do so for the first time on November 10, 2007, in Allentown.

DATA AND THE NARRATIVE

I present each Moravian-and-Muhlenberg football game in terms of distinguishing features that are recognizable in time and over time. The importance of some game statistics is clear soon after the game ends. Yardage totals and lost fumbles are two apt examples. I refer to both in my interpretations of annual chapters in the relationship.

Other parts of the historical record are relevant one year later, when returning players reunite on the playing field. Two apt examples are penalty yardage and the fourth-quarter scoring flow. Players remember a "rough" game when many penalties are assessed. Coaches remember fourth-quarter rallies and collapses, and remind their players of these precedents inherited from the recent past.

Still other parts of the historical record are meaningful over a long sweep of time. This is particularly true for such "once in a lifetime" events as a game-winning field goal and a 95-yard return of the opening kickoff for a touchdown. Both events are part of the Moravian-and-Muhlenberg historical record.

As I locate each historical record in time, I necessarily look beyond the aggregate numbers in search of plays and flows of action that sum into those numbers. Those who inherit an historical record might want to know whether the 17 Muhlenberg passing attempts in the 1958 Moravian-and-Muhlenberg game were made in steady increments throughout the game, or after the Muhlenberg team fell behind. Likewise, inheritors might want to know which team scored first in the fourth quarter in the 1958 game. (In the lower section of Table 4.1, see the fourth column of numbers in the line score.) For someone reflecting on the flow of a game, it makes a big difference whether Moravian scored first, to build on a 22-14 lead, or whether Muhlenberg scored to narrow its deficit to 22-20, foreshadowing a suspenseful final quarter.

In weaving this data into the narrative, I make a lasting place for players and their feats. In this spirit, I conclude each chapter by recognizing a specific performance that spans several games. For most games, I focus on the end of a player's career, when his accomplishments in the relationship become fixed in time for all to see.

I add one touch to reinforce the point that inheritors can choose how to interpret the historical record. I begin each chapter with commentary about performance of the two defense units. Defense often takes a backseat to offense in what is recorded and reported about a football game. Moreover, reports of offense performance often accentuate the positive. It is not often that a game report begins, "The defenses achieved a combined 24 changes of ball possession, including 16 punts." I do just this for each chapter of the modern Moravian-and-Muhlenberg football relationship. Using the aggregate team statistics, I add the number of offense turnovers (interceptions thrown and fumbles lost) and punts to report how many times the defense took possession of the ball from the offense. Only then do I get around to summarizing the aggregate offense performances.

A Word to Readers

There is repetition in the narrative that follows. This is necessary. This chapter is an introduction to a different way of talking about intercollegiate football

competition. It takes practice to talk in new ways. There are forty-eight opportunities here—forty-eight games played in the modern Moravian-and-
Muhlenberg football relationship—to practice talking about football competitors leaving something meaningful for their successors. Be patient. Immerse
yourself in the narrative. Eventually, I streamline it in subtle ways.

FORTY-EIGHT LEGACIES IN THE PLAYING RELATIONSHIP

The Muhlenberg defense and the Moravian defense achieved a combined 16
changes of ball possession on November 22, 1958. The Muhlenberg offense
relinquished possession on 5 turnovers (2 interceptions and 3 fumbles) and 2
punts. The Moravian offense relinquished possession on 2 fumbles and 7
punts. Muhlenberg's offense, directed by Ralph Borneman, gained sufficient
yardage for 13 first downs, one more than did the Moravian offense, directed
by Tony Matz and Russ DeVore. These statistics are listed in the upper section of Table 4.1.

Newcomers to the playing relationship in 1959 joined with returning players who helped create two precedents in the 1958 game at Moravian Field.[3]
First, the 1958 participants played nearly penalty-free football. Compared to
the 432 yards combined total offense, the two teams were penalized only 30
yards. Team penalty yardage is shown in the upper section of Table 4.1. Second, the decisive scoring plays occurred in the fourth quarter.

The first quarter was scoreless, as shown in the line score in the lower section of Table 4.1. At halftime, Moravian led Muhlenberg, 14-8. After Muhlenberg tied the game at 14-all, Moravian took the lead after three quarters,
22-14. The scoring flow in the fourth quarter was:
    Muhlenberg—Wargo 4 run (run failed)
    Moravian—Safety (Borneman tackled in end zone)
    Moravian—Hollendersky 1 run (pass failed)
After Tom Wargo scored the Muhlenberg touchdown, the Moravian defense
prevented the game-tying two-point conversion run. After the Moravian
safety, with the score 24-20 in Moravian's favor, the Muhlenberg offense was
still within a touchdown of taking the lead. The late rushing touchdown by
George Hollendersky sealed the game outcome.

In other ways, the 1958 chapter is available for all members of the playing
relationship since 1958. The Moravian defense scored 8 points. Johnny Olson
returned a pass interception 64 yards for a touchdown. The Moravian line
tackled Borneman in the Muhlenberg end zone for a two-point safety. After
the safety, Muhlenberg attempted an onside kick from its own 20-yard line.
The ball was recovered by the Moravian team. The two starting quarterbacks

played multiple roles. Borneman attempted an extra-point kick. On defense, he recovered a Moravian fumble. Matz returned punts and played defensive back. Borneman and Matz were not alone as "two-way" performers. Thirty Muhlenberg players played in the game. Only twenty Moravian players took part.

Lastly, Matz, Hollendersky, and others participating in their only Moravian-and-Muhlenberg game joined in ending a twelve-year hiatus in the playing relationship and in establishing a single-game rushing benchmark: Hollendersky's 104 yards.

The Moravian defense and the Muhlenberg defense achieved a combined 16 changes in ball possession on November 21, 1959. The Muhlenberg offense relinquished ball possession on 4 turnovers and 3 punts. The Moravian offense relinquished ball possession on 2 turnovers and 7 punts. The two offenses performed comparably in retaining ball possession. The Muhlenberg offense, guided by Rollie Houseknecht and Ralph Borneman, achieved 14 first downs, two more than did the Moravian offense. These team statistics are listed in Table 4.2.

Newcomers to the playing relationship in 1960 joined with returning players who helped create two precedents in the 1959 game at Muhlenberg Field. First, Moravian players were assessed 55 of the 70 penalty yards. (Penalty yardage is listed in Table 4.2.) Second, the game outcome was clinched in the fourth quarter.

Earlier, after a scoreless first quarter, Muhlenberg led Moravian at halftime, 12-8. (The line score is shown in Table 4.2.) The third quarter was scoreless. The lone scoring play in the fourth quarter was:

Muhlenberg—Yost 1 run (Owens run)

The touchdown by Ed Yost sealed the Muhlenberg win and Moravian loss.

Table 4.2. Team Statistics and Line Score for 1959 Game

1959		Moravian		Muhlenberg	
First downs		12		14	
Yards rushing		82		315	
Yards passing		111		90	
Passes completed-attempted		10-19		3-12	
Pass attempts intercepted		1		2	
Fumbles lost		1		2	
Punts		7		3	
Yards penalized		55		15	
Moravian	0	8	0	0	—8
Muhlenberg	0	12	0	8	—20

In other ways, the 1959 chapter is available for all members of the playing relationship, before and since. On the fourth-quarter Muhlenberg touchdown drive, Muhlenberg rushers exceeded Moravian's rushing output for the entire game (91 yards to 82 yards). Jim Orr of Muhlenberg recorded multiple quarterback sacks. The two starting quarterbacks played multiple roles. Houseknecht played on defense and intercepted a Moravian pass. John Williams of Moravian played as a defensive back. Numerous players on both teams were two-way participants. Thirty-two Muhlenberg players appeared in the game. Twenty-two Moravian players played.

Lastly, players participating in their final Moravian-and-Muhlenberg game joined to conclude an era in the playing relationship: Herb Owens of Muhlenberg participated in scoring plays in both the 1958 and 1959 games and rushed for 131 yards.

The Muhlenberg defense and the Moravian defense achieved a combined 16 changes of ball possession on November 19, 1960. The Muhlenberg defense achieved 5 Moravian turnovers and, in all, 12 possession changes.[4] The Muhlenberg offense, guided by Rollie Houseknecht, gained yardage for 25 first downs, while relinquishing possession on 3 turnovers and only one punt. The Moravian defense yielded over 400 yards. Team statistics are listed in Table 4.3.

Newcomers to the playing relationship in 1961 joined with returning players who helped create two precedents in the 1960 game at Moravian Field. First, the 66 total penalty yards were indicative of a "clean" game. Second, neither team scored in the fourth quarter.

Earlier, Muhlenberg stretched a 7-0 first-quarter lead to a 19-8 halftime lead (Table 4.3). After three quarters of play, Muhlenberg led Moravian, 33-

Table 4.3. Team Statistics and Line Score for 1960 Game

1960	Muhlenberg	Moravian
First downs	25	10
Yards rushing	314	144
Yards passing	87	32
Passes completed-attempted	6-17	4-13
Pass attempts intercepted	1	2
Fumbles lost	2	3
Punts	1	7
Yards penalized	26	40

Muhlenberg	7	12	14	0	—33
Moravian	0	8	8	0	—16

16. The three scoring plays in the third quarter turned out to be the final scoring of the game:

Muhlenberg—Yost 3 run (Butz pass from Houseknecht)

Muhlenberg—Houseknecht 1 plunge (pass failed)

Moravian—Coe 3 plunge (Kelyman pass from Ritter)

Trailing 33-8 in the third quarter, the Moravian offense could do little to erase the deficit.

In other ways, the 1960 chapter is available for all members of the playing relationship, before and since. Ed Yost of Muhlenberg and Andy Semmel of Moravian were among several players who made contributions on both offense and defense. In addition to rushing for two touchdowns, Yost played defense and recovered a Moravian fumble. Quarterback Semmel also played defensive back. Before halftime, the Moravian defense stopped Muhlenberg on a goal-line stand.

Lastly, players participating in their final Moravian-and-Muhlenberg game joined to conclude an era in the playing relationship. Ed Yost of Muhlenberg scored touchdowns in all three games in which he played and rushed for 208 yards.

The Moravian defense and the Muhlenberg defense achieved a combined 17 changes of ball possession on November 18, 1961. The Muhlenberg defense achieved 3 Moravian turnovers and induced 8 punts. Rollie Houseknecht guided the Muhlenberg offense to 17 first downs. Muhlenberg lost possession on one interception and 5 punts. Team statistics are listed in Table 4.4.

Newcomers to the playing relationship in 1962 joined with returning players who helped create two precedents in the 1961 game at Muhlenberg Field.

Table 4.4.   Team Statistics and Line Score for 1961 Game

1961		*Moravian*		*Muhlenberg*	
First downs		13		17	
Yards rushing		164		173	
Yards passing		22		141	
Passes completed-attempted		2-12		12-20	
Pass attempts intercepted		1		1	
Fumbles lost		2		0	
Punts		8		5	
Yards penalized		57		90	
Moravian	0	0	0	8	—8
Muhlenberg	0	14	6	13	—33

First, officials assessed 147 penalty yards, more than twice the yardage in any of the three previous games. Second, the only question in the fourth quarter was whether the Moravian offense would avoid a shutout.

Earlier, after a scoreless first quarter, Muhlenberg led 14-0 at halftime and 20-0 after three quarters (see Table 4.4). The scoring flow in the fourth quarter was:

Muhlenberg—Donmoyer 1 run (pass failed)

Muhlenberg—Kuntzleman 55 punt return (Houseknecht kick)

Moravian—Riccardi 13 pass from Semmel (Semmel run)

The score was 33-0 before the Moravian offense unit scored a touchdown. Andy Semmel quarterbacked the Moravian offense to a touchdown in the final minute of the game.

In other ways, the 1961 chapter is available for all members of the playing relationship, before and since. One punt by John Donmoyer of Muhlenberg traveled 61 yards. The Moravian defense contained Muhlenberg for one quarter.

Lastly, players participating in their final Moravian-and-Muhlenberg game joined to conclude an era in the playing relationship: Charlie Kuntzleman of Muhlenberg scored three touchdowns in two games, doing so in three different ways. Kuntzleman scored on a rushing play, a pass play, and a punt return. In two games, he rushed for 224 yards.

The Muhlenberg defense and the Moravian defense achieved a combined 20 changes of ball possession on November 17, 1962. The Muhlenberg defense achieved 6 Moravian turnovers and induced 7 punts. The Muhlenberg offense, guided by Terry Haney, retained possession with 14 first downs, one more than did the Moravian offense. Team statistics are listed in Table 4.5.

Newcomers to the playing relationship in 1964 joined with returning players who helped create two precedents in the 1962 game at Moravian Field.[5]

Table 4.5.   Team Statistics and Line Score for 1962 Game

1962	Muhlenberg	Moravian		
First downs	14	13		
Yards rushing	66	120		
Yards passing	233	83		
Passes completed-attempted	13-24	7-19		
Pass attempts intercepted	0	4		
Fumbles lost	2	2		
Punts	5	7		
Yards penalized	15	32		
Muhlenberg	6	0	12	14	—32
Moravian	0	0	0	8	—8

First, only 47 yards in penalties were assessed. Second, for the second straight year, the only question in the fourth quarter was whether Moravian would avoid a shutout.

Earlier, Muhlenberg led Moravian, 6-0, after one quarter and at halftime (Table 4.5). Muhlenberg extended the lead to 18-0 by the end of the third quarter. The scoring flow in the fourth quarter was:

Muhlenberg—Hiller 69 pass interception (Woginrich pass from Haney)

Moravian—Morganstine 1 plunge (P. Mazza pass from Mushrush)

Muhlenberg—Barlok 12 pass interception (pass failed)

The Moravian touchdown was sandwiched between two costly turnovers.

In other ways, the 1962 chapter is available for all members of the playing relationship, before and since. The Muhlenberg defense put 12 points on the scoreboard. Gary Hiller and Ron Barlok each returned a pass interception for a touchdown. In the first half, the Moravian defense held Muhlenberg rushers to minus-10 yards. Undeterred, Haney directed Muhlenberg to an 18-0 lead on touchdown passes covering 40, 17, and 37 yards. Pat Mazza of Moravian played both ways and caught a two-point conversion pass.

Lastly, players participating in their final Moravian-and-Muhlenberg football game joined to conclude an era in the playing relationship: Dean Lowe of Muhlenberg caught touchdown passes in consecutive years.

The Muhlenberg defense and the Moravian defense achieved a combined 22 changes of ball possession on November 21, 1964. The Muhlenberg defense achieved 5 Moravian turnovers. Each offense ceded the ball 7 times on punts. The Muhlenberg offense, guided by Terry Haney and Ron Henry, recorded 10 first downs, one more than did the Moravian offense. Team statistics are listed in Table 4.6.

Table 4.6.   Team Statistics and Line Score for 1964 Game

1964	Muhlenberg	Moravian
First downs	10	9
Yards rushing	141	160
Yards passing	9	21
Passes completed-attempted	2-9	1-11
Pass attempts intercepted	2	2
Fumbles lost	1	3
Punts	7	7
Yards penalized	25	75

Muhlenberg	0	7	0	14	—21
Moravian	0	0	6	0	—6

Newcomers to the playing relationship in 1965 joined with returning players who helped create two precedents in the 1964 game at Moravian Field. First, much of the penalty yardage (75 yards) was assessed to
Moravian players. Second, the fourth quarter was decisive in the game
outcome.

Earlier, after a scoreless first quarter, Muhlenberg led Moravian at halftime, 7-0. By the end of the third quarter, Moravian had closed the deficit to
one point, a 7-6 Muhlenberg lead (Table 4.6). The scoring flow in the fourth
quarter was:

Muhlenberg—Capobianco 19 run (Binder pass from Henry)

Muhlenberg—Gould 10 run (pass failed)

More points were scored in the closing quarter than in the first three quarters
combined.

In other ways, the 1964 chapter is available to all members of the playing relationship, before and since. A Moravian player was ejected from the
game. The two defense units shut down the passing game, intercepting
more passes (4) than there were pass completions (3). A Moravian drive
stalled at the Muhlenberg 15-yard line in the third quarter. The Muhlenberg
rushing offense gained 101 yards on two fourth-quarter scoring drives. A
Muhlenberg player (this time Charlie Woginrich) returned a punt for a
touchdown for the second time in three games. Two linemen played multiple roles. Dave Binder of Muhlenberg caught a two-point conversion pass
and played defense. Besides playing center and defensive line, Bill Silcox
of Moravian did the punting.

Lastly, players participating in their final Moravian-and-Muhlenberg game
joined to conclude an era in the playing relationship: In three straight games,
the Muhlenberg team scored two fourth-quarter touchdowns.

The Moravian defense and the Muhlenberg defense achieved a combined
17 changes of ball possession on November 20, 1965. Each defense forced 6
punts. Meanwhile, the Moravian offense, guided by John Petley, retained possession with 17 first downs, rushing for much of the necessary yardage. Team
statistics are listed in Table 4.7.

Newcomers to the playing relationship in 1966 joined with returning players who helped create two precedents in the 1965 game at Muhlenberg Field.
First, most of the penalty yardage (75 of 90) was assessed to Moravian. Second, the Muhlenberg offense rallied late in the game.

Earlier, Moravian led Muhlenberg by 7-0 at the end of the first quarter and
by 10-0 at halftime. The third quarter was scoreless (Table 4.7). The scoring
flow in the fourth quarter was:

Muhlenberg—Woginrich 41 pass from Henry (Henry run)

Moravian—Nehilla 3 run (Parry kick)

Table 4.7. Team Statistics and Line Score for 1965 Game

1965		Moravian		Muhlenberg	
First downs		17		11	
Yards rushing		205		13	
Yards passing		70		170	
Passes completed-attempted		5-13		16-36	
Pass attempts intercepted		0		3	
Fumbles lost		2		0	
Punts		6		6	
Yards penalized		75		15	
Moravian	7	3	0	7	—17
Muhlenberg	0	0	0	8	—8

The Muhlenberg touchdown and two-point conversion cut the Moravian lead to 10-8. The Moravian touchdown drive and PAT kick squelched the Muhlenberg comeback.

In other ways, the 1965 chapter is available for all members of the playing relationship, before and since. The Moravian defense scored a touchdown when John Shipley blocked a punt and returned the ball 30 yards for a touchdown. "Special teams" accounted for all the first-half scoring. The field goal by Brian Parry of Moravian was the first in the modern Moravian-and-Muhlenberg football relationship. Unlike in previous years, Moravian rushing (205 yards) was nearly unstoppable, and Muhlenberg rushing was almost non-existent (13 yards) in the same game. Twice in the third quarter, the Muhlenberg defense stopped the Moravian offense inside the Muhlenberg 5-yard line. The 36 passing attempts by Ron Henry of Muhlenberg were the most thus far in the modern Moravian-and-Muhlenberg relationship.

The game marked the third straight year of change in the Moravian quarterback position. John Petley played in his only Moravian-and-Muhlenberg game in 1965.

Lastly, Petley and other players participating in their final Moravian-and-Muhlenberg game joined to conclude an era in the playing relationship: Charlie Woginrich of Muhlenberg scored a touchdown in each of three games.

The Muhlenberg defense and the Moravian defense achieved a combined 20 changes of ball possession on November 19, 1966. The Muhlenberg defense achieved 4 Moravian turnovers, 3 on fumbles. The Moravian defense forced 9 Muhlenberg punts, while the Muhlenberg offense, guided by Paul Fischer, could gain only 8 first downs. Meanwhile, the Moravian offense was guided by Greg Seifert and Jim Dietz to 17 first downs, rushing for much of the necessary yardage. Team statistics are listed in Table 4.8.

Table 4.8.   Team Statistics and Line Score for 1966 Game

1966	Muhlenberg	Moravian
First downs	8	17
Yards rushing	124	266
Yards passing	57	62
Passes completed-attempted	4-15	2-9
Pass attempts intercepted	0	1
Fumbles lost	1	3
Punts	9	6
Yards penalized	20	45

Muhlenberg	7	0	0	0	—7
Moravian	7	0	0	7	—14

Newcomers to the playing relationship in 1967 joined with returning players who helped create two precedents in the 1966 game at Moravian Field. First, the participants joined to play a comparatively "clean" game. Only 65 yards of penalties were assessed. Second, suspense built in the fourth quarter about whether the game would end in a tie.

Earlier, Muhlenberg and Moravian concluded the first quarter in a 7-7 tie. The second quarter was scoreless, as was the third quarter (Table 4.8). The scoring in the fourth quarter was:

Moravian—Horn fumble recovery in end zone (N. Linker kick)

The scoreless middle quarters were a first in modern Moravian-and-Muhlenberg football.

In other ways, the 1966 chapter is available for all members of the playing relationship, before and since. Both defenses stifled the passing game; only 25% of the passing attempts were completed. Moravian rushers overcame 3 lost fumbles to more than double the yardage gained by Muhlenberg rushers. The game-winning touchdown was scored on a fumble recovery. Walt Horn of Moravian fell on a teammate's fumble in the Muhlenberg end zone. It was Horn's final game and his first collegiate touchdown.

Lastly, Horn and other players participating in their final Moravian-and-Muhlenberg game joined to conclude an era in the playing relationship: Hank Nehilla of Moravian carried the ball 62 times for 209 yards in two games.

The Moravian defense and the Muhlenberg defense achieved a combined 20 changes of ball possession on November 18, 1967. Each defense forced 8 punts and achieved 2 turnovers. The two offenses were evenly matched in ball possession. The Moravian offense, guided by Jim Dietz and Greg Seifert, gained 14 first downs, one more than did the Muhlenberg offense that was guided by Ron Henry and Bill Evans. Team statistics are listed in Table 4.9.

Table 4.9. Team Statistics and Line Score for 1967 Game

1967		Moravian		Muhlenberg	
First downs		13		14	
Yards rushing		214		143	
Yards passing		131		120	
Passes completed-attempted		5-11		10-32	
Pass attempts intercepted		1		2	
Fumbles lost		1		0	
Punts		8		8	
Yards penalized		73		85	
Moravian	7	0	6	6	—19
Muhlenberg	0	0	0	8	—8

Newcomers to the playing relationship in 1968 joined with returning players who helped create two precedents in the 1967 game at Muhlenberg Field. First, they played in the most penalty-filled game thus far. The officials assessed 158 yards of penalties in the 1967 game. Second, the fourth quarter was anticlimactic in the game outcome.

Earlier, Moravian led Muhlenberg at the end of the first quarter, 7-0. After a scoreless quarter, Moravian extended the lead to 13-0 by the end of the third quarter (Table 4.9). The scoring flow in the fourth quarter was:

Moravian—Wilson 2 run with blocked kick (kick failed)

Muhlenberg—Saeger 32 pass from Evans (DiPanni run)

The Moravian team built a 19-0 lead in the fourth quarter before the Muhlenberg scoring play.

In other ways, the 1967 chapter is available for all members of the playing relationship, before and since. The Moravian defense scored a touchdown when Jeff Wilson returned a blocked kick 2 yards for a touchdown. It was the second time in three years that a blocked punt resulted in a touchdown. Dave Kemmerer, Ed Zaninelli, and Steve Markovich of Moravian recorded 17, 12, and 12 tackles, respectively. Henry and Evans of Muhlenberg attempted nearly three times the number of passes (32) attempted by Dietz and Seifert of Moravian (11). Only eight Moravian backs played in the game. Nineteen Muhlenberg backs played.

Lastly, players participating in their final Moravian-and-Muhlenberg game joined to conclude an era in the playing relationship: Ron Henry of Muhlenberg concluded three years in the playing relationship. In this period, he played quarterback, running back and defensive back.

The Muhlenberg defense and the Moravian defense achieved a combined 18 changes of ball possession on November 23, 1968. The Moravian defense induced 10 Muhlenberg punts. Meanwhile, the Moravian offense was guided

Table 4.10.   Team Statistics and Line Score for 1968 Game

1968		Muhlenberg		Moravian		
First downs		13		24		
Yards rushing		96		369		
Yards passing		65		140		
Passes completed-attempted		8-19		9-11		
Pass attempts intercepted		2		0		
Fumbles lost		0		2		
Punts		10		4		
Yards penalized		60		55		
Muhlenberg	0	7	0	8	—15	
Moravian	7	14	13	13	—47	

by Jim Dietz to retain possession with 24 first downs. Team statistics are listed in Table 4.10.

Newcomers to the playing relationship in 1969 joined with returning players who helped create two precedents in the 1968 game at Steel Field. First, they played a penalty-filled game. Officials assessed 115 penalty yards. Second, the fourth quarter was anticlimactic.

Earlier, Moravian led Muhlenberg 21-7 at halftime and 34-7 at the end of three quarters of play (Table 4.10). The scoring flow in the fourth quarter was:

Muhlenberg—Gonzalez 3 run (Harding pass from Uhrich)

Moravian—Martinelli 24 pass from Dietz (Regan kick)

Moravian—Smith 3 run (run failed)

The closest Muhlenberg would get was 34-15 after the two-point conversion pass.

In other ways, the 1968 chapter is available for all members of the playing relationship, before and since. Hugh Gratz of Moravian intercepted two passes and also played running back. The 369 Moravian rushing yards was a single-game high. The disparity in touchdowns, seven for Moravian and two for Muhlenberg, was also the largest thus far. Player participation was far greater than a decade earlier. In 1968, forty Muhlenberg players and forty-four Moravian players played in the game.

Lastly, players participating in their final Moravian-and-Muhlenberg game joined to conclude an era in the playing relationship: Jim Dietz quarterbacked the Moravian offense in three straight Moravian wins and Muhlenberg losses. Moravian Quarterback Greg Seifert played in the 1966 and 1967 games, but missed the 1968 game due to injury.

The Moravian defense and the Muhlenberg defense achieved a combined 14 changes of ball possession on November 22, 1969. The Moravian defense achieved 9 possession changes, 6 on Muhlenberg punts. Meanwhile, the

Table 4.11. Team Statistics and Line Score for 1969 Game

1969		Moravian		Muhlenberg	
First downs		18		10	
Yards rushing		420		106	
Yards passing		83		79	
Passes completed-attempted		5-10		7-26	
Pass attempts intercepted		0		2	
Fumbles lost		2		1	
Punts		3		6	
Yards penalized		50		0	
Moravian	0	6	12	19	—37
Muhlenberg	0	0	0	0	—0

Moravian offense, guided by Gary Martell, Joe Dowling, and Steve Markovich, had little difficulty maintaining possession. The 18 Moravian first downs far exceeded the 5 times that the offense unit relinquished possession. Team statistics are listed in Table 4.11.

Newcomers to the playing relationship in 1970 joined with returning players who helped create two precedents in the 1969 game at Muhlenberg Field. First, all 50 penalty yards were charged to the Moravian team. Second, the Muhlenberg offense was within three scoring plays (plus extra points) of at least tying the game as the fourth quarter began.

Earlier, the two teams played a scoreless first quarter. Moravian led Muhlenberg by 6-0 at halftime and by 18-0 after three quarters (Table 4.11). The scoring flow in the fourth quarter was:

Moravian—H. Gratz 4 run (kick failed)

Moravian—Overk 42 run (run failed)

Moravian—Smith 31 run (Schedler kick)

The Moravian rushing game wore down the Muhlenberg defense in the fourth quarter.

In other ways, the 1969 chapter is available for all members of the playing relationship, before and since. Moravian rushers gained 420 yards. Ed Zaninelli of Moravian tackled Muhlenberg ball carriers 15 times. The game was Ray Whispell's eleventh and final as Muhlenberg Head Coach.

Lastly, players participating in their final Moravian-and-Muhlenberg game joined to conclude an era in the playing relationship: Hugh Gratz of Moravian rushed for 264 yards, intercepted 3 passes, and scored 5 touchdowns in three games.

The Muhlenberg defense and the Moravian defense achieved a combined 16 changes of ball possession on November 18, 1970. The Moravian defense induced 10 punts and achieved 3 Muhlenberg turnovers. The Moravian offense,

Table 4.12.   Team Statistics and Line Score for 1970 Game

1970	*Muhlenberg*	*Moravian*			
First downs	9	22			
Yards rushing	−2	362			
Yards passing	125	94			
Passes completed-attempted	8-21	10-16			
Pass attempts intercepted	2	0			
Fumbles lost	1	1			
Punts	10	2			
Yards penalized	23	66			
Muhlenberg	0	7	0	0	—7
Moravian	7	20	21	7	—55

guided by Joe Dowling and Gary Martell, gained 22 first downs and relinquished possession 3 times. Meanwhile, the Muhlenberg offense, guided by
Randy Uhrich, gained only 9 first downs. Team statistics are listed in Table 4.12

Newcomers to the playing relationship in 1971 joined with returning players who helped create two precedents in the 1970 game at Steel Field. First,
Moravian drew 66 of 89 penalty yards. Second, Muhlenberg trailed by 41
points as the fourth quarter began.

Earlier, Moravian led Muhlenberg at the end of one quarter, 7-0. Moravian
stretched the lead to 27-7 by halftime. After three quarters, Moravian led
Muhlenberg, 48-7 (Table 4.12). The lone scoring play in the fourth quarter
was:

Moravian—Youmans 1 run (Marish kick)

The final Moravian touchdown was scored by freshman Art Youmans.

In other ways, the 1970 chapter is available for all members of the playing
relationship, before and since. Bill Gastmeyer of Moravian returned an interception 47 yards for a touchdown. The Moravian defense held Muhlenberg
rushers to minus-2 yards. The Muhlenberg offense entered Moravian territory
only three times. The game became the de facto Middle Atlantic Conference
South championship game, because the two teams entered the game in a tie
for first place in the league.

Lastly, players participating in their final Moravian-and-Muhlenberg football game joined to conclude an era in the playing relationship: Jack Iannantuono of Moravian rushed for 531 yards and 6 touchdowns in four games.
Three times, he rushed for more yards than did the entire Muhlenberg team.

The Moravian defense and the Muhlenberg defense achieved a combined
23 changes of ball possession on November 20, 1971. Each defense forced 8
punts. The Muhlenberg defense achieved 4 Moravian turnovers. Meanwhile,

Table 4.13.   Team Statistics and Line Score for 1971 Game

1971		Moravian		Muhlenberg	
First downs		12		6	
Yards rushing		236		50	
Yards passing		91		62	
Passes completed-attempted		4-19		5-28	
Pass attempts intercepted		2		3	
Fumbles lost		2		0	
Punts		8		8	
Yards penalized		61		36	
Moravian	0	0	14	0	—14
Muhlenberg	0	7	0	0	—7

the Moravian defense limited the Muhlenberg offense, guided by Ed DiYanni, to 6 first downs. Team statistics are listed in Table 4.13.

Newcomers to the playing relationship in 1972 joined with returning players who helped create two precedents in the 1971 game at Muhlenberg Field. First, Moravian drew 61 of 97 penalty yards. Second, the outcome was in doubt at the start of the fourth quarter.

Earlier, after a scoreless first quarter, Muhlenberg led Moravian at halftime, 7-0. After three quarters, Moravian had taken the lead, 14-7 (Table 4.13). The scoring flow in the third quarter was:

Moravian—Marish 1 run (Marish kick)

Moravian—Martell 5 run (Marish kick)

The scoreless fourth quarter was the first since 1960.

In other ways, the 1971 chapter is available for all members of the playing relationship, before and since. The Muhlenberg offense did not score. The Muhlenberg defense scored a touchdown when Don Dufford returned a pass interception 41 yards in the second quarter. The passing game was poorly executed by both teams. Only 9 of 47 pass attempts were completed. In the scoreless final quarter, the Muhlenberg offense moved far into Moravian territory three times. The Moravian defense stopped Muhlenberg at the Moravian 20-yard line in the final two minutes.

Lastly, players participating in their final Moravian-and-Muhlenberg football game joined to conclude an era in the playing relationship: Quarterback Joe Dowling of Moravian led the Moravian offense to three straight wins and Muhlenberg losses.

The Muhlenberg defense and the Moravian defense achieved a combined 20 changes of ball possession on November 18, 1972. The Moravian defense induced 10 punts and limited the Muhlenberg offense to 6 first downs. Meanwhile,

Table 4.14. Team Statistics and Line Score for 1972 Game

1972	Muhlenberg	Moravian			
First downs	6	26			
Yards rushing	2	326			
Yards passing	144	80			
Passes completed-attempted	7-26	8-19			
Pass attempts intercepted	2	2			
Fumbles lost	1	1			
Punts	10	4			
Yards penalized	23	55			
Muhlenberg	0	7	0	7	—14
Moravian	17	9	6	6	—38

Gary Martell and Fred Ferratti guided the Moravian offense to retain possession through 26 first downs. Team statistics are listed in Table 4.14.

Newcomers to the playing relationship in 1973 joined with returning players who helped create two precedents in the 1972 game at Steel Field. First, Moravian players were assessed the bulk of penalty yardage (55 of 78 yards). Second, the fourth quarter began with Muhlenberg facing a 25-point deficit.

Earlier, Moravian held a 17-0 lead over Muhlenberg at the end of the first quarter. At halftime, Moravian led Muhlenberg, 26-7 (Table 4.14). The Moravian lead grew after three quarters, 32-7. The scoring flow in the fourth quarter was:

Muhlenberg—Hedden 55 pass from Shirvanian (Kleppinger kick)
Moravian—Ferratti 2 run (kick failed)

The Moravian reserve offense unit scored the final touchdown of the game.

In other ways, the 1972 chapter is available for all members of the playing relationship, before and since. Moravian "special teams" scored two touchdowns. Bob Porcarro's punt return touchdown was the first for Moravian in the modern playing relationship. Mark Steinberger's 30-yard return of the blocked punt was the fourth Moravian defensive touchdown in eight games. Three scoring plays covered more than 50 yards. Porcarro ran 72 yards on his touchdown. Muhlenberg touchdown passes covered 53 and 55 yards. The Moravian defense held Muhlenberg rushers to 2 yards.

Lastly, players participating in their final Moravian-and-Muhlenberg football game joined to conclude an era in the playing relationship: Gary Martell of Moravian rushed for 237 yards in three games and scored a rushing touchdown in each game.

The Moravian defense and the Muhlenberg defense achieved a combined 21 changes of ball possession on November 17, 1973. Each defense induced

Table 4.15.   Team Statistics and Line Score for 1973 Game

1973		*Moravian*		*Muhlenberg*	
First downs		14		10	
Yards rushing		126		190	
Yards passing		131		100	
Passes completed-attempted		10-27		4-8	
Pass attempts intercepted		0		0	
Fumbles lost		1		2	
Punts		9		9	
Yards penalized		25		15	

Moravian	0	0	7	6	—13
Muhlenberg	7	7	0	7	—21

9 punts. Turnovers were few (3). No passes were intercepted. The Muhlenberg offense retained possession fewer times (10 first downs) than it relinquished possession (11) to Moravian. Team statistics are listed in Table 4.15.

Newcomers to the playing relationship in 1974 joined with returning players who helped create two precedents in the 1973 game at Muhlenberg Field. First, only 40 penalty yards were assessed. Second, Muhlenberg extended a slim lead by scoring first in the fourth quarter.

Earlier, Muhlenberg led Moravian at halftime, 14-0 (Table 4.15). Moravian scored in the third quarter to pare the Muhlenberg lead to 14-7. The scoring flow in the fourth quarter was:

Muhlenberg—Boll fumble recovery in end zone (Stovall kick)
Moravian—Ferratti 1 run (kick failed)
Randy Boll recovered a teammate's fumble in the Moravian end zone.

In other ways, the 1973 chapter is available for all members of the playing relationship, before and since. Frank McCants and Jon Light of Muhlenberg each made 5 tackles. Light assisted on 15 tackles. For the first time in four games, Muhlenberg rushers exceeded 50 yards. Muhlenberg rushers had not been so productive since 1960. For the first time since 1965, the Moravian offense gained fewer than 300 yards. The two passing offenses performed differently. Jon Van Valkenburg and Fred Ferratti of Moravian combined to throw 17 incomplete passes. Of the 4 passes completed by Bob Shirvanian of Muhlenberg, his 73-yard touchdown pass to Eric Butler was game-changing. The score came on the final play of the first half and doubled the Muhlenberg lead.

Lastly, players participating in their final Moravian-and-Muhlenberg football game joined to conclude an era in the playing relationship: Ron Salley of Muhlenberg rushed for 112 yards in his final game.

The Muhlenberg defense and the Moravian defense achieved a combined 20 changes of ball possession on November 23, 1974. Each defense achieved 3 turnovers. Meanwhile, the Moravian offense, guided by Jon Van Valkenburg, retained possession with 21 first downs, relinquishing the ball on 6 punts and the 3 turnovers. Team statistics are listed in Table 4.16.

Newcomers to the playing relationship in 1975 joined with returning players who helped create two precedents in the 1974 game at Steel Field. First, more penalty yardage was assessed Muhlenberg players (47 of 81 yards) for the first time since 1968. Second, the Muhlenberg offense had the momentum as the fourth quarter began.

Earlier, the game was tied at halftime, 14-14. After Moravian built a 28-14 lead early in the third quarter, the Muhlenberg offense reduced the deficit to one point (Table 4.16). There were four scoring plays in the third quarter:

Moravian—King 11 run (Richards kick)
Moravian—Van Valkenburg 1 run (Richards kick)
Muhlenberg—Mill 20 pass from Reid (Stovall kick)
Muhlenberg—Boll 14 pass from Reid (Stovall kick)

The scoring flow for the fourth quarter was:

Moravian—King 40 run (Richards kick)
Moravian—Gratz 1 run (Richards kick)

The two Moravian scoring drives in the fourth quarter covered 79 yards and 45 yards.

In other ways, the 1974 chapter is available for all members of the playing relationship, before and since. Two overworked defenses yielded the most total yardage in any Moravian-and-Muhlenberg game thus far in the modern playing relationship. The Moravian defense stopped an 83-yard Muhlenberg drive on the Moravian 8-yard line in the closing minutes. As in every game

Table 4.16.   Team Statistics and Line Score for 1974 Game

1974		Muhlenberg		Moravian	
First downs		14		21	
Yards rushing		71		368	
Yards passing		270		86	
Passes completed-attempted		17-30		5-11	
Pass attempts intercepted		1		1	
Fumbles lost		2		2	
Punts		8		6	
Yards penalized		47		34	
Muhlenberg	7	7	13	0	—27
Moravian	0	14	14	14	—42

since 1964, the Muhlenberg offense unit attempted more passes. This time, over half were completed. Mike Reid led the most productive Muhlenberg passing game since Terry Haney's performance in the 1962 game. Four of the six Moravian scoring drives covered at least 57 yards.

Lastly, players participating in their final Moravian-and-Muhlenberg football game joined to conclude an era in the playing relationship: Bob Gratz of Moravian rushed for 221 yards and 2 touchdowns in three games.

The Moravian defense and the Muhlenberg defense achieved a combined 21 changes of ball possession on November 22, 1975. The Moravian defense achieved 7 Muhlenberg turnovers, including 4 pass interceptions. Meanwhile, Jon Van Valkenburg guided the Moravian offense to 17 first downs. Moravian relinquished possession on 6 punts and 3 turnovers. Team statistics are listed in Table 4.17.

Newcomers to the playing relationship in 1976 joined with returning players who helped create two precedents in the 1975 game at Muhlenberg Field. First, the two teams were assessed comparable penalty yardage. Second, the game outcome was in doubt after three quarters.

Earlier, Moravian led Muhlenberg at halftime, 3-0, and extended the lead to 9-0 after three quarters (Table 4.17). The scoring play in the fourth quarter was:

Moravian—G. Feinberg 16 pass from Van Valkenburg (Finch kick)
This Moravian touchdown concluded a 61-yard drive.

In other ways, the 1975 chapter is available for all members of the playing relationship, before and since. Muhlenberg defenders tackled Moravian rushers for losses 11 times. Joe Hoffman of Moravian intercepted a pass thrown by Mike Reid of Muhlenberg at the Moravian 5-yard line in the third quarter. Two plays after Hoffman's 14-yard return and a 15-yard penalty against Muhlenberg, Bob

Table 4.17.   Team Statistics and Line Score for 1975 Game

1975		Moravian		Muhlenberg	
First downs		17		12	
Yards rushing		241		151	
Yards passing		70		117	
Passes completed-attempted		7-13		9-23	
Pass attempts intercepted		1		4	
Fumbles lost		2		3	
Punts		6		5	
Yards penalized		64		60	
Moravian	0	3	6	7	—16
Muhlenberg	0	0	0	0	—0

Ternosky of Moravian scored on a 64-yard run to stretch the Moravian lead to 9-0. In the second quarter, Leon Finch of Moravian kicked a field goal that caromed off the upright and the crossbar.

Lastly, players participating in their final Moravian-and-Muhlenberg football game joined to conclude an era in the playing relationship: Mike Reid of Muhlenberg completed 26 of 53 passes for 387 yards and 2 touchdowns as a starter in the 1974 and 1975 games. In the 1972 game, he completed a 53-yard touchdown pass.

The Muhlenberg defense and the Moravian defense achieved a combined 9 changes of ball possession on November 20, 1976. The Moravian defense induced 6 Muhlenberg punts. None of the 42 passes was intercepted. The Moravian offense was guided by Jon Van Valkenburg, to retain possession with 25 first downs. There were no Moravian punts. Team statistics are listed in Table 4.18.

Newcomers to the playing relationship in 1977 joined with returning players who helped create two precedents in the 1976 game at Steel Field. First, officials assessed 140 penalty yards in almost equal proportion. Second, the fourth quarter began with a 22-point Moravian lead.

Earlier, Moravian led Muhlenberg after one quarter, 14-0. Moravian extended the lead by halftime, 26-7 (Table 4.18). The scoring flow in the third quarter was:

Moravian—Finch 29 FG

Muhlenberg—Sartori 8 pass from Schlecter (Stovall kick)

Moravian—VanValkenburg 33 run (Finch kick)

There was no scoring in the fourth quarter.

In other ways, the 1976 chapter is available for all members of the playing relationship, before and since. For the second time in four games, neither de-

Table 4.18.   Team Statistics and Line Score for 1976 Game

1976		Muhlenberg	Moravian		
First downs		16	25		
Yards rushing		63	450		
Yards passing		180	43		
Passes completed-attempted		18-35	3-7		
Pass attempts intercepted		0	0		
Fumbles lost		1	2		
Punts		6	0		
Yards penalized		66	74		
Muhlenberg	0	7	7	0	—14
Moravian	14	12	10	0	—36

fense intercepted a pass. Mike Brichta of Moravian forced a bad pass by Muhlenberg QB John Schlechter in the fourth quarter. The Moravian rushing game was virtually unstoppable for the third straight game.

Lastly, players participating in their final Moravian-and-Muhlenberg football game joined to conclude an era in the playing relationship: Kenny King and Jon Van Valkenburg of Moravian rushed for 390 and 247 yards, respectively, in three games. King rushed for 4 touchdowns, and Van Valkenburg rushed for 3 touchdowns.

The Moravian defense and the Muhlenberg defense achieved a combined 16 changes of ball possession on November 19, 1977. The Muhlenberg defense induced 8 Moravian punts and limited the Moravian offense, guided by Jack Bradley, to 10 first downs. Meanwhile the Muhlenberg offense was guided by Don Sommerville to 20 first downs and only 6 losses of possession. Team statistics are listed in Table 4.19.

Newcomers to the playing relationship in 1978 joined with returning players who helped create two precedents in the 1977 game at Muhlenberg Field. First, officials assessed 52 of the 87 penalty yards to Moravian. Second, the fourth quarter was the scene of the most dramatic offense comeback thus far in the Moravian-and-Muhlenberg playing relationship.

Earlier, Moravian led Muhlenberg at halftime, 21-6. Muhlenberg trailed by nine points, 21-12, entering the fourth quarter (Table 4.19). The scoring flow in the fourth quarter was:

Muhlenberg—Sules 5 run (Weller kick)

Muhlenberg—Sules 1 run (run failed)

John Sules of Muhlenberg scored the second touchdown of the quarter in the closing minute.

Table 4.19.　Team Statistics and Line Score for 1977 Game

1977	Moravian	Muhlenberg
First downs	10	20
Yards rushing	233	140
Yards passing	36	272
Passes completed-attempted	4-10	15-24
Pass attempts intercepted	1	0
Fumbles lost	1	3
Punts	8	3
Yards penalized	52	35

Moravian	0	21	0	0	—21
Muhlenberg	6	0	6	13	—25

In other ways, the 1977 chapter is available for all members of the playing relationship, before and since. John Sanford of Muhlenberg recorded 14 solo tackles. The game-winning Muhlenberg touchdown drive covered 80 yards.

Lastly, players participating in their final Moravian-and-Muhlenberg football game joined to conclude an era in the playing relationship: Bob Ternosky of Moravian rushed for over 325 yards and 2 touchdowns in three games. Three of his rushes covered distances of 64, 52, and 57 yards.

The Muhlenberg defense and the Moravian defense achieved a combined 19 changes of possession on November 11, 1978. The Muhlenberg defense achieved 4 Moravian turnovers and induced 8 punts. Meanwhile, the Muhlenberg offense, guided by John Schlechter, had little difficulty retaining possession. Muhlenberg gained yardage sufficient for 21 first downs, while losing possession on 6 punts and a pass interception. Team statistics are listed in Table 4.20.

Newcomers to the playing relationship in 1979 joined with returning players who helped create two precedents in the 1978 game at Steel Field. First, penalties interrupted the flow of the game. Officials assessed 216 penalty yards, the most thus far in the modern playing relationship. Second, the outcome was still in doubt at the start of the fourth quarter.

Earlier, Muhlenberg led Moravian at halftime, 14-0. The third quarter was scoreless (Table 4.20). The scoring flow in the fourth quarter was:

Muhlenberg—Bodine 1 run (Hiller kick)

Muhlenberg—Sules 1 run (kick failed)

Muhlenberg—Albanese 20 run (Hiller kick)

Two Muhlenberg touchdowns in the final five minutes ended any doubts about the outcome.

Table 4.20.   Team Statistics and Line Score for 1978 Game

1978		Muhlenberg		Moravian	
First downs		21		8	
Yards rushing		176		65	
Yards passing		116		60	
Passes completed-attempted		12-22		6-23	
Pass attempts intercepted		1		2	
Fumbles lost		0		2	
Punts		6		8	
Yards penalized		86		130	
Muhlenberg	7	7	0	20	—34
Moravian	0	0	0	0	—0

In other ways, the 1978 chapter remains available to all who belong to the playing relationship, before and since. Muhlenberg sacked Moravian quarterbacks three times. A short Moravian punt in the second quarter set up the second Muhlenberg touchdown.

Lastly, players participating in their final Moravian-and-Muhlenberg football game joined to conclude an era in the playing relationship: The final score marked the first Muhlenberg win and the first Moravian loss at Steel Field.

The Muhlenberg defense and the Moravian defense achieved a combined 18 changes of possession on November 10, 1979. The Moravian offense relinquished possession on 3 turnovers and 7 punts. The Moravian offense, guided by Jack Bradley and Ed Stange, gained yardage sufficient for 15 first downs, two more occasions than did the Muhlenberg offense, guided by Brian Schulte. Team statistics are listed in Table 4.21.

Newcomers to the playing relationship in 1980 joined with returning players who helped create two precedents in the 1979 game at Muhlenberg Field. First, the players exceeded the one-year-old benchmark for most penalty yardage. Officials assessed 243 penalty yards, more than one-half the combined 406 yards gained in total offense. Second, Muhlenberg held a slim lead entering the fourth quarter.

Earlier, Muhlenberg led Moravian at the end of one quarter, 7-6. The second quarter was scoreless (Table 4.21). The scoring play in the third quarter was:

Muhlenberg—Sartori 10 pass from Schulte (Hiller kick)
The Muhlenberg defense preserved the lead in the scoreless final quarter.

In other ways, the 1979 chapter remains available to all who belong to the playing relationship, before and since. Muhlenberg attempted an onside kick

Table 4.21. Team Statistics and Line Score for 1979 Game

1979		Moravian		Muhlenberg	
First downs		15		13	
Yards rushing		67		66	
Yards passing		99		174	
Passes completed-attempted		14-37		14-29	
Pass attempts intercepted		2		2	
Fumbles lost		1		0	
Punts		7		6	
Yards penalized		119		124	
Moravian	6	0	0	0	—6
Muhlenberg	7	0	7	0	—14

on the opening kickoff. The kick by Mike Hiller was recovered by teammate Bill Kolano. The first Muhlenberg touchdown came less than two minutes later. Moravian Quarterback Jack Bradley left the game with an injury in the second quarter. He did not return. Bradley and Ed Stange combined to throw 23 incomplete passes. The substantial penalty yardage, 13 punts, and 38 incomplete passes summed into offense futility for both teams.

Lastly, players participating in their final Moravian-and-Muhlenberg football game joined to conclude an era in the playing relationship: John Sartori of Muhlenberg caught 15 passes for 154 yards and 2 touchdowns in the 1977, 1978, and 1979 games. In his other game, he caught 2 touchdown passes as a freshman.

The Muhlenberg defense and the Moravian defense achieved a combined 26 changes of ball possession on November 15, 1980. The Muhlenberg defense achieved 8 turnovers, including 5 pass interceptions. The Moravian defense achieved 5 turnovers, including 4 pass interceptions. Meanwhile, the Moravian offense, guided by Jack Bradley, recorded slightly better numbers in retaining the ball. Moravian relinquished possession 14 times, and gained yardage sufficient for 18 first downs. Team statistics are listed in Table 4.22.

Newcomers to the playing relationship in 1981 joined with returning players who helped create two precedents in the 1980 game at Steel Field. First, officials assessed nearly 100 yards in penalties to each team. Second, the fourth quarter was a thrilling conclusion to the game.

Earlier, Muhlenberg and Moravian played to a halftime tie, 10-10. The game was tied after three quarters, too, 17-17 (Table 4.22). The scoring flow in the fourth quarter was:

Muhlenberg—Smith 25 pass interception (Lea kick)
Moravian—Nimphius 23 pass from Bradley (run failed)

Table 4.22.   Team Statistics and Line Score for 1980 Game

1980	Muhlenberg	Moravian				
First downs	13	18				
Yards rushing	123	90				
Yards passing	54	232				
Passes completed-attempted	8-23	22-50				
Pass attempts intercepted	4	5				
Fumbles lost	1	3				
Punts	7	6				
Yards penalized	97	90				
Muhlenberg	0	10	7	7	—24	
Moravian	10	0	7	6	—23	

Bradley of Moravian was tackled short of the goal line on the two-point conversion attempt. The game clock showed 2:08 remaining.

In other ways, the 1980 chapter is available for all members of the playing relationship, before and since. The Muhlenberg defense scored a touchdown when Jamie Smith returned a pass interception 25 yards.[6] Chris Horton of Muhlenberg made the game-saving tackle on Bradley's fourth-quarter conversion try. Despite gaining 499 yards combined, both offenses were erratic. Two statistics were telling: 26 lost possessions and 43 incomplete passes. The game was Frank Marino's eleventh and final as Muhlenberg Head Coach.

Lastly, players participating in their final Moravian-and-Muhlenberg football game joined to conclude an era in the playing relationship: Jack Bradley of Moravian threw 3 touchdown passes and rushed for one touchdown, but went winless as a starter.

The Muhlenberg defense and the Moravian defense achieved a combined 21 changes of ball possession on November 14, 1981. The Muhlenberg defense achieved 5 Moravian turnovers. Meanwhile, the Muhlenberg offense, guided by Gary Greb, recorded slightly better numbers in retaining the ball. Muhlenberg relinquished possession 9 times, and gained yardage sufficient for 15 first downs. The Moravian offense relinquished the ball as many times (12) as it gained first downs. Team statistics are listed in Table 4.23.

Newcomers to the playing relationship in 1982 joined with returning players who helped create two precedents in the 1981 game at Muhlenberg Field. First, each team was assessed comparable penalty yardage. Second, the fourth quarter was once again a thrilling conclusion.

Earlier, Muhlenberg led Moravian at halftime, 3-0. At the end of three quarters, the game was tied, 3-3 (Table 4.23). The scoring flow in the fourth quarter was:

Table 4.23.   Team Statistics and Line Score for 1981 Game

1981	Moravian	Muhlenberg
First downs	12	15
Yards rushing	86	177
Yards passing	73	99
Passes completed-attempted	6-17	8-24
Pass attempts intercepted	3	2
Fumbles lost	2	2
Punts	7	5
Yards penalized	76	73

Moravian	0	0	3	6	—9
Muhlenberg	0	3	0	7	—10

Muhlenberg—Hiller 5 pass from Greb (Lea kick)
Moravian—T. Ulicny 1 run (pass failed)
On the two-point conversion attempt, Dave Kaercher of Moravian threw an incomplete pass under pressure. Fewer than 6 minutes remained on the game clock.

In other ways, the 1981 chapter is available for all members of the playing relationship, before and since. For the second year in a row, it was Chris Horton of Muhlenberg who stopped the Moravian two-point conversion attempt that would have given Moravian the lead. Lou Sorrentino of Moravian prevented a touchdown by tackling Mike Bailey of Muhlenberg after the latter gained 47 yards on the play. Two-thirds of the passing attempts fell incomplete or were intercepted. Moravian ended the season winless.

Lastly, players participating in their final Moravian-and-Muhlenberg football game joined to conclude an era in the playing relationship: Lou Sorrentino of Moravian intercepted 3 passes in his final two games.

The Muhlenberg defense and the Moravian defense achieved a combined 20 changes of ball possession on November 13, 1982. The Muhlenberg defense achieved 5 Moravian turnovers. Meanwhile, the Muhlenberg offense was guided by Gary Greb to retain possession with 17 first downs. They relinquished possession 10 times, including 8 punts. Team statistics are listed in Table 4.24.

Newcomers to the playing relationship in 1983 joined with returning players who helped create two precedents in the 1982 game at Steel Field. First, officials assessed Moravian players 137 of the 166 penalty yards. Second, the fourth quarter was pivotal.

Earlier, Moravian led Muhlenberg at halftime, 6-0. The third quarter was scoreless (Table 4.24). The scoring flow in the fourth quarter was:

Table 4.24. **Team Statistics and Line Score for 1982 Game**

1982	Muhlenberg	Moravian
First downs	17	16
Yards rushing	122	331
Yards passing	111	28
Passes completed-attempted	9-28	2-5
Pass attempts intercepted	0	2
Fumbles lost	2	3
Punts	8	5
Yards penalized	29	137

Muhlenberg	0	0	0	6	—6
Moravian	0	6	0	10	—16

Muhlenberg—Mottola 11 run (kick blocked)
Moravian—Roberts 29 FG
Moravian—Rhinehart 6 run (Roberts kick)
Moravian scored quickly after the game-tying touchdown run by Mickey Mottola.

In other ways, the 1982 chapter is available to all who belong to the playing relationship, before and since. The Moravian rushing game returned after an absence of five years. The 5 Moravian passing attempts were the fewest since 1977. After Muhlenberg tied the game at 6-6, Tim Williams of Moravian made a substantial kickoff return. Later in that possession, David Latourette gained 46 yards on a rushing play. The Moravian touchdown drive in the fourth quarter covered 86 yards.

Lastly, players participating in their final Moravian-and-Muhlenberg football game joined to conclude an era in the playing relationship: Gary Greb of Muhlenberg threw 3 touchdown passes and went 2-1 as the quarterback. Chris Horton stopped two fourth-quarter two-point conversion attempts, and recorded a quarterback sack in the 1982 game. Jim Roberts of Moravian kicked 3 field goals in four games.

The Moravian defense and the Muhlenberg defense achieved a combined 18 changes of ball possession on November 12, 1983. Moravian achieved 5 Muhlenberg turnovers. There were no Moravian turnovers. Each defense induced at least 6 punts. The Moravian offense was guided to 15 first downs by Frank Godshall, more than twice the number of Muhlenberg first down gains. Team statistics are listed in Table 4.25.

Newcomers to the playing relationship in 1984 joined with returning players who helped create two precedents in the 1983 game at Muhlenberg Field.

Table 4.25. Team Statistics and Line Score for 1983 Game

1983	Moravian	Muhlenberg		
First downs	15	7		
Yards rushing	221	52		
Yards passing	61	57		
Passes completed-attempted	6-16	6-14		
Pass attempts intercepted	0	3		
Fumbles lost	0	2		
Punts	7	6		
Yards penalized	25	26		
Moravian	7	3	0	14	—24
Muhlenberg	7	0	0	0	—7

First, penalty yardage was the least (51) since 1973. Second, Moravian took a slim lead into the fourth quarter.

Earlier, Muhlenberg and Moravian were tied after one quarter, 7-7. Moravian led at halftime, 10-7 (Table 4.25). The third quarter was scoreless. The scoring flow in the fourth quarter was:

Moravian—Joseph 6 run (Messemer kick)

Moravian—Joseph 2 run (Messemer kick)

The first Moravian touchdown drive in the fourth quarter covered 54 yards.

In other ways, the 1983 chapter is available for all members of the playing relationship, before and since. Kurt Montz of Moravian intercepted a pass thrown by John Hobby of Muhlenberg to begin the final Moravian touchdown drive. Kevin Mei of Muhlenberg returned the opening kickoff 95 yards for a touchdown. The Muhlenberg offense sputtered after starting quarterback Pete Broas left the game with an injury.

Lastly, players participating in their final Moravian-and-Muhlenberg football game joined to conclude an era in the playing relationship: The Moravian offense gained more rushing yardage in consecutive games for the first time since 1976 and 1977.

The Muhlenberg defense and the Moravian defense achieved a combined 14 changes of ball possession on November 10, 1984. The two offenses committed only 3 turnovers. The Moravian offense was guided by Scott Rhinehart to 17 first downs, while relinquishing possession on 5 punts. Team statistics are listed in Table 4.26.

Newcomers to the playing relationship in 1985 joined with returning players who helped create two precedents in the 1984 game at Steel Field. First, officials assessed Moravian players 142 penalty yards, 95 more than the

Table 4.26. Team Statistics and Line Score for 1984 Game

1984		Muhlenberg		Moravian	
First downs		11		17	
Yards rushing		33		170	
Yards passing		237		131	
Passes completed-attempted		15-25		9-18	
Pass attempts intercepted		0		1	
Fumbles lost		1		1	
Punts		6		5	
Yards penalized		47		142	
Muhlenberg	0	0	7	7	—14
Moravian	14	0	0	3	—17

yardage assessed to Muhlenberg. Second, the final quarter was the scene of a "first" in the modern playing relationship.

Earlier, Moravian led Muhlenberg at halftime, 14-0. After three quarters, Moravian held the lead, 14-7 (Table 4.26). The scoring flow in the fourth quarter was:

Muhlenberg—Mann 2 run (Mulroy kick)

Moravian—Phillips 33 FG

Shawn Phillips of Moravian kicked the field goal with 22 seconds remaining in the game.

In other ways, the 1984 chapter is available for all members of the playing relationship, before and since. After Phillips kicked the field goal, Moravian received multiple penalties. Thus, Phillips kicked off from deep in Moravian territory. Pete Broas guided the Muhlenberg offense to the Moravian 28-yard line as time expired. Earlier in the game, John Motko of Moravian took part in two sacks of Broas. Tim Williams of Moravian blocked a punt to set up the second Moravian touchdown in the first quarter.

Lastly, players participating in their final Moravian-and-Muhlenberg football game joined to conclude an era in the playing relationship: Two-way player John Hobby of Muhlenberg played QB in the 1983 game and intercepted a pass in the 1984 game.

The Moravian defense and the Muhlenberg defense achieved a combined 21 changes of ball possession on November 16, 1985. The Moravian defense achieved 5 turnovers, all pass interceptions. Meanwhile, the Moravian offense retained possession (10 first downs) as many times as it relinquished possession. Team statistics are listed in Table 4.27.

Table 4.27. Team Statistics and Line Score for 1985 Game

1985	Moravian	Muhlenberg
First downs	10	16
Yards rushing	114	53
Yards passing	87	166
Passes completed-attempted	8-22	15-35
Pass attempts intercepted	2	5
Fumbles lost	0	0
Punts	8	6
Yards penalized	75	60

Moravian	0	7	0	8	—15
Muhlenberg	0	0	10	0	—10

Newcomers to the playing relationship in 1986 joined with returning players who helped create two precedents in the 1985 game at Muhlenberg Field.
First, officials assessed Moravian players 75 of the 135 penalty yards. Second, Muhlenberg led at the end of three quarters for the first time since the
1980 game.

Earlier, Moravian led Muhlenberg at halftime, 7-0. Muhlenberg moved into
the lead after three quarters, 10-7 (Table 4.27). The scoring play in the fourth
quarter was:

Moravian—McLaughlin 9 pass from Godshall (Lasko run)

The fourth-quarter comeback was Moravian's first in the modern playing relationship.

In other ways, the 1985 chapter is available for all members of the playing
relationship, before and since. In the touchdown drive that culminated in the
15-10 Moravian lead, the Moravian offense faced a first-and-35 situation.
Frank Godshall then led Moravian to a first down. Muhlenberg regained possession with 33 seconds left. Chris Giordano guided the offense to the Moravian 48-yard line as time expired.

Lastly, players participating in their final Moravian-and-Muhlenberg football game joined to conclude an era in the playing relationship: Jim Joseph of
Moravian rushed 97 times for 455 yards and 6 rushing touchdowns in four
games. He rushed for a touchdown in each game.

The Muhlenberg defense and the Moravian defense achieved a combined
26 changes of ball possession on November 15, 1986. The Moravian defense
achieved 5 Muhlenberg turnovers, 4 on pass interceptions. Each defense induced at least 9 punts. Team statistics are listed in Table 4.28.

Newcomers to the playing relationship in 1987 joined with returning players who helped create two precedents in the 1986 game at Steel Field. First,

Table 4.28. Team Statistics and Line Score for 1986 Game

1986		Muhlenberg		Moravian	
First downs		10		14	
Yards rushing		24		218	
Yards passing		176		92	
Passes completed-attempted		13-34		9-24	
Pass attempts intercepted		4		1	
Fumbles lost		1		1	
Punts		9		10	
Yards penalized		55		96	
Muhlenberg	0	0	0	0	—0
Moravian	0	0	7	7	—14

officials assessed nearly 100 yards (96) in penalties to Moravian players and 55 yards to Muhlenberg. Second, the game outcome was up for grabs at the start of the fourth quarter.

Earlier, there was no scoring in the first half. Moravian led Muhlenberg after three quarters, 7-0 (Table 4.28). The scoring play in the fourth quarter was:

Moravian—Masessa 4 run (Perry kick)

Mark Masessa scored the Moravian touchdown midway through the fourth quarter.

In other ways, the 1986 chapter is available for all members of the playing relationship, before and since. The Moravian defense stopped three late Muhlenberg drives. Thirty-six passes fell incomplete. Scott Stanilious of Moravian intercepted a pass that set up the first touchdown. Moravian defenders forced a 20-yard punt that set up the other score. Rocco Calvo coached his 23rd and final game as Moravian Head Coach.

Lastly, players participating in their final Moravian-and-Muhlenberg football game joined to conclude an era in the playing relationship: Scott Stanilious of Moravian intercepted 2 passes each in consecutive games.

The Moravian defense and the Muhlenberg defense achieved a combined 16 changes of ball possession on November 14, 1987. There were no lost fumbles. All 5 turnovers came on pass interceptions, 3 by the Moravian defense. The Muhlenberg offense, guided by Chris Elser, relinquished the ball 9 times while gaining 24 first downs. The Moravian offense, guided by Rob Light, relinquished the ball 7 times while gaining 17 first downs. The 41 first downs were the most in the modern playing relationship. Team statistics are listed in Table 4.29.

Newcomers to the playing relationship in 1988 joined with returning players who helped create two precedents in the 1987 game at Muhlenberg Field.

Table 4.29.   Team Statistics and Line Score for 1987 Game

1987	Moravian	Muhlenberg
First downs	17	24
Yards rushing	154	115
Yards passing	108	214
Passes completed-attempted	9-18	22-37
Pass attempts intercepted	2	3
Fumbles lost	0	0
Punts	5	6
Yards penalized	105	20

Moravian	0	6	6	0	—12
Muhlenberg	0	0	7	7	—14

First, Moravian players were assessed most (105 of 125 total yards) of the penalty yardage. Second, the Muhlenberg offense accomplished a comeback after being shut out in the first half.

Earlier, Moravian led Muhlenberg at halftime, 6-0. Moravian led 12-7 after three quarters (Table 4.29). The scoring flow in the third quarter was:

Moravian—Light 1 run (pass failed)

Muhlenberg—Concordia 9 pass from Elser (Hartman kick)

The scoring play in the fourth quarter was:

Muhlenberg—Potkul 2 pass from Elser (Hartman kick)

With the Muhlenberg defense containing the Moravian offense after the touchdown run by Light, Elser directed the come-from-behind touchdown drives.

In other ways, the 1987 chapter is available for all members of the playing relationship, before and since. John Patrignani of Moravian returned a punt 48 yards to set up the Moravian touchdown in the third quarter. After Moravian intercepted 3 of his passes in the first half, Elser completed 9 of 11 passes on the two touchdown drives. The Muhlenberg offense held possession of the ball for the final five minutes of the game.

Lastly, players participating in their final Moravian-and-Muhlenberg football game joined to conclude an era in the playing relationship: The outcome marked an end to a five-game Moravian win streak and Muhlenberg losing streak.

The Muhlenberg defense and the Moravian defense achieved a combined 14 changes of ball possession on November 12, 1988. The defenses achieved 3 turnovers. The Moravian offense was guided by Rob Light to 17 first downs. The Muhlenberg offense, guided by Chris Elser, retained possession with 13 first downs and relinquished possession 9 times, 7 on punts. Team statistics are listed in Table 4.30.

Table 4.30.   Team Statistics and Line Score for 1988 Game

1988	Muhlenberg	Moravian
First downs	13	17
Yards rushing	86	151
Yards passing	238	218
Passes completed-attempted	16-27	13-22
Pass attempts intercepted	2	0
Fumbles lost	0	1
Punts	7	5
Yards penalized	41	69

Muhlenberg	0	13	6	6	—25
Moravian	14	10	20	0	—44

Newcomers to the playing relationship in 1989 joined with returning players who helped create two precedents in the 1988 game at Steel Field. First, officials assessed Moravian players 8 penalties for 69 of the 110 penalty yards. Second, Moravian held a 25-point lead entering the fourth quarter.

Earlier, Moravian led Muhlenberg at halftime, 24-13. After three quarters, Moravian led, 44-19 (Table 4.30). The scoring play in the fourth quarter was:

Muhlenberg—Aniello 27 pass from Elser (pass failed)
The Muhlenberg touchdown was anticlimactic.

In other ways, the 1988 chapter is available for all members of the playing relationship, before and since. Moravian "special teams" scored two touchdowns. In the first quarter, John Patrignani returned a punt 51 yards for a score. In the third quarter, Mike Obert blocked a punt, and Mike Reinhard fell on the ball in the end zone. The two offenses amassed 693 total yards. The 25 Muhlenberg points were the second-highest total for a losing team; Muhlenberg scored 27 points in the 1974 game.

Lastly, players participating in their final Moravian-and-Muhlenberg football game joined to conclude an era in the playing relationship: Chris Elser of Muhlenberg threw 5 touchdown passes. Tony Concordia of Muhlenberg caught 3 touchdown passes. Jeff Potkul of Muhlenberg rushed for more than 140 yards and threw a touchdown pass.

The Moravian defense and the Muhlenberg defense achieved a combined 13 changes of possession on November 11, 1989. There were 4 turnovers. Meanwhile, the Moravian offense, guided by Rob Light, achieved 20 first downs and lost possession 5 times (4 punts). The Muhlenberg offense, guided by Mickey Rowe, retained possession with 14 first downs, lost 3 turnovers, and was forced to punt on 5 occasions. Team statistics are listed in Table 4.31.

Table 4.31.   Team Statistics and Line Score for 1989 Game

1989	*Moravian*	*Muhlenberg*			
First downs	20	14			
Yards rushing	162	146			
Yards passing	213	109			
Passes completed-attempted	13-20	7-19			
Pass attempts intercepted	1	2			
Fumbles lost	0	1			
Punts	4	5			
Yards penalized	54	55			
Moravian	7	0	7	0	—14
Muhlenberg	0	9	0	0	—9

Newcomers to the playing relationship in 1990 joined with returning players who helped create two precedents in the 1989 game at Muhlenberg Field. First, the penalty yardage was nearly identical. Second, Muhlenberg trailed by five points as the fourth quarter began.

Earlier, Muhlenberg led Moravian at halftime, 9-7. After three quarters, Moravian led, 14-9 (Table 4.31). The scoring play in the third quarter was:

Moravian—Light 8 run (Cunniff kick)

The two defenses achieved a fourth-quarter shutout.

In other ways, the 1989 chapter is available for all members of the playing relationship, before and since. Despite permitting over 600 yards in total offense, the two defenses permitted only four scoring plays. Wayne Caton of Muhlenberg tackled Moravian ball carriers 15 times. Russ Parsons of Moravian tackled Muhlenberg ball carriers 18 times, 3 during a fourth-quarter goal line stand. After Rob Lyons of Moravian intercepted a Rowe pass, the Moravian offense controlled the ball for the final 4 minutes. The game was Ralph Kirchenheiter's ninth and final as Muhlenberg Head Coach.

Lastly, players participating in their final Moravian-and-Muhlenberg football game joined to conclude an era in the playing relationship: Rob Light of Moravian completed 44 of 84 passes for 631 yards and 2 touchdowns. He rushed for 4 touchdowns.

The Muhlenberg defense and the Moravian defense achieved 32 possession changes on November 10, 1990. The Muhlenberg defense achieved 4 turnovers. Each defense induced at least 12 punts. Each offense retained possession with 7 first downs. Team statistics are listed in Table 4.32.

Newcomers to the playing relationship in 1991 joined with returning players who helped create two precedents in the 1990 game at Steel Field. First, Moravian players were assessed 8 penalties and Muhlenberg players were as-

Table 4.32.   **Team Statistics and Line Score for 1990 Game**

1990		Muhlenberg		Moravian	
First downs		7		7	
Yards rushing		20		143	
Yards passing		112		19	
Passes completed-attempted		10-27		2-15	
Pass attempts intercepted		1		2	
Fumbles lost		3		1	
Punts		12		13	
Yards penalized		65		85	
Muhlenberg	0	3	0	0	—3
Moravian	0	7	0	0	—7

sessed 10 penalties. Second, for the thirteenth straight year, the outcome was unclear as the teams began the fourth quarter.

Earlier, Moravian led Muhlenberg at halftime, 7-3. The third quarter was scoreless (Table 4.32). The fourth quarter was scoreless, too. The two defenses controlled the final quarter.

In other ways, the 1990 chapter is available for all members of the playing relationship, before and since. In the fourth quarter, Paul Woodling of Moravian tackled Eric Slaton of Muhlenberg after Slaton had gained 43 yards on a pass from Doug Donovan. Moravian tacklers sacked Donovan for minus-50 rushing yards. Neither passing game got untracked in the rain. Of the 42 attempts, 30 fell incomplete. Donovan was the third Muhlenberg Quarterback in three years.

Lastly, players participating in their final Moravian-and-Muhlenberg football game joined to conclude an era in the playing relationship: Rob Paessler of Muhlenberg rushed 40 times for 152 yards and one touchdown in two games.

The Moravian defense and the Muhlenberg defense achieved a combined 18 changes of ball possession on November 16, 1991. The Muhlenberg defense achieved 5 Moravian turnovers, 4 on fumbles. The Moravian defense permitted 13 first downs, while inducing 9 Muhlenberg punts. Mike Harth and Sean Keville guided the Moravian offense to retain possession with 19 first downs, compared to only 2 punts. Team statistics are listed in Table 4.33.

Newcomers to the playing relationship in 1992 joined with returning players who helped create two precedents in the 1991 game at Muhlenberg Field. First, each team was assessed 9 penalties for a combined 180 yards. Second, the fourth quarter was the scene of the most dramatic offense comeback thus far in the Moravian-and-Muhlenberg playing relationship.

Table 4.33.   Team Statistics and Line Score for 1991 Game

1991		*Moravian*		*Muhlenberg*	
First downs		19		13	
Yards rushing		166		114	
Yards passing		219		193	
Passes completed-attempted		19-32		11-36	
Pass attempts intercepted		1		1	
Fumbles lost		4		1	
Punts		2		9	
Yards penalized		80		100	
Moravian	6	0	8	14	—28
Muhlenberg	7	14	6	0	—27

Earlier, Muhlenberg led Moravian at halftime, 21-6. Moravian still trailed by 13 points, 27-14, after three quarters (Table 4.33). The scoring flow in the third quarter was:

Moravian—Iasparro 64 punt return (Bagnaturo pass from Harth)
Muhlenberg—Slaton 56 pass from McCullough (Gorman kick)
The scoring flow in the fourth quarter was:
Moravian—Durepo 26 pass from Keville (kick blocked)
Moravian—Hahn 13 pass from Keville (Durepo pass from Keville)

Freshman Quarterback Keville was a principal figure in the fourth quarter Moravian comeback. The winning points were scored with 1:21 remaining in the game.

In other ways, the 1991 chapter is available for all members of the playing relationship, before and since. Chris Iasparro of Moravian returned a punt 64 yards for a touchdown. Jacob Massenoir and Craig Stump of Muhlenberg recorded 15 and 13 tackles, respectively. Six touchdown passes were thrown by the two offenses.

Lastly, players participating in their final Moravian-and-Muhlenberg football game joined to conclude an era in the playing relationship: Eric Slaton of Muhlenberg caught 6 passes for 154 yards and a touchdown in two games.

The Muhlenberg defense and the Moravian defense achieved a combined 16 changes of ball possession on November 14, 1992. The Moravian defense accomplished 9 Muhlenberg losses of possession. Meanwhile, John Mattes guided the Moravian offense to 26 first downs. Moravian relinquished possession 4 times, 3 on interceptions. Team statistics are listed in Table 4.34.

Newcomers to the playing relationship in 1993 joined with returning players who helped create two precedents in the 1992 game at Steel Field. First, Moravian players were whistled for 13 penalties totaling 116 yards, twice the

Table 4.34.   Team Statistics and Line Score for 1992 Game

1992		Muhlenberg		Moravian	
First downs		11		26	
Yards rushing		59		108	
Yards passing		238		349	
Passes completed-attempted		15-34		26-38	
Pass attempts intercepted		1		3	
Fumbles lost		1		1	
Punts		7		3	
Yards penalized		58		116	
Muhlenberg	0	0	7	7	—14
Moravian	7	21	0	7	—35

Muhlenberg yardage (5 penalties). Second, Moravian held a wide lead starting the fourth quarter.

Earlier, Moravian led Muhlenberg at halftime, 28-0. Muhlenberg trailed after three quarters, 28-7. The scoring flow in the fourth quarter was:

Moravian—Cubbin 11 run (Koy kick)

Muhlenberg—Lokerson 60 pass from McCullough (Scott kick)

The touchdown pass by Sean McCullough came too late to affect the game outcome.

In other ways, the 1992 chapter is available for all members of the playing relationship, before and since. The Moravian defense sacked Sean McCullough of Muhlenberg three times. The shortest of the five Moravian touchdown drives covered 41 yards. Two drives covered 81 yards each.

Lastly, players participating in their final Moravian-and-Muhlenberg football game joined to conclude an era in the playing relationship: Craig Cubbin of Moravian rushed 28 times for 97 yards and 3 touchdowns in two games. He also threw a touchdown pass.

The Muhlenberg defense and the Moravian defense achieved a combined 22 changes of ball possession on November 13, 1993. Each defense induced at least 6 punts. There were only 3 turnovers in the game. The two offenses were comparably capable of retaining possession; each gained 19 first downs. Team statistics are listed in Table 4.35.

Newcomers to the playing relationship in 1994 joined with returning players who helped create two precedents in the 1993 game at Muhlenberg Field. First, officials penalized Muhlenberg players twice the number of times (6) and for more than twice the yardage assessed on the 3 Moravian penalties. Second, the fourth quarter began with Moravian having extended a slim lead.

Table 4.35. Team Statistics and Line Score for 1993 Game

1993		*Moravian*		*Muhlenberg*	
First downs		19		19	
Yards rushing		166		50	
Yards passing		281		287	
Passes completed-attempted		15-25		22-54	
Pass attempts intercepted		1		1	
Fumbles lost		0		1	
Punts		6		8	
Yards penalized		29		64	
Moravian	10	7	7	0	—24
Muhlenberg	0	7	7	0	—14

Earlier, Moravian led Muhlenberg at halftime, 17-7. After three quarters, Moravian held onto a ten-point lead, 24-14 (Table 4.35). The scoring flow in the third quarter was:

Muhlenberg—Bokus 37 pass from McCullough (Habash kick)

Moravian—Natale 55 run (Kurtz kick)

The Moravian defense withstood the Muhlenberg passing game in the scoreless final period.

In other ways, the 1993 chapter is available for all members of the playing relationship, before and since. Twice in the fourth quarter, Muhlenberg drives ended inside the Moravian 10-yard line. John D'Angelo of Muhlenberg tackled 16 Moravian ball carriers. Bob Hennessy of Moravian recorded 10 tackles. The Moravian offense used the rushing game to control the ball for 10 minutes more than did the Muhlenberg offense. The 54 Muhlenberg passing attempts were the most in the modern playing relationship.

Lastly, players participating in their final Moravian-and-Muhlenberg football game joined to conclude an era in the playing relationship: Sean McCullough of Muhlenberg completed 46 of 120 passes for 715 yards and 7 touchdowns in three Muhlenberg losses. Jud Frank of Moravian rushed 56 times for 208 yards in four games. He also caught a touchdown pass.

The Moravian defense and the Muhlenberg defense achieved a combined 18 changes of ball possession on November 12, 1994. The Muhlenberg defense achieved 6 Moravian turnovers. Offsetting the 6 turnovers and 3 punts, the Moravian offense was guided by Sean Keville to 21 first downs. The Muhlenberg offense, guided by Jason Jack, retained possession with 17 first downs and relinquished possession 9 times. Team statistics are listed in Table 4.36.

Newcomers to the playing relationship in 1995 joined with returning players who helped create two precedents in the 1994 game at Steel Field. First,

Table 4.36.   **Team Statistics and Line Score for 1994 Game**

1994		Muhlenberg		Moravian	
First downs		17		21	
Yards rushing		32		221	
Yards passing		278		290	
Passes completed-attempted		17-37		18-33	
Pass attempts intercepted		2		3	
Fumbles lost		2		3	
Punts		5		3	
Yards penalized		63		106	
Muhlenberg	3	14	0	0	—17
Moravian	7	22	7	14	—50

Moravian players were assessed 12 penalties for 106 of the 169 penalty yards. Second, the fourth quarter began with Moravian holding a 19-point lead after a comparatively quiet third quarter.

Earlier, Moravian led Muhlenberg at halftime, 29-17. After three quarters, the Moravian lead had grown, 36-17 (Table 4.36). The scoring flow in the fourth quarter was:

Moravian—Bonsall 2 run (Stasiak kick)

Moravian—Paciulli 56 pass interception (Stasiak kick)

The final touchdown came in the first four minutes of the fourth quarter.

In other ways, the 1994 chapter is available for all members of the playing relationship, before and since. Each defense scored a touchdown. Dan Terpstra of Muhlenberg recovered a blocked punt in the Moravian end zone. Mike Paciulli of Moravian returned a pass interception 56 yards for a touchdown. Moravian pass rushers tackled Jack of Muhlenberg for 35 yards in losses. Trailing 10-7 in the second quarter, Moravian took the lead on an 87-yard kickoff return touchdown by Chad Breidinger.

Lastly, players participating in their final Moravian-and-Muhlenberg football game joined to conclude an era in the playing relationship: Sean Keville of Moravian completed 35 of 63 passes for 585 yards and 5 touchdowns in three games. He also completed 2 touchdown passes as a freshman. He rushed for a touchdown, too. Rob Lokerson of Muhlenberg caught 19 passes for 353 yards and a touchdown in three games.

The Moravian defense and the Muhlenberg defense achieved a combined 16 changes of ball possession on November 11, 1995. The Moravian defense achieved 10 of the changes, on 4 turnovers and 6 Muhlenberg punts. Meanwhile, the Moravian offense was guided by Joe Schroeder to 20 first downs while relinquishing the ball 6 times. Team statistics are listed in Table 4.37.

Table 4.37. Team Statistics and Line Score for 1995 Game

1995		*Moravian*		*Muhlenberg*	
First downs		20		17	
Yards rushing		303		160	
Yards passing		112		81	
Passes completed-attempted		9-23		11-31	
Pass attempts intercepted		1		3	
Fumbles lost		0		1	
Punts		5		6	
Yards penalized		78		10	
Moravian	6	15	10	7	—38
Muhlenberg	0	7	0	0	—7

Newcomers to the playing relationship in 1996 joined with returning players who helped create two precedents in the 1995 game at Muhlenberg Field.
First, officials called 8 of the 10 penalties on Moravian. Second, Moravian led
by 24 points as the fourth quarter began.

Earlier, Moravian led Muhlenberg at halftime, 21-7. After three quarters,
Moravian led, 31-7 (Table 4.37). The scoring play in the fourth quarter was:

Moravian—Scobo 1 run (Kurtz kick)

Rob Scobo of Moravian scored the final touchdown with under 6 minutes remaining.

In other ways, the 1995 chapter is available for all members of the playing
relationship, before and since. The Moravian defense scored a touchdown
when Jeff Pukszyn returned a pass interception 11 yards in the second quarter. Shawn Storm of Moravian accomplished two quarterback sacks.

Lastly, players participating in their final Moravian-and-Muhlenberg football game joined to conclude an era in the playing relationship: Bill Van Dyke
of Muhlenberg caught 23 passes for 289 yards in four games.

The Muhlenberg defense and the Moravian defense achieved a combined
16 changes of ball possession on November 16, 1996. The Moravian defense
induced 8 Muhlenberg punts, while permitting only 6 first downs. Meanwhile, Mike Harrison guided the Moravian offense to retain possession with
20 first downs. Team statistics are listed in Table 4.38.

Newcomers to the playing relationship in 1997 joined with returning players who helped create two precedents in the 1996 game at Steel Field. First,
officials called only 9 penalties for 62 yards. Few of the penalties exceeded 5
yards. Second, for the second straight year, the fourth quarter began with
Moravian holding a 24-point lead.

Table 4.38. Team Statistics and Line Score for 1996 Game

1996		Muhlenberg		Moravian	
First downs		6		20	
Yards rushing		−2		218	
Yards passing		128		170	
Passes completed-attempted		9-19		11-18	
Pass attempts intercepted		1		2	
Fumbles lost		1		0	
Punts		8		4	
Yards penalized		32		30	
Muhlenberg	0	3	0	0	—3
Moravian	3	7	17	0	—27

Earlier, Moravian led Muhlenberg at halftime, 10-3. Moravian led after three quarters, 27-3 (Table 4.38). The Moravian offense controlled the ball in the scoreless final period.

In other ways, the 1996 chapter is available for all members of the playing relationship, before and since. Dan Terpstra of Muhlenberg tackled Moravian ball carriers 10 times. The Moravian defense held Muhlenberg rushers to minus-2 yards. George Fosdick of Muhlenberg threw 10 incomplete passes and was sacked 4 times.

Lastly, players participating in their final Moravian-and-Muhlenberg football game joined to conclude an era in the playing relationship: Brad Lower of Moravian rushed 49 times for 272 yards in two games. Chad Breidinger of Moravian rushed 39 times for 200 yards and 2 touchdowns in three games. Breidinger also scored on a kickoff return.

The Moravian defense and the Muhlenberg defense achieved a combined 17 changes of ball possession on November 15, 1997. Each defense induced 6 punts. Team statistics are listed in Table 4.39.

Newcomers to the playing relationship in 1998 joined with returning players who helped create two precedents in the 1997 game at Muhlenberg Field. First, officials assessed equal penalty yardage. Second, the outcome was in doubt as the fourth quarter began.

Earlier, Muhlenberg led Moravian at halftime, 13-7. After three quarters, Moravian held the lead, 14-13 (Table 4.39). The scoring flow in the fourth quarter was:

Muhlenberg—Sapir 18 FG

Moravian—Campbell 21 pass interception (Smith kick)

The Moravian touchdown was scored midway through the final period.

Table 4.39. Team Statistics and Line Score for 1997 Game

1997	Moravian	Muhlenberg
First downs	15	17
Yards rushing	122	164
Yards passing	137	213
Passes completed-attempted	9-18	19-41
Pass attempts intercepted	0	1
Fumbles lost	3	1
Punts	6	6
Yards penalized	63	63

Moravian	0	7	7	7	—21
Muhlenberg	7	6	0	3	—16

In other ways, the 1997 chapter is available for all members of the playing relationship, before and since. The Moravian defense scored the game-winning touchdown. Kevin Campbell returned a pass interception 21 yards for the score. Kevin Greenberg of Moravian tackled Muhlenberg ball carriers 12 times. Muhlenberg once led by 13-0. The Muhlenberg offense controlled the ball with 81 plays.

Lastly, players participating in their final Moravian-and-Muhlenberg football game joined to conclude an era in the playing relationship: The final score marked the tenth straight Moravian win and Muhlenberg loss.

The Muhlenberg defense and the Moravian defense achieved a combined 19 changes of ball possession on November 14, 1998. The Muhlenberg defense achieved 6 Moravian turnovers, including 4 fumble recoveries. Meanwhile, Mike McCabe guided the Muhlenberg offense to 19 first down ball retentions. The Muhlenberg offense relinquished possession 7 times, 5 times on punts. Team statistics are listed in Table 4.40.

Newcomers to the playing relationship in 1999 joined with returning players who helped create two precedents in the 1998 game at Steel Field. First, officials called 9 penalties on Muhlenberg players for 103 yards. Moravian was assessed 5 penalties. Second, Moravian trailed Muhlenberg by a touchdown as the fourth quarter began.

Earlier, Muhlenberg and Moravian concluded the first quarter in a 14-14 tie. Muhlenberg led at halftime, 17-14, and after three quarters, 20-14 (Table 4.40). The scoring flow in the fourth quarter was:

Muhlenberg—Arcuri 34 pass interception (run failed)

Muhlenberg—Brader 5 run (Dickinson kick)

The interception return by Arcuri changed the game.

Table 4.40.   Team Statistics and Line Score for 1998 Game

1998	Muhlenberg	Moravian		
First downs	19	17		
Yards rushing	210	155		
Yards passing	199	127		
Passes completed-attempted	11-30	12-27		
Pass attempts intercepted	0	2		
Fumbles lost	2	4		
Punts	5	6		
Yards penalized	103	60		
Muhlenberg	14	3	3	13	—33
Moravian	14	0	0	0	—14

In other ways, the 1998 chapter is available for all members of the playing relationship, before and since. Greg Arcuri scored a touchdown for the Muhlenberg defense, when he returned an interception 34 yards. Moravian twice led by 7 points in the first quarter.

Lastly, players participating in their final Moravian-and-Muhlenberg football game joined to conclude an era in the playing relationship: Jason Brader of Muhlenberg rushed 67 times for 320 yards and one touchdown in two games.

The Moravian defense and the Muhlenberg defense achieved a combined 13 changes of ball possession on November 13, 1999. The Muhlenberg offense, guided by Mike McCabe and Justin Jones, retained possession with 20 first downs and relinquished possession only 3 times. Team statistics are listed in Table 4.41.

Newcomers to the playing relationship in 2000 joined with returning players who helped create two precedents in the 1999 game at Scotty Wood Stadium. First, officials called 10 of the 12 penalties on Muhlenberg players. Second, the fourth quarter began with Muhlenberg holding a 42-point lead, the largest in the modern playing relationship.

Earlier, Muhlenberg led Moravian after one quarter, 21-7. The Muhlenberg halftime lead was 42-13 (Table 4.41). After three quarters, Muhlenberg led Moravian, 45-13. The scoring flow in the fourth quarter was:

Moravian—Fick 19 run (McIntyre kick)

Muhlenberg—Reed 19 FG

Moravian—Fick 55 run (kick failed)

Two touchdown runs by freshman Josh Fick gave the Moravian team some reason to celebrate.

Table 4.41.   Team Statistics and Line Score for 1999 Game

1999		Moravian		Muhlenberg	
First downs		17		20	
Yards rushing		189		175	
Yards passing		241		352	
Passes completed-attempted		13-30		21-37	
Pass attempts intercepted		1		1	
Fumbles lost		3		0	
Punts		6		2	
Yards penalized		20		90	
Moravian	7	6	0	13	—26
Muhlenberg	21	21	7	3	—52

In other ways, the 1999 chapter is available for all members of the playing relationship, before and since. Joshua Carter of Muhlenberg returned a kickoff 78 yards for a touchdown in the second quarter. Carter crossed the goal line six times. Four times, the touchdowns counted for scores. His apparent scores on another kickoff return and a punt return were nullified, due to Muhlenberg penalties. Steve DiRenzo of Moravian tackled Muhlenberg ball carriers 14 times.

Lastly, players participating in their final Moravian-and-Muhlenberg football game joined to conclude an era in the playing relationship: Rob Petrosky of Moravian completed 31 of 70 pass attempts for 474 yards and 2 touchdowns in three games. He also rushed for 2 touchdowns.

The Muhlenberg defense and the Moravian defense achieved a combined 13 changes of ball possession on November 11, 2000. Each defense achieved 3 turnovers. Meanwhile the Muhlenberg offense was guided by Mike McCabe to 24 first downs, while relinquishing the ball only twice on punts. Charlie Bowden guided the Moravian offense to 23 first downs, in contrast to the 8 times that Moravian relinquished possession. Team statistics are listed in Table 4.42.

Newcomers to the playing relationship in 2001 joined with returning players who helped create two precedents in the 2000 game at Steel Field. First, officials called 8 of the 13 penalties on Muhlenberg. Second, despite trailing all afternoon, the Moravian team was within a touchdown and a two-point play of tying the game as the fourth quarter began.

Earlier, Muhlenberg led Moravian at halftime, 28-12. After three quarters, Muhlenberg continued to hold the lead, 28-20 (Table 4.42). The scoring flow in the fourth quarter was:

Muhlenberg—Bernardo 2 run (Dickinson kick)
Muhlenberg—Bernardo 1 run (Dickinson kick)
Muhlenberg—Dickinson 28 FG

Three Muhlenberg drives were productive in the final period.

Table 4.42. Team Statistics and Line Score for 2000 Game

2000		Muhlenberg		Moravian	
First downs		24		23	
Yards rushing		317		155	
Yards passing		159		250	
Passes completed-attempted		11-24		16-33	
Pass attempts intercepted		3		2	
Fumbles lost		0		1	
Punts		2		5	
Yards penalized		60		50	
Muhlenberg	14	14	0	17	—45
Moravian	0	12	8	0	—20

In other ways, the 2000 chapter is available for all members of the playing relationship, before and since. Joshua Carter of Muhlenberg turned the game around in the second quarter with a 90-yard kickoff return touchdown. Moravian had just scored to close the deficit to 21-12. Mike Burke of Muhlenberg intercepted two Bowden passes.

Lastly, players participating in their final Moravian-and-Muhlenberg football game joined to conclude an era in the playing relationship: P. J. Jankowicz of Moravian rushed 76 times for 298 yards and one touchdown in four games.

The Moravian defense and the Muhlenberg defense achieved a combined 16 changes of ball possession on November 10, 2001. The Moravian defense intercepted 6 Muhlenberg passes. Meanwhile, the Moravian offense was guided by Will Seng and Charlie Bowden to 17 first downs. Moravian relinquished possession 6 times. Team statistics are listed in Table 4.43.

Newcomers to the playing relationship in 2002 joined with returning players who helped create two precedents in the 2001 game at Scotty Wood Stadium. First, officials assessed 11 of the 16 penalties to Muhlenberg. Second, the Moravian lead entering the fourth quarter was the first since a one-point lead in 1997.

Earlier, Moravian led Muhlenberg at halftime, 10-7. Moravian extended the lead after three quarters, 17-7 (Table 4.43). In a scoreless fourth quarter, the Moravian pass defense sealed the win and the Muhlenberg loss.

In other ways, the 2001 chapter is available for all members of the playing relationship, before and since. Jarrod Pence of Moravian intercepted 3 passes thrown by Justin Jones of Muhlenberg. On the first Muhlenberg possession of the game, Jones led a 51-yard touchdown drive. The Moravian pass defense and rushing offense (52 rushes) then took control. Mike Koth of Muhlenberg tackled Moravian ball carriers 10 times.

Table 4.43.   Team Statistics and Line Score for 2001 Game

2001		Moravian		Muhlenberg	
First downs		17		9	
Yards rushing		117		72	
Yards passing		120		111	
Passes completed-attempted		10-22		11-22	
Pass attempts intercepted		0		6	
Fumbles lost		1		1	
Punts		5		3	
Yards penalized		44		82	
Moravian	0	10	7	0	—17
Muhlenberg	7	0	0	0	—7

Lastly, players participating in their final Moravian-and-Muhlenberg football game joined to conclude an era in the playing relationship: Joshua Carter of Muhlenberg scored 8 touchdowns in four games in three different ways: 2 rushes, 4 pass receptions, and 2 kickoff returns. Carter caught 11 passes for 265 yards in the four games.

The Muhlenberg defense and the Moravian defense achieved a combined 21 changes of ball possession on November 16, 2002. Each defense induced 8 punts. The Muhlenberg pass defense intercepted 3 Moravian passes and permitted 3 Moravian pass completions. Meanwhile, Justin Jones guided the Muhlenberg offense to 14 first downs while relinquishing possession 10 times. In the rain and mud, there was one lost fumble. Team statistics are listed in Table 4.44.

Newcomers to the playing relationship in 2003 joined with returning players who helped create two precedents in the 2002 game at Steel Field. First, 5 of the 6 penalties were assessed to Muhlenberg. Second, it was anybody's game as the fourth quarter began.

Earlier, Muhlenberg led Moravian at halftime, 6-0. Muhlenberg led after three quarters, 8-0 (Table 4.44). The Muhlenberg rushing offense controlled the scoreless final period.

In other ways, the 2002 chapter is available for all members of the playing relationship, before and since. The Muhlenberg defense put 2 points on the scoreboard with the safety in the third quarter. The safety came after Nate Pogue of Moravian intercepted a pass and threw a lateral to teammate Jarrod Pence. Pence was then tackled in his own end zone. Steve Doll of Muhlenberg intercepted a Moravian pass in the final minute. His teammate Dan Miller accomplished 4 solo tackles and 4 assisted tackles.

Table 4.44.   Team Statistics and Line Score for 2002 Game

2002		Muhlenberg		Moravian	
First downs		14		9	
Yards rushing		163		98	
Yards passing		44		27	
Passes completed-attempted		4-18		3-17	
Pass attempts intercepted		1		3	
Fumbles lost		1		0	
Punts and average		8		8	
Yards penalized		60		15	
Muhlenberg	0	6	2	0	—8
Moravian	0	0	0	0	—0

Lastly, players participating in their final Moravian-and-Muhlenberg football game joined to conclude an era: The outcome was the first shutout since the 1986 game.

The Moravian defense and the Muhlenberg defense achieved a combined 21 changes of ball possession on November 15, 2003. The Muhlenberg defense achieved 13 of the changes, inducing 10 punts. Meanwhile, Ryan Newman guided the Muhlenberg offense to hold possession with 17 first downs. The Muhlenberg offense relinquished possession 8 times. Team statistics are listed in Table 4.45.

Newcomers to the playing relationship in 2004 joined with returning players who helped create two precedents in the 2003 game at Scotty Wood Stadium. First, only 7 penalties were assessed for a total of 44 yards. Second, by the start of the fourth quarter, Moravian offense units had not scored a point for eight consecutive quarters (in 2001, 2002, and 2003).

Earlier, Muhlenberg led Moravian at halftime, 10-0. Muhlenberg led after three quarters, 17-0 (Table 4.45). The scoring play in the fourth quarter was:

Muhlenberg—Bernardo 2 run (Hendershot kick)

The Muhlenberg defense extended the Moravian scoreless streak.

In other ways, the 2003 chapter is available for all members of the playing relationship, before and since. Joe Getz of Muhlenberg intercepted two passes thrown by Jerry Venturino. The first came in the Muhlenberg end zone on the opening Moravian possession. Two punts by Getz were downed inside the Moravian 5-yard line. John Panikiewsky of Moravian tackled Muhlenberg ball carriers 11 times.

Lastly, players participating in their final Moravian-and-Muhlenberg football game joined to conclude an era in the playing relationship: Matt

Table 4.45.   Team Statistics and Line Score for 2003 Game

2003		Moravian		Muhlenberg	
First downs		12		17	
Yards rushing		85		201	
Yards passing		142		185	
Passes completed-attempted		13-31		16-30	
Pass attempts intercepted		3		0	
Fumbles lost		0		2	
Punts		10		6	
Yards penalized		24		20	
Moravian	0	0	0	0	—0
Muhlenberg	0	10	7	7	—24

Table 4.46.   Team Statistics and Line Score for 2004 Game

2004		Muhlenberg		Moravian	
First downs		13		11	
Yards rushing		171		94	
Yards passing		63		100	
Passes completed-attempted		9-18		9-31	
Pass attempts intercepted		1		3	
Fumbles lost		2		1	
Punts		6		4	
Yards penalized		89		70	
Muhlenberg	6	14	0	8	—28
Moravian	2	0	0	12	—14

Bernardo of Muhlenberg rushed 103 times for 555 yards and 6 touchdowns in four games.

The Muhlenberg defense and the Moravian defense achieved a combined 17 changes of possession on November 13, 2004. The two offenses gained 24 first downs (13 by Muhlenberg). Team statistics are listed in Table 4.46.

Newcomers to the playing relationship in 2005 joined with returning players who helped create two precedents in the 2004 game at Steel Field. First, Muhlenberg players were penalized 7 times for 89 yards, while Moravian players were called for 8 infractions for fewer total yards. Second, the Muhlenberg defense held the Moravian offense scoreless for the first three quarters, running the scoreless streak to twelve quarters since the 2001 game.

Earlier, Muhlenberg led Moravian at halftime, 20-2. The third quarter was scoreless (Table 4.46). The scoring flow in the fourth quarter was:

Moravian—Jacoubs 9 run (kick blocked)

Muhlenberg—Merrill blocked PAT return

Muhlenberg—Gasker 85 kickoff return (pass failed)

Moravian—Garr fumble recovery in end zone (run failed)

The Jacoubs touchdown narrowed the Muhlenberg lead to 20-8. Less than a minute later, the score was 28-8, in Muhlenberg's favor.

In other ways, the 2004 chapter is available for all members of the playing relationship, before and since. The game contained several oddities. A safety was scored by Moravian when a Muhlenberg offense player was called for a penalty in his own end zone. A failed extra-point attempt was converted into a two-point defensive conversion; Ryan Merrill of Muhlenberg ran the length of the field with the blocked PAT attempt. Phil Gasker of Muhlenberg returned the ensuing Moravian kickoff 85 yards for a touchdown.

Muhlenberg scored in the first half after a successful onside kick and then again after Dustin Martin blocked a Moravian punt. Muhlenberg also pulled a trick play in the first half. With the offense set at the line of scrimmage, Quarterback Nick Rosetti strolled toward his coaches, as if to seek guidance about the play. Meanwhile, the ball was snapped to Muhlenberg back Matt Johnson who completed a pass for a first down at the Moravian 5-yard line.

More conventionally, Ryan Peer of Muhlenberg tackled Moravian ball carriers 7 times. Cliff Garr of Moravian tackled Muhlenberg ball carriers 13 times.

Lastly, players participating in their final Moravian-and-Muhlenberg football game joined to conclude an era in the playing relationship: The safety scored by Moravian was the first since the 2002 game and only the third safety ever scored.

The Moravian defense and the Muhlenberg defense achieved a combined 15 changes of ball possession on November 12, 2005. Each defense achieved 2 turnovers. Jerry Venturino guided the Moravian offense to 17 first downs. Moravian punted 6 times. Team statistics are listed in Table 4.47.

Newcomers to the playing relationship in 2006 joined with returning players who helped create two precedents in the 2005 game at Scotty Wood Stadium. First, Muhlenberg was penalized 9 times for 90 yards. Eight penalties were called on Moravian players. Second, Moravian entered the fourth quarter with a lead for the first time since 2001.

Earlier, after a scoreless first quarter, Moravian led Muhlenberg at halftime, 10-7. Moravian led after three quarters, 24-7 (Table 4.47). The scoring flow in the fourth quarter was:

Muhlenberg—Santagato 4 run (kick failed)

Muhlenberg—Douglass 45 pass from Santagato (pass failed)

Table 4.47. Team Statistics and Line Score for 2005 Game

2005		Moravian		Muhlenberg	
First downs		17		14	
Yards rushing		193		111	
Yards passing		206		172	
Passes completed-attempted		12-21		13-26	
Pass attempts intercepted		1		1	
Fumbles lost		1		1	
Punts		6		5	
Yards penalized		59		90	
Moravian	0	10	14	0	—24
Muhlenberg	0	7	0	12	—19

Eric Santagato almost pulled off the largest Muhlenberg fourth-quarter come-back in the modern playing relationship.

In other ways, the 2005 chapter is available for all members of the playing relationship, before and since. Alex Miller of Muhlenberg accomplished 9 solo tackles and 4 assisted tackles. Phil Gasker of Muhlenberg put his team in the lead in the second quarter when he returned a kickoff 94 yards for a touchdown.

Lastly, players participating in their final Moravian-and-Muhlenberg foot-ball game joined to conclude an era in the playing relationship: Phil Gasker of Muhlenberg returned a kickoff for a touchdown in consecutive years.

The Muhlenberg defense and the Moravian defense achieved a combined 19 changes of ball possession on November 21, 2006. Each defense achieved 4 turnovers. Guided by Eric Santagato, the Muhlenberg offense recorded 17 first downs and was stopped on 8 occasions. Guided by Ben Rempe and Marc Braxmeier, the Moravian offense recorded 12 first downs and was stopped on 11 occasions. Team statistics are listed in Table 4.48.

Newcomers to the playing relationship in 2007 will join with returning players who helped create two precedents in the 2006 game at Calvo Field. First, officials called 5 penalties on Moravian players and 4 on Muhlenberg players. Second, the score was tied before a Muhlenberg touchdown with 1:49 remaining in the third quarter.

Earlier, Muhlenberg and Moravian were tied at halftime, 3-3. After three quarters, Muhlenberg led Moravian, 17-10 (Table 4.48). The scoring play in the fourth quarter was:

Muhlenberg—Santagato 4 run (Hughes kick)

The Muhlenberg touchdown was scored with 37 seconds remaining in the game.

Table 4.48.   Team Statistics and Line Score for 2006 Game

2006		Muhlenberg		Moravian	
First downs		17		12	
Yards rushing		182		118	
Yards passing		171		131	
Passes completed-attempted		14-20		10-24	
Pass attempts intercepted		2		3	
Fumbles lost		2		1	
Punts		4		7	
Yards penalized		39		43	
Muhlenberg	3	0	14	7	—24
Moravian	0	3	7	0	—10

In other ways, the 2006 chapter is available for all members of the playing relationship, before and since. For the first time since the 1986 game, no touchdowns were scored in the first half. The 3-3 halftime tie was a first in the Moravian-and-Muhlenberg relationship. Cameron Ahouse of Muhlenberg intercepted a Moravian pass at the goal line with less than 6 minutes remaining, launching the final Muhlenberg touchdown drive that covered 85 yards. Ahouse tackled 8 Moravian ball carriers.

Lastly, players participating in their final Moravian-and-Muhlenberg football game joined to conclude an era in the playing relationship: Shawn Martell of Moravian caught a pass in each of his four games, 8 passes in all, as he walked in the footsteps of his father, Gary Martell of Moravian (1969–72).

CONCLUSION

This chapter culminates my project of reinterpreting an intercollegiate football competition as a place where human beings do things together in one another's company. In this chapter, the place is the relationship among players on a given day and across the years. I reinterpreted each of forty-eight games in the modern Moravian-and-Muhlenberg football relationship as a chapter written jointly by the competitors who played a football game. Each chapter marks a place in time that the competitors can claim as their own. Each chapter then becomes available for competitors who follow in the footsteps of their predecessors on the Moravian-and-Muhlenberg playing field. Each group of competitors, simply by playing their game in their unique way, thus contributes a legacy to their successors. This is a thoroughly ethical act, because each game provides material with which subsequent competitors can take a measure of what they accomplished together.

This meaning of *place* complements the relational place and the natural places in which I located the Moravian-and-Muhlenberg football playing relationship in the three preceding chapters. The ethical accomplishment that I interpret in this chapter is an impressive one, because it reaches beyond a bilateral relationship between competitors who join in the present in their civil act of creating a football game. By playing the game as they do, any one group of competitors make a contribution available to human beings they might never meet. The elasticity of this contribution, in time and stretching into relationships among third parties, creates a civil space that expands in time. The participants in the 2007 Moravian-and-Muhlenberg football game can benefit together from what the historical records that predecessors created in 1967, 1977, 1987, and 1997, for example. Moreover, participants in the

1977 game can gain a new appreciation of what they accomplished, as inheritors of the game played in 1997. This is a story of civic engagement that emanates from the routine playing of a football game. The human ties last long after the wins and losses are recorded.

NOTES

1. There are, of course, numerous metaphors for "teacher." The list includes expert, lecturer, informant, and disciplinarian. What I have in mind here is someone whose acts inspire students to gain increasing proficiency in asking their own questions.

2. P. A. Peters, "Moravian Trips Berg in Uphill Battle," *Bethlehem Globe-Times*, 22 November 1971, 21.

3. The reference to 1959 is not a typographical error. It is a device for identifying the most immediate inheritors from the 1958 game: namely, the 1959 participants.

4. Hereafter, I leave it to the reader to add the number of pass interceptions, fumbles lost, and punts, to arrive at the number of possession changes.

5. Cancellation of the 1963 games accounts for the two-year gap.

6. Another source listed the run at 30 yards.

Conclusion

There have been no tie scores in the modern Moravian-and-Muhlenberg football relationship. In the forty-eight games played from 1958 through 2006, the two teams nearly played to a tie score three times: 1980, 1981, and 1991. In each of those games, the victorious team scored one more point than did the losing team. This is a football conclusion that I make available with the data that I gathered and reported in this book.

There are four distinct layers of human ties that the members of forty-nine Moravian football teams and the members of forty-nine Muhlenberg football teams have woven into the modern Moravian-and-Muhlenberg football relationship. Forty-eight times, these human beings joined on the field of play and made room for one another's expressions of distinctiveness (Chapter 1). Forty-nine times, these human beings, already parties to multiple playing relationships, specifically sought one another's company to meet on the field of play (Chapter 2). Forty-eight times, Moravian team members and Muhlenberg team members moved together in the natural world as affirmation of their belonging together to the Moravian-and-Muhlenberg football relationship (Chapter 3). Forty-eight times, these human beings jointly wrote a chapter in an accumulating history that became available to their successors in the playing relationship (Chapter 4). Forty-eight times, Moravian team members and Muhlenberg team members joined to create a win and a loss embedded in these four layers of human ties. This is an ethical, historical conclusion that I made available with the data that I gathered and reported in this book.

This book contains an historical record of ethical accomplishment in an intercollegiate athletic competition. Two groups of human beings, one representing Moravian College and one representing Muhlenberg College, their football interests in sharp opposition, have found ways to stay together for a

half-century. Their ethical accomplishment has been the voluntary, joint cre-
ation of a civic association. As new members joined each group annually, vet-
erans and newcomers alike have taken their places in sustaining this mani-
festation of civic life. These human beings have achieved wins, losses, *and
human ties.* This is an ethical accomplishment worth celebrating.

In telling this story of civic engagement, I accomplish something that other
observers of American intercollegiate athletics have had difficulty accomplishing. I demonstrate that we can logically and empirically insert *accomplishment* into sentences and narratives about *ethics* and *intercollegiate athletic competition.* Modern discourse about ethics and American intercollegiate
athletic competition is mired in complaint about human moral failing. Such a
discourse about scandal, excess, and moral hypocrisy is a familiar one. It is the
starting point for thoughtful critiques of intercollegiate athletics, such as the
one argued by Peter A. French in *Ethics and College Sports.*

This discourse is stunted. It is a discourse in which ethical accomplishment
can rise no further than the temporary absence of scandal, excess, and moral
hypocrisy. If we ordinary citizens hold out hope for civil society, we must do
better than accept such a cynical perspective on ethical accomplishment in
competition. I show that we can.

Writing as a pragmatist, I sketch the outline of a new vocabulary about
ethics and intercollegiate athletic competition. I do not take the interconnec-
tion of ethics and athletic competition to be a settled matter. Susan Sontag
wrote elegantly of the "struggle for rhetorical ownership" of illness.[1] I draw
inspiration from Sontag's argument to propose a parallel struggle for "ownership" of *ethics and intercollegiate athletic competition.*

Critics of intercollegiate athletic competition in the United States often
proceed from the assumption that competition is the sum of simultaneous individual pursuits by human beings who covet a limited set of outcomes. If
competition is intense individual striving, then the critic of intercollegiate
athletics can readily draw on historical evidence of human fallibility to spin
a story about the inevitable transgressions by competitors. Such a story about
ethically deficient competitors is easy to create and to sustain.[2]

I start instead with the assumption that competition begins in a relationship. For any two human beings to engage in play toward some prize, I propose, they must agree to join, to play somewhere, and to play by some set of
agreements about how they will play. This depiction of competition is no less
credibly grounded in everyday experience than is the discourse about competitors' moral failings. I start where any school-age child starts when she
wants to arrange a game. She must find a place to play. That place is first a
human relationship; someone must agree to play the game with her. That
place is also a physical space where the players meet, such as someone's back

yard. In time, in these two places, the parties create an historical place that is their shared experience of competing.

In sum, there is more unfolding ethically in a competitive relationship than can be conveyed in the simple double negative: the temporary absence of scandal. The mythology that competition is a breeding ground for ethical scandal now has a competitor. The Moravian-and-Muhlenberg football relationship is a case in point.

What can we imagine doing with *wins, losses, and human ties* in practice? I close with two observations. One pertains to the Moravian-and-Muhlenberg football playing relationship. The other pertains to the undergraduate college curriculum.

One implication of this research is that we would do well to begin honoring those who have encouraged the Moravian-and-Muhlenberg football relationship. Raymond Whispell coached Muhlenberg football teams in the first eleven games in the modern playing relationship while serving as Director of Athletics. His counterpart at Moravian College in those years was Director of Athletics Harvey Gillespie. They were joined by Moravian Football Coach Rocco Calvo. Recently, the Moravian home football field has been renamed Rocco Calvo Field. In the spirit of their joint efforts to renew annually the Moravian-and-Muhlenberg football relationship, Calvo, Whispell, and Gillespie deserve some form of joint, public recognition. One place to start could be the Calvo Whispell Gillespie entrance gate at both the Moravian home field and the Muhlenberg home field.

Beyond the Moravian-and-Muhlenberg playing relationship, there is argument to be made that *wins, losses, and human ties* can be transformed into an undergraduate program of study in a liberal arts curriculum. There is a companion argument to be made that college coaches can play a central role in activating such a curriculum. Peter French, for one, gives up on connecting college sports and academic mission of the modern university. I do not think that the list of connections has been exhausted. Stay tuned.

NOTES

1. Susan Sontag, *AIDS and Its Metaphors* (New York: Farrar, Straus and Giroux, 1989), 93.

2. For a description of a pedagogical endeavor built on such a premise, see Brad Wolverton, "Morality Play," *Chronicle of Higher Education*, 4 August 2006, A32–35. My point is that such a premise is optional.

Bibliography

I draw on seven kinds of sources: books; newspaper articles; National Collegiate Athletic Association publications; Moravian College and Muhlenberg College yearbooks; Moravian and Muhlenberg online sports information; National Weather Service data; and other articles.

BOOKS

Bateson, Mary Catherine. *Composing a Life*. New York: Plume, 1990.

Berry, Wendell. *The Wild Birds: Six Stories of the Port William Membership*. San Francisco: North Point Press, 1986.

Bowen, William G., and Sarah A. Levin. *Reclaiming the Game: College Sports and Educational Values*. Princeton, N.J.: Princeton University Press, 2003.

Carse, James P. *Finite and Infinite Games*. New York: Random House, 1986.

Conroy, Pat. *My Losing Season*. New York: Nan A. Talese, 2002.

Donaldson, Thomas, and Thomas W. Dunfee. *Ties that Bind: A Social Contracts Approach to Business Ethics*. Boston: Harvard Business School Press, 1999.

Feinstein, John. *A Civil War: Army vs. Navy*. Boston: Little, Brown and Company, 1996.

Feinstein, John. *A March to Madness*. Boston: Little, Brown and Company, 1998.

French, Peter A. *Ethics and College Sports: Ethics, Sports, and the University*. Lanham, Md.: Rowman & Littlefield, 2004.

Gilligan, Carol, Nona Lyons, and Trudy Hanmer, eds. *Making Connections: The Relational Worlds of Adolescent Girls at Emma Willard School*. Cambridge, Mass.: Harvard University Press, 1990.

Goldstein, Richard. *Ivy League Autumns: An Illustrated History of College Football's Grand Old Rivalries*. New York: St. Martin's Press, 1996.

Gough, Russell W. *Character is Everything: Promoting Ethical Excellence in Sports*. Fort Worth, Tex.: Harcourt Brace, 1997.

Grundy, Pamela. *Learning to Win: Sports, Education, and Social Change in Twentieth-Century North Carolina*. Chapel Hill, N.C.: University of North Carolina Press, 2001.

Hall, Donald. *Life Work*. Boston: Beacon, 1993.

Hough, John, Jr. *The Conduct of the Game*. New York: Warner, 1987.

Hunt, Shelby D. *A General Theory of Competition: Resources, Competences, Productivity, Economic Growth*. Thousand Oaks, Calif.: Sage Publications, 1999.

Leopold, Aldo. *A Sand County Almanac*. New York: Ballantine, 1970.

Miller, Jean Baker. *Toward a New Psychology of Women*. 2d ed. Boston: Beacon, 1987.

O'Connell, Brian. *Civil Society: The Underpinnings of American Democracy*. Hanover, N.H.: University Press of New England, 1999.

Putnam, Robert D. *Bowling Alone: The Collapse and Revival of American Community*. New York: Simon & Schuster, 2000.

Rorty, Richard. *Contingency, Irony, and Solidarity*. Cambridge: Cambridge University Press, 1989.

Rosen, Charley. *Scandals of '51: How the Gamblers Almost Killed College Basketball*. New York: Seven Stories Press, 1999.

Rosenau, Pauline Vaillancourt. *The Competition Paradigm: America's Romance with Conflict, Contest, and Commerce*. Lanham, Md.: Rowman & Littlefield, 2003.

Shulman, James L., and William G. Bowen. *The Game of Life: College Sports and Educational Values*. Princeton, N.J.: Princeton University Press, 2001.

Sontag, Susan. *AIDS and Its Metaphors*. New York: Farrar, Straus and Giroux, 1989.

West, Elliott. *The Way to the West*. Albuquerque, N. Mex.: University of New Mexico Press, 1995.

Wideman, John Edgar. *Hoop Roots: Playground Basketball, Love, and Race*. Boston: Houghton Mifflin Company, 2001.

Watterson, John Sayle. *College Football: History, Spectacle, Controversy*. Baltimore, Md.: Johns Hopkins University Press, 2000.

NEWSPAPER ARTICLES

The main sources for this book are newspaper accounts of the Moravian-and-Muhlenberg football games in 1946 and from 1958 through 2006. These accounts were published in three newspapers in the Lehigh Valley region: *Bethlehem Globe-Times*, (Allentown) *Morning Call*, and (Easton) *Express-Times*. Over the years, names of these publications changed. From 1958 through 1984, the Allentown Sunday newspaper was the *Sunday Call-Chronicle* (hereafter *Call-Chronicle*). In 1985, the *Morning Call* weekday name was extended to the Sunday edition. By the time of the 1991 game, the *Globe-Times* and *Easton Express* had merged. The *Express-Times* was the result. The *Globe-Times* was a Monday-through-Saturday newspaper, except for the *Sunday Globe* edition from 1982–1985. The *Express-Times* is published seven days a week.

The *Globe-Times* and *Express-Times* editions from 1958–2006 are available on microfilm in the Bethlehem Public Library. The *Sunday Call-Chronicle* and *Morning Call* editions from 1958–2006 are available on microfilm in the Allentown Public Library.

The newspaper articles are listed by year, then alphabetically by author.

1946

"Mules Whip Moravian, 47-0," *Call-Chronicle*, 17 November 1946, 17.

1958

Aubrey, Coulter. "Fired-up 'Hounds Trip Mules," *Call-Chronicle*, 23 November 1958, 41, 43.

Cressman, Don. "Moravian Belts Muhlenberg for Calvo, 30-20," *Bethlehem Globe-Times*, 24 November 1958, 24, 32.

1959

Cressman, Don. "Owens, Yost Too Much for Moravian," *Bethlehem Globe-Times*, 23 November 1959, 19–20.

McCarron, Joe. "Mules' Long Runs Submerge Moravian," *Call-Chronicle*, 22 November 1959, 41–42.

1960

Buss, Jim. "Mules Jar Moravian," *Call-Chronicle*, 20 November 1960, 45–46.

Cressman, Don. "Mules Maul Hounds in Finale," *Bethlehem Globe-Times*, 21 November 1960, 22, 28.

1961

Collins, Jack. "Mules' Shotgun Rips Moravian," *Bethlehem Globe-Times*, 20 November 1961, 24, 36.

McCarron, Joe. "Muhlenberg Surprises Moravian, 33-8," *Call-Chronicle*, 19 November 1961, D1, 4.

1962

Collins, Jack. "Muhlenberg's Air Attack Riddles Moravian," *Bethlehem Globe-Times*, 19 November 1962, 24.

Gray, Jack. "Haney Passes for 3 Touchdowns as Mules Upset Moravian, 32-8,"*Call-Chronicle*, 18 November 1962, D1, 8.

1963

"What Do You Say? What Can You Say?" *Bethlehem Globe-Times*, 23 November 1963, 16.

1964

Collins, Jack. "'Berg Extends Mastery Over Greyhounds," *Bethlehem Globe-Times*, 23 November 1964, 24, 26.
DeLong, Dave. "Mules Erupt in 4th Period, Deal Moravian 21-6 Loss," *Call-Chronicle*, 22 November 1964, D1.

1965

DeLong, Dave. "Moravian Raps Mules, 17-8, Behind Running of Nehilla," *Call-Chronicle*, 21 November 1965, D2-3.
Gray, Jack. "Muhlenberg Coach Says Game One of Best Yet," *Call-Chronicle*, 21 November 1965, D3.
Wildblood, Alan. "Win-Hungry Moravian Trips Mules, 17-8," *Bethlehem Globe-Times*, 22 November 1965, 23.

1966

Aubrey, Coult. "Moravian Tabs TD on Fumble, Turns Back Muhlenberg, 14-7," *Call-Chronicle*, 20 November 1966, D1-2.
Vass, Jack. "Unheralded Senior Stars in Moravian Victory," *Bethlehem Globe-Times*, 21 November 1966, 24, 28.

1967

Aubrey, Coult. "Gratz Leads Moravian Over Mules, 19-8," *Call-Chronicle*, 19 November 1967, C1-2.
Harris, Bill. "Enthusiasm Name of the Game for Mules and Greyhounds," *Call-Chronicle*, 19 November 1967, C2.
Peters, P.A. "Gratz Leads Moravian Hero List in 19-8 Win," *Bethlehem Globe-Times*, 20 November 1967, 26.

1968

Aubrey, Coult. "When Opposition is Muhlenberg, Hugh Gratz Turns Into Super-Star," *Call-Chronicle*, 24 November 1968, C3.
Larimer, Terry. "Startled Mules Drubbed 47-15," *Call-Chronicle*, 24 November 1968, C1, 3.

Peters, P.A. "Moravian's String of Touchdowns Stuns 'Berg," *Bethlehem Globe-Times*, 25 November 1968, 22–23.

1969

Aubrey, Coult. "'Hounds Roll Over Mules 37-0," *Call-Chronicle*, 23 November 1969, C1, 2.

Peters, P.A. "Moravian Juggernaut Demolishes Mules, 37-0," *Bethlehem Globe-Times*, 24 November 1969, 22.

1970

Aubrey, Coult. "Moravian's Bonisese An Unexpected Hero," *Call-Chronicle*, 22 November 1970, C3.

Buss, Jim. "Greyhounds Capture Title," *Call-Chronicle*, 22 November 1970, C1, 3.

Peters, P.A. "Moravian Mauls Mules 55-7 for MAC Crown," *Bethlehem Globe-Times*, 23 November 1970, 22.

1971

Aubrey, Coult. "Moravian Holds Off Mules' Threat 14-7," *Call-Chronicle*, 21 November 1971, C1-2.

Buss, Jim. "Moravian 'Fortunate' at Times," *Call-Chronicle*, 21 November 1971, C2.

McCallum, Jack. "Big Defensive Plays Won for 'Hounds," *Bethlehem Globe-Times*, 22 November 1971, 21.

Peters, P.A. "Moravian Trips Berg in Uphill Battle," *Bethlehem Globe-Times*, 22 November 1971, 21.

1972

Aubrey, Coult. "Martell Settles for Satisfaction," *Call-Chronicle*, 19 November 1972, C2.

Buss, Jim. "'Frustration Battle' Won by Moravian 38-14," *Call-Chronicle*, 19 November 1972, C1-2.

McCallum, Jack. "Records Don't Bother Martell," *Bethlehem Globe-Times*, 20 November 1972, 31.

Peters, P.A. "Greyhounds Finally Get Big Plays to Crush Mules," *Bethlehem Globe-Times*, 20 November 1972, 31.

1973

Aubrey, Coult. "Muhlenberg Halts Trend," *Call-Chronicle*, 18 November 1973, C1, 5.

Buratti, Bruce. "Mules Regain Big Kick In Short Span of 1 Year," *Bethlehem Globe-Times*, 19 November 1973, 23.

Buss, Jim. "Mules' Season a 'Family Affair'," *Call-Chronicle*, 18 November 1973, C5.

Peters, P.A. "Muhlenberg Ends Greyhound Reign," *Bethlehem Globe-Times*, 19 November 1973, 23–24.

1974

Aubrey, Coult. "Offensive Linemen Run the Show," *Call-Chronicle*, 24 November 1974, C2.

Buss, Jim. "'Hounds' 42-27 Win a 'Delight'," *Call-Chronicle*, 24 November 1974, C1.

Peters, P.A. "Moravian Grinds Out 42-27 Win Over Mules," *Bethlehem Globe-Times*, 25 November 1974, 22, 26.

1975

Aubrey, Coult. "Moravian Zips the Mules 16-0," *Call-Chronicle*, 23 November 1975, C1-2.

Peters, P.A. "Moravian Outkicks Mules in Season Final 16-0," *Bethlehem Globe-Times*, 24 November 1975, 23.

1976

Concevitch, John. "The Difference in This Game? CONTACT," *Bethlehem Globe-Times*, 22 November 1976, 26.

Peters, P.A. "Muhlenberg Brings Out the Best in Moravian," *Bethlehem Globe-Times*, 22 November 1976, 26, 28.

Wismer, Ted. "Mules Routed, 36–14," *Call-Chronicle*, 21 November 1976, C1, 3.

1977

Aubrey, Coult, "Mules Win in Final 3 Seconds," *Call-Chronicle*, 20 November 1977, C1-2.

McCallum, Jack. "Key Trap Play Leads Mules to Last-Second Victory," *Bethlehem Globe-Times*, 21 November 1977, 27–28.

1978

Aubrey, Coult. "Muhlenberg Thunders to 34-0 Rout of Moravian," *Call-Chronicle*, 12 November 1978, C1-2.

McCallum, Jack. "This Time, Muhlenberg Was the Bully," *Bethlehem Globe-Times*, 13 November 1978, 18.

1979

Aubrey, Coult. "Mules Cool Moravian Early, 14-6," *Call-Chronicle*, 11 November 1979, C1, 6.

Curtis, Jake. "Muhlenberg Makes it 0-9 for Moravian 11," *Bethlehem Globe-Times*, 12 November 1979, 17.

1980

Curtis, Jake. "Mules' Victory Over Moravian Symbolic of Season," *Bethlehem Globe-Times*, 17 November 1980, C1, 3.

Lapos, Jack. "Mules Hold Off Moravian," *Call-Chronicle*, 16 November 1980, C1, 4.

1981

Lapos, Jack. "History Repeats as Mules Get 10-9 Victory," *Call-Chronicle*, 15 November 1981, C1, 4.

Rhodin, Tony. "Moravian 11 Denied First Victory When Two-Point Conversion Fails," *Bethlehem Globe-Times*, 16 November 1981, C1, 4.

1982

Fox, John Jay. "Moravian Ends Muhlenberg Jinx with 16-6 Win," *Call-Chronicle*, 14 November 1982, C1, 4.

Williams, Ted. "Greyhounds Send Mules Packing," *Sunday Globe*, 14 November 1982, C1, 8.

1983

Lapos, Jack. "Joseph Scores 3 TDs as Moravian Rolls 24-7," *Call-Chronicle*, 13 November 1983, C1, 4.

Williams, Ted. "Moravian Closes with a Rush," *Sunday Globe*, 13 November 1983, C1, 11.

1984

Fox, John Jay. "Moravian Wins 17-14 on First FG of Season," *Call-Chronicle*, 11 November 1984, C1, 8.

Hoffman, Joe. "It's Moravian—-by a Foot," *Sunday Globe*, 11 November 1984, C1, 8.

Lapos, Jack. "Mules Fail to Get Off Tying FG in Waning Seconds," *Call-Chronicle*, 11 November 1984, C8
Williams, Ted. "Punter Fills the Bill," *Sunday Globe*, 11 November 1984, C1, 8.

1985

Hoffman, Joe. "'Hounds Rain on Mules' Parade," *Sunday Globe*, 17 November 1985, C1, 12.
Lapos, Jack. "Moravian Defense Saves the Day," *Morning Call*, 17 November 1985, C1, 4.

1986

Fox, John Jay. "Moravian Gets a Total Team Effort," *Morning Call*, 16 November 1986, C1, 11.
Hoffman, Joe. "Greyhound 'D' Puts the Clamps on Muhlenberg," *Bethlehem Globe-Times*, 17 November 1986, C1, 5.

1987

Aubrey, Coult. "Mules' Elser Disconnects Moravian," *Morning Call*, 15 November 1987, C1, 15.
Fox, John Jay. "Bolesky Typified Moravian Tenacity," *Morning Call,* 15 November 1987, C3.
Schlottman, Jack. "Mules End Moravian Mastery," *Bethlehem Globe-Times*, 16 November 1987, C1, 7.

1988

Blockus, Gary R. "Moravian Meets Challenge," *Morning Call*, 13 November 1988, C1, 12.
Groller, Keith. "Dapp: Team Effort No Overused Cliché," *Morning Call*, 13 November 1988, C1, 12.
Hoffman, Joe. "And It Gets Better for Moravian," *Bethlehem Globe-Times*, 14 November 1988, C1, 5.

1989

Blockus, Gary R. "Moravian Edges Mules 14-9," *Morning Call*, 12 November 1989, C1, 12.
Groller, Keith. "Greyhounds May Have Set Record for Tense Finishes," *Morning Call*, 12 November 1989, C1.
Heilig, John. "'Hounds Stop Mules," *Bethlehem Globe-Times*, 13 November 1989, C1, 15.

Williams, Ted. "Just Another Frantic Finish," *Bethlehem Globe-Times*, 13 November 1989, C1, 15.

1990

Heilig, John. "Mudville Joy," *Bethlehem Globe-Times*, 12 November 1990, C1, 4.

Long, Ernie. "Moravian Needs Late Stand to Down Muhlenberg 7-3," *Morning Call*, 11 November 1990, C1, 11.

Williams, Ted. "One Win Makes a Season," *Bethlehem Globe-Times*, 12 November 1990, C1, 4.

1991

Deeb, Monica. "Moravian Conversion Tops Mules," *Express-Times*, 17 November 1991, F1, 8.

Groller, Keith. "Star is Born as 'Hounds Rally to Nip Mules 28–27," *Morning Call*, 17 November 1991, C1, 11.

Long, Ernie. "'Big Play' Just Wasn't There for Mules," *Morning Call*, 17 November 1991, C11.

1992

Groller, Keith. "Moravian's Mattes Goes Out on High (319 Yards) Note," *Morning Call*, 15 November 1992, C12.

Hoffman, Joe. "Hounds Feast on the Mules," *Express-Times*, 15 November 1992, D1, 5.

Long, Ernie. "'Hounds Finish Off Season with Victory over Mules," *Morning Call*, 15 November 1992, C1, 12.

1993

Groller, Keith. "Scoreboard-Watching Pays Off for 'Hounds," *Morning Call*, 14 November 1993, C1, 13.

Hinkel, Tom. "NCAA Bid May Await 'Hounds," *Express-Times*, 14 November 1993, D1, 5.

Long, Ernie. "Record-Setting Keville Leads Moravian over Mules 24–14," *Morning Call*, 14 November 1993, C1, 13.

1994

Hinkel, Tom. "'Hounds Go Out with a Bang," *Express-Times*, 13 November 1994, D1-2.

Long, Ernie. "Keville Comes Up Big," *Morning Call*, 13 November 1994, C1, 10.

1995

Groller, Keith. "Moravian Punishes Mules in Finale," *Morning Call*, 12 November 1995, C1, 12.
Hinkel, Tom. "Running Out on a Positive Note," *Express-Times*, 12 November 1995, C3.

1996

Hinkel, Tom. "Greyhounds Lower Boom in Season Finale," *Express-Times*, 17 November 1996, C5.
Williams, Andre. "Greyhounds-Mules Lacked That Certain Electricity," *Morning Call*, 17 November 1996, C4.
Williams, Andre. "Moravian Continues Its Domination of Muhlenberg," *Morning Call*, 17 November 1996, C4.

1997

Brown, Andy. "Muhlenberg Forgets to Win," *Express-Times*, 16 November 1997, C1, 5.
Deeb, Monica. "Campbell Pick Leads 'Hounds over Mules," *Morning Call*, 16 November 1997, C1, 7.

1998

Hinkel, Tom. "Brader's Effort Lifts the Mules," *Express-Times*, 15 November 1998, C1-2.
Williams, Andre. "Brader, Mules Complete Memorable Season with a Win over Moravian," *Morning Call*, 15 November 1998, C1, 10.

1999

Groller, Keith. "Muhlenberg Scores 42 Points in First Half, Coasts over Moravian," *Morning Call*, 14 November 1999, C1, 12.
Hinkel, Tom. "Carter Kick-Starts Mules," *Express-Times*, 14 November 1999, D1, 3.

2000

Fox, John Jay. "Bernardo Answers the Call, Lifts Muhlenberg to 45-20 Rout," *Morning Call*, 12 November 2000, C1-2.
Hinkel, Tom. "Freshman Runs for 251, Mules Hammer 'Hounds," *Express-Times*, 12 November 2000, C1-2.

2001

Hinkel, Tom. "Greyhounds Play Takeaway to Kick Mules," *Express-Times*, 11 November 2001, C1, 14.

Hudson, Beth. "Greyhounds Rebound to Beat Muhlenberg, 17-7," *Morning Call*, 11 November 2001, C1, 5.

2002

Hinkel, Tom. "Mules' Bernardo Continues to Run Strong on Steel Field," *Express-Times*, 17 November 2002, C1, 4.
Reinhard, Paul. "For Mules' Koth, A Beautifully Muddy Day," *Morning Call*, 17 November 2002, C11.
Schuler, Jeff. "Muhlenberg Blanks Moravian, Earns NCAA Berth," *Morning Call*, 17 November 2002, C11.

2003

Hinkel, Tom. "McGowan, Santini Step Up," *Express-Times*, 16 November 2003, C2.
Hinkel, Tom. "Mules Deliver in the Clutch," *Express-Times*, 16 November 2003, C1-2.
Schuler, Jeff. "A Game to Remember for Getz, As Mules Romp," *Morning Call*, 16 November 2003, C6.

2004

Hinkel, Tom. "Mules Get Playoff Bid; Moravian Must Wait," *Express-Times*, 14 November 2004, C2.
Schuler, Jeff. "With Win and Luck, Mules Get NCAA Nod," *Morning Call*, 14 November 2004, C1, 6.

2005

Meixell, Ted. "Seniors Get Only Win over Mules," *Morning Call*, 13 November 2005, mcall.com.

2006

Heilig, John. "Mules End Season on Good Note, Beat Rival Moravian," *Morning Call*, 12 November 2006, CC8.
Hinkel, Tom. "Mules Keep on Knocking," *Express-Times*, 12 November 2006, C2.

NCAA FOOTBALL GUIDES, CHRONOLOGICAL

Official National Collegiate Athletic Association Football Guide 1958. New York: National Collegiate Athletic Bureau, 1958.
Official National Collegiate Athletic Association Football Guide 1959. New York: National Collegiate Athletic Bureau, 1959.

Official National Collegiate Athletic Association Football Guide 1960. New York: National Collegiate Athletic Bureau, 1960.

Official National Collegiate Athletic Association Football Guide 1961. New York: National Collegiate Athletic Bureau, 1961.

Official National Collegiate Athletic Association Football Guide 1962. New York: National Collegiate Athletic Bureau, 1962.

Official National Collegiate Athletic Association Football Guide 1963. 73rd Annual Edition. New York: National Collegiate Athletic Bureau, 1963.

Official National Collegiate Athletic Association Football Guide 1964. 74th Annual Edition. New York: National Collegiate Athletic Bureau, 1964.

Official National Collegiate Athletic Association Football Guide 1965. 75th Annual Edition. New York: National Collegiate Athletic Bureau, 1965.

Official National Collegiate Athletic Association Football Guide 1966. 76th Annual Edition. New York: National Collegiate Athletic Bureau, 1966.

Official National Collegiate Athletic Association Football Guide 1967. 77th Annual Edition. Phoenix, Ariz.: College Athletics Publishing Service, 1967.

Official National Collegiate Athletic Association Football Guide 1968. Phoenix, Ariz.: College Athletics Publishing Service, 1968.

Official National Collegiate Athletic Association Football Guide 1969. Centennial Celebration Edition. Phoenix, Ariz.: College Athletics Publishing Service, 1969.

Official NCAA Football Guide 1970. Phoenix, Ariz.: College Athletics Publishing Service, 1970.

Official NCAA Football Guide 1971. Phoenix, Ariz.: College Athletics Publishing Service, 1971.

Official NCAA Football Guide 1972. Phoenix, Ariz.: College Athletics Publishing Service, 1972.

Official NCAA Football Guide 1973. Shawnee Mission, Kans.: NCAA Publishing Service, 1973.

Official NCAA Football Guide 1974. Shawnee Mission, Kans.: NCAA Publishing Service, 1974.

Official NCAA Football Guide 1975. Shawnee Mission, Kans.: NCAA Publishing Service, 1975.

Official NCAA Football Guide 1976. Shawnee Mission, Kans.: NCAA Publishing Service, 1976.

Official NCAA Football Guide 1977. Shawnee Mission, Kans.: NCAA Publishing Service, 1977.

Official NCAA Football Guide 1978. Shawnee Mission, Kans.: NCAA Publishing Service, 1978.

1979 NCAA Football. Shawnee Mission, Kans.: NCAA Publishing Service, 1979.

1980 NCAA Football. Shawnee Mission, Kans.: NCAA Publishing Service, 1980.

1981 NCAA Football Records. Shawnee Mission, Kans.: NCAA Publishing Service, 1981.

1982 NCAA Football. Mission, Kans.: NCAA, 1982.

1983 NCAA Football. Mission, Kans.: NCAA, 1983.

1984 NCAA Football. Mission, Kans.: NCAA, 1984.

1985 NCAA Football. Mission, Kans.: NCAA, 1985.
1986 NCAA Football. Mission, Kans.: NCAA, 1986.
1987 NCAA Football. Mission, Kans.: NCAA, 1987.
1988 NCAA Football. Mission, Kans.: NCAA, 1988.
1989 NCAA Football. Mission, Kans.: NCAA, 1989.
1990 NCAA Football. Overland Park, Kans.: NCΛΛ, 1990.
Official 1991 NCAA Football. Overland Park, Kans.: NCAA, 1991.
Official 1992 NCAA Football. Overland Park, Kans.: NCAA, 1992.
Official 1993 NCAA Football. Overland Park, Kans.: NCAA, 1993.
NCAA Football: The Official 1994 College Football Records Book. Overland Park, Kans.: NCAA, 1994.
NCAA Football: The Official 1995 College Football Records Book. Overland Park, Kans.: NCAA, 1995.
NCAA Football: The Official 1996 College Football Records Book. Overland Park, Kans.: NCAA, 1996.
NCAA Football: The Official 1997 College Football Records Book. Overland Park, Kans.: NCAA, 1997.
NCAA Football: The Official 1998 College Football Records Book. Overland Park, Kans.: NCAA, 1998.
The Official 1999 Football Records Book. Indianapolis, Ind.: NCAA, 1999.
NCAA Official 2000 Football Records Book. Indianapolis, Ind.: NCAA, 2000.
NCAA Football Records 2001. Indianapolis, Ind.: NCAA, 2001.

YEARBOOKS

Benigna, Moravian College yearbook, 1958–2007, in Reeves Library, Moravian College.
Ciarla, Muhlenberg College yearbook, 1959–2002, in Trexler Library, Muhlenberg College.

MORAVIAN AND MUHLENBERG SPORTS INFORMATION ONLINE

Moravian College Athletics 2002–06 schedules and game statistics: moravian.edu/athletics.
Muhlenberg College 2002–06 football schedules: muhlenberg.edu/athletics.

METEOROLOGICAL DATA

Surface Weather Observations, Allentown-Bethlehem-Easton Airport (later Lehigh Valley International Airport), collected by the Weather Bureau (U.S. Department of

Commerce), 1958–1971, and by the National Weather Service (National Oceanic and Atmospheric Administration, Department of Commerce), 1972–2006, for the day of each scheduled game.

OTHER ARTICLES

Brady, Erik. "Small Schools' Promised Land." *USA Today*, 14 December 2006, 3C.

Gumbrecht, Hans Ulrich. "They Have a Powerful Aesthetic Appeal." *Chronicle of Higher Education*, 23 June 2006, B10-11.

Suggs, Welch. "The Role of Sports in Small-College Life." *Chronicle of Higher Education*, 8 July 2005, A32-33.

Washington Post, 23 November 1963, D1.

Wolfe, Richard A., Karl E. Weick, John M. Usher, James R. Terborg, Laura Poppo, Audrey J. Murrell, Janet M. Dukerich, Deborah Crown Core, Kevin E. Dickson, and Jessica Simmons Jourdan. "Sport and Organizational Studies: Exploring Synergy." *Journal of Management Inquiry* 14, no. 2 (June 2005): 182–210.

Wolverton, Brad. "Morality Play." *Chronicle of Higher Education*, 4 August 2006, A32-35.

Index

About the Author

Daniel R. Gilbert, Jr., teaches Gettysburg College students about ethics, organized endeavor, competition, and civil society. He grew up in Bethlehem, Pennsylvania, dreaming of one day taking his place in uniform on an intercollegiate athletic playing field. He fulfilled that dream, although not as a football player. Dr. Gilbert earned degrees from Dickinson College (B.A., and Phi Beta Kappa), Lehigh University (M.B.A.), and the University of Minnesota (Ph.D.).